# Breaking the Impasse

*Electoral Politics, Mass Action, and
the New Socialist Movement in the United States*

Kim Moody

Haymarket Books
Chicago, Illinois

Published in 2022 by
Haymarket Books
P.O. Box 180165
Chicago, IL 60618
773-583-7884
www.haymarketbooks.org
info@haymarketbooks.org

ISBN: 978-1-642597-01-1

Distributed to the trade in the US through Consortium Book Sales and Distribution (www.cbsd.com) and internationally through Ingram Publisher Services International (www.ingramcontent.com).

This book was published with the generous support of Lannan Foundation and Wallace Action Fund.

Special discounts are available for bulk purchases by organizations and institutions. Please email info@haymarketbooks.org for more information.

Cover design by Eric Kerl.

Printed in Canada by union labor.

Library of Congress Cataloging-in-Publication data is available.

10 9 8 7 6 5 4 3 2 1

# Praise for *Breaking the Impasse*

"Kim Moody's latest book promises to be a major contribution to the renewed debates on socialist strategy in the US. Moody expertly demolishes the analytic and historical arguments for strategies to either transform the Democratic Party into a social-democratic party or use its 'ballot line' to prepare for an independent working-class party in an undefined future. He demonstrates that it has always been mass, disruptive working-class movements, in workplaces and in the streets, that are the source of popular power and radicalism—the key to winning concessions from capital and the state and creating the conditions for working-class political independence and power." —CHARLES POST, editor of *Spectre*

"Kim Moody breaks new ground in his brilliant, readable, breathtakingly comprehensive analysis that upends conventional thinking about this fraught moment in history. He draws on encyclopedic knowledge of labor, movements for social justice, politics, electoral activity, and debates about the Democratic Party, making an inspiring, persuasive case about how to build a mass social upsurge to break the stranglehold of billionaires over our daily existence." —LOIS WEINER, author of *The Future of Our Schools: Teachers Unions and Social Justice*

"Essential reading for those interested in understanding and joining the mass upsurge of workers and others oppressed by the predatory global capitalist system. In addition to his usual detailed, empirically rich, and wide-ranging documentation of labor struggles and the changing structure of capitalist employment, Kim Moody's analysis of the constraining structure of the Democratic Party and its role as a graveyard for democratic and radical politics is nuanced, detailed, and breaks new ground." —MICHAEL GOLDFIELD, author of *The Southern Key: Class, Race, and Radicalism in the 1930s and 1940s*

# CONTENTS

# Introduction

In the last few years, a new socialist movement has taken shape in the United States on a scale not seen since the 1930s or 1940s. While it has been in the making for much longer, with many of its future members moving through the inspiration and frustration of the multiple social movements of the last decade or so, it is only relatively recently that it has exploded on the political scene. The high-profile 2016 presidential primary campaign of self-defined democratic socialist Bernie Sanders gave a boost to the idea of socialism none of the prior movements had perhaps because of its high visibility and perceived proximity to political power. The organizational expression of this new socialist movement has been the Democratic Socialists of America (DSA) which has soared from a few thousand members in 2015 to ninety thousand and growing as of early 2021. It has transformed from an older social democratic organization into a more radical, multi-tendency, and dynamic democratic socialist movement.

The political context into which this new movement was born is a complex and contradictory one. On the one hand, the increasingly morbid symptoms of a crisis-ridden capitalism have produced worldwide but mostly sporadic up-surges, while on the other hand, conventional politics across much of the world has been trapped in an impasse characterized by a rising right and a traditional electoral left retreating toward the center mostly in the form of neoliberalism. No matter what party or coalition sits in government, it appears unable to deal effectively with the crises or to meet the needs and demands of the majority. Naturally, this impasse differs in its specifics from country to country. In the US, it is characterized most visibly by a Republican Party moving ever rightward and a Democratic Party defending itself by moving toward the political center, far from even the reforms of the New Deal or the Great Society. While in compari-son to the Trump era, even Joe Biden's limited first moves have the feel of a wave of relief, in relation to the crises facing the majority of Americans and, indeed, people the world over, they are more a ripple in a stagnant pool. This book elaborates on this political impasse as the context in which DSA and the new socialist movement has arisen, and argues for the means of breaking through it.

On the one hand, the spectacular growth of DSA has been drawn from activists in a wide variety of social movement and political activities, most of which have experienced serious difficulty in winning major advances. Even where some gains are won, the "big" issues that provide the framework in which movements struggle—issues such as economic inequality, police violence, mass incarceration, climate change, and even so basic a matter as organizing a union—seem beyond reach as corporate giants and governments refuse to budge or even offer symbolic concessions. On the other hand, the 2016 Sanders campaign for the presidential nomination of the Democratic Party drew in tens of thousands of volunteers and millions of voters in an effort that commanded national attention and for a time altered the political debate. Electoral action now seemed to many like a viable path forward.

The organizational site of its birth in DSA and its legacy as well as the electoral context that helped it grow so rapidly, however, threw this new socialist left into the very political impasse that paralyzes electoral politics in the US. The political legacy of DSA stems largely from the work of Michael Harrington and his analysis of American politics in the 1960s and 1970s, which, drawing on mainstream political science, limited left electoral politics to the United States' seemingly immutable two-party system. The task of socialists, Harrington famously argued, was to be "the left wing of the possible"; that is, of Democratic Party liberalism. When Harrington and others first advocated the strategy of "realignment" in the Democratic Party beginning in the early 1960s, that party and liberalism in general were moving—reluctantly, to be sure—to the left, driven above all by the civil rights movement of that era. Today, after years of retreat the opposite is true. Liberalism, the Democratic Party, and its various wings have retreated to and are stuck in the political center, partially as a result of their own electoral direction. The expectations of the party's progressives have been lowered and the fight for reforms limited to symbolic resolutions, alternative budgets that get no attention, and campaigns that lack the force of real opposition. Even the boldest of proposals such as a Green New Deal and Medicare for All for the most part fall short of undermining capitalist property relations or the soaring inequality of the era.

And even these come up against a wall of centrist resistance. Today the "left wing of the possible" in this party of capital is very limited indeed.

Few in DSA today cite Harrington, fewer still claim to want to revive the failed project of "realignment" of the Democratic Party, mostly understood as its reform into a social democratic party. For some he even represents a position from which to distance one's self. In his place, as we will see in chapter 4, Bayard Rustin, who by the mid-1960s tragically moved even farther toward the right of social democracy than Harrington, has been revived by some to promote a version of "coalition" politics in the Democratic Party, even though most of the proposed coalition members already vote for this party to little avail. Thus, in the matter of the two-party system as the unavoidable default framework for socialist electoral politics, Harrington, with an inadvertent boost from Rustin, and the analytical tradition they did much to develop and popularize on the left cast a long shadow.

Bernie Sanders's spectacular challenge to the Democratic Party's complacent centrism gave new life not only to the socialist movement, but to this older political framework as well. That, unlike previous challenges, it was done in the name of democratic socialism and the programmatic spirit of the New Deal only solidified the Democratic Party, its supposedly open ballot line, and its allegedly permeable nature in the minds of many as the unavoidable path of electoral politics for many in this new generation of socialists.

It is for this reason that *Breaking the Impasse* takes a new and different look at the US electoral system as well as the Democratic Party and proposes an alternative analysis of the roots of today's electoral impasse. It critically examines some of the major proposals for working in or through this party that has no members or internal democracy. It analyzes the 2020 elections and the trends that led to it in order to assess the internal dynamics of the Democratic Party that have held it to its centrist course even in the face of the multiple crises facing the US and the world. It argues that the political impasse that blocks even modest progressive reforms, let alone any real solutions to today's crises, can only be broken by a mass social upsurge in which the organization of millions of workers currently outside of organized labor is central. That, in turn, requires transforming most of today's unions and transcending the current system of labor relations. It is through this alternative path that the new socialist movement can become a major force in US politics.

The classic Marxist assumption of this argument is that socialism can only come about through the independent organization, self-activity, and political power of the working class. This class is understood here not as an undifferentiated mass, but as a diverse, divided, and contradictory product of the social relations of capitalism always in formation. In this actually existing working class, race and gender play central roles in its subordination to *and* in dialectical fashion resistance to the demands of capital. The analysis presented here rejects the counterposition of class and race in particular, which is featured in much of the current debate about political strategy. Racism may have been born in slavery and colonialism, but it was adopted almost from birth by a rampant and expanding international capitalist system.

Most of what I have written about in the past has focused on organized labor, the conditions of and changes in the working class, and the developments in capitalism that both limit and enable working-class resistance and struggle. Along the way, however, I managed to pick up a master's degree in political science. So, after nearly a quarter of a century working at *Labor Notes*, which provided me with a real "graduate" course in unions and working-class life, I later taught political science and US politics in the City University of New York system for several years. After moving to London, where I taught industrial relations for a while, I eventually earned a PhD in American studies, which furthered my interest in and research of US electoral politics. My experience and interest in this side of politics increasingly propelled me into the debate on political action that has intensified with the growth of DSA. *Breaking the Impasse* is an attempt to pull together some of the analysis and research in electoral politics that resulted from this history.

Most of the material in this book is original to *Breaking the Impasse*. Some of it, however, appeared in various publications before the book's publication. Some of the analysis of chapter 3 on the 2020 election appeared in *Against the Current*. The section of racial policing appeared on the website of the Marxist journal *Spectre*, while most of the critique of Jane McAlevey's organizing "model" in chapter 6 appeared in the second issue of that journal. Much of the section on workplace technology and logistics infrastructure in chapter 7 appeared in the Winter 2021 issue of *New Politics*. I thank these publications for permission to use those materials in this book.

The people who have influenced my thinking on these issues over the years are too numerous to list. For the most part they are activists and thinkers associated with a broad revolutionary Marxist current known as "socialism from below" or "third camp" socialism. This a tendency that has always put democracy and working-class self-activity and organization at the center of its politics. These activists and thinkers will not be found in any single organization over the years, though many belonged to the International Socialists, Solidarity, or the International Socialist Organization, and today many belong to DSA. Of course, the influences on my thinking go far beyond this to many of the classic and more recent Marxist theorists; working-class activists and organizers; the many past and current writers for publications such as *Labor Notes, New Politics, Against the Current, Historical Materialism, New Left Review, Spectre,* and *Jacobin;* and many more.

Putting things together in a book involves a lot of work and support. The folks at *Haymarket* have, as always, been very helpful, as have the various people in the US and elsewhere I correspond with. My thanks to all these sources of ideas, help, and inspiration past and present. Special thanks to my partner and comrade, Sheila Cohen, for her support and patience while I worked on this book through serial lockdowns in what seemed like the never-ending pandemic of 2020–21.

CHAPTER 1

# The Impasse

*The multiplication of parties, which arises as a result of other factors, is facilitated by one type of electoral system and hindered by another. Ballot procedure, however, has no driving power. The most decisive influences in this respect are the aspects of the life of the nation such as ideologies and particularly the socio-economic structure.*[1]

—Maurice Duverger, *Political Parties*

For the past three decades, since the end of the "Reagan Revolution" of the 1980s when politics shifted dramatically to the right, electoral politics in the US have been at an impasse. By "impasse" I mean a political situation defined in part by legislative gridlock between the country's two major parties, and in part by the economic limitations and class dependencies perceived by the leaders and actors in both parties, in which no major reforms have been possible. Drawing on Brookings Institution analyst William Galston, Mike Davis has perceptively described this impasse as political "trench warfare" with its stalemate and "immobile line of battle."[2]

This impasse, however, is not only a matter of legislative gridlock, as persistent as that is, but of a partisan and ideological polarization that was not typical of twentieth century US politics. This polarization and impasse is rooted in deep divisions within the capitalist class as it faces its own crises, on the one hand, and underlying class and racial dimensions that are more familiar but also more intertwined, on the other. It has been characterized by what political scientists call an "asymmetrical polarization," in that it has been stuck in a context that cannot go beyond right versus center.[3]

This impasse is not unique to the US. It is found around the world where the traditional parties of the left have moved toward the center, while new forces on the right push politics toward more irrational, often authoritarian, frequently racist, but always deeply pro-capitalist policies and trends. This acceptance of the system by both sides is not only intellectual, but above all in the US based in the presence of capital and its contesting factions within each party funding the entire political process—party organizations, all but a handful of candidates and office holders, and the legions of expensive specialists and consultants that typically run political campaigns these days. Thus, the impasse is internal to both major parties. For the Democrats, however, the internal impasse is enforced by the increased role of super-wealthy individual donors, on the one hand, and a strategic orientation to wealthy and more prosperous voters, on the other.

This political framework is itself embedded in and limited by capitalism's recurring crises spurred by the ups and downs *and* secular tendency of falling profit rates. Marxist economist Michael Roberts has called this the "long depression."[4] This has meant that the capitalist class is itself engaged in an internal struggle over such economic surplus as this crippled system provides. The impasse itself is thus primarily the result of the conflict of capitalist elites caught in what Dylan Riley characterizes as a "a zero-sum redistributive conflict" at the top and bottom of society.[5] It is a clash between organized sections of finance and production, new industries and old, corporate giants and upstart privateers, *and* the largely disorganized mass of the population and electorate that finds itself more and more removed from any influence over the political process.

The crises facing capitalism today, however, go beyond even this limiting economic context. There is the now unavoidable climate crisis that is the result of capitalism's relentless exploitation of Earth's resources and reliance on fuels and materials that further damage the environment. On top of this has come a series of epidemics, the latest of which has proved deadly on a massive scale and difficult to confine. The COVID-19 virus spread rapidly across the corridors of travel and trade that capitalism has refined and accelerated in the last few decades far faster than the 1918 influenza pandemic. It was the first "just in time" plague clashing with neoliberalism's costly, understaffed, wholly or partly privatized health systems. These triple crises have, in turn, deepened the ongoing crisis of social reproduction experienced in various ways by the world's growing and still largely impoverished working class.

Because the most active elements in this near zero-sum conflict are sections of capital and their immediate social and political allies, the result is a politically limited polarization among frustrated sections of the population, from the petty bourgeoisie longing for the old white United States to sections of the working class for whom the old palliatives of the New Deal and Great Society are beyond reach. For the vast majority of people in the US, the current political choices are limited to the increasing irrationality of the right embodied in the Republican Party or the cautious centrism of the remnants of American liberalism represented by the Democratic Party. This is the political form of the impasse.

It is, however, not a regime of stability. On the contrary, as the deepening of the multiple crises upends the lives of millions, a president claims the 2020 election was rigged with no evidence, the far right emerges from the shadows in full violent "extra-parliamentary" form, the police flout any level of civilian regulation, the financial markets become more irrational, and slumps become more frequent, the impasse itself becomes a cause of instability, anger, and frustration through the inability of the nation's political leaders to deal with the symptoms, much less their causes.

At the same time, a new socialist movement is on the rise in the United States. The Bernie Sanders presidential campaigns, the election of publicly declared socialists to a variety of offices, the spectacular growth of the Democratic Socialists of America (DSA) to ninety thousand members as 2021 opened, and even a number of polls all point to an embrace of this political idea not seen for generations. The new socialist movement has arisen in the context of an era of multiple systemic crises since 2008, repeated mass demonstrations, an upheaval in women's actions in the Women's March and #MeToo movements, the teachers' upsurge, an uptick of general worker self-activity, new forms of rebellion in the context of the pandemic, and the explosion of the second phase of the Black Lives Matter movement. Yet, the first widely visible public debut of this new socialist sentiment, as a version of socialism per se, has been an electoral one primarily through Bernie Sanders's two runs for the presidential nomination of the Democratic Party that inspired many activists to see electoral action as a viable road to relevance and even socialism.

Given the persistent impasse of American politics, the anticlimactic nature of the Sanders 2020 campaign and its absorption into the Democratic Party's centrist presidential campaign at almost indecent speed and the relative silence of most Democratic "progressives" in the face of an avalanche of Obama and Clinton administration veterans and other centrist administration appointments, however, one might question socialists' continued emphasis on electoral politics altogether. Surely, as much as we were glad to see the back of Trump at least as president, in the face of this electoral move to the middle of the road by what passes as the political alternative, the more palpable resistance in the streets and workplaces demands the active intervention and energy of the United States' new socialist movement. It is mass action that will be the most effective way to push the political agenda away from the center and toward the needs of those at the sharp end of today's multiple crises. This will be a major theme in this book.

Nevertheless, as many socialists are being drawn into mainstream politics whether reluctantly or enthusiastically, a growing number of DSA members have had local and state election victories as well as defeats on the Democratic ballot line, and some opportunities for independent political action are emerging. It remains necessary to debate the very nature of socialist electoral activity for the foreseeable future. Whatever place we give it in relation to the mass movements of the day, electoral action by socialists is now part of the political landscape. The debate as to whether socialist electoral activity should be conducted within the Democratic Party, and if so how, or on an independent class basis is an old one. But like many "old" debates in the socialist movement, in a new context it takes on a new relevance, sometimes with a new twist. And the post-2008 context is, indeed, new.

Jared Abbott and Dustin Guastella (A&G) have presented one of the most sophisticated arguments for why socialists should pursue electoral work along the Democratic Party ballot line.[6] Rejecting a third-party approach as unrealistic under the US "winner-take-all" electoral system, they propose a "a medium-term road to building a party-surrogate and a mass working-class constituency for democratic-socialist politics." This is the new twist on the old argument. At the same time, the authors reject the old social democratic idea of "realigning" or reforming the Democratic Party advocated by Michael Harrington, Bayard Rustin, and others to no effect years ago.

In addition to arguing against a third party, A&G also reject "movementist" (non-electoral) approaches, as well as the "organize first, build political (i.e., electoral) power later" approaches. They even spurn any effort to break with the Democrats. Instead they propose building "a powerful mass organization— what we call a party-surrogate—that is independent of the two major parties and can shield candidates from their outsize influence." I will return to the nature of this surrogate and its claims to shield socialists from the influence of the major parties later, but first we must rehearse yet again the arguments for why we are supposedly compelled by the American two-party system to operate within the framework of the Democratic Party ballot line.

## Districts as Destiny: Duverger's Law

The notion that the United States' two-party system is anchored in the "winner-take-all" or "first-past-the-post" single-member district system of representation is a staple of American mainstream political science found in virtually every textbook on US politics.[7] Ironically, this foundational American notion that "first-past-the-post" single-member districts (henceforth FPTP-SMD) impose a two-party electoral system was most thoroughly researched and formulated by a French Communist academic at the height of the Cold War. In the 1950s Maurice Duverger, an ardent supporter of the Soviet Union, where there were no contested elections to speak of, studied different systems of representation across multiple nations. He discovered a high correlation between systems of representation based on the FPTP-SMD method in which the candidate with the largest vote or plurality was the victor, on the one hand, and two-party systems which discouraged third-party success, on the other. This became "Duverger's Law." Indeed, A&G cite Duverger's classic work.[8]

Under these circumstances third-party candidates create a "spoiler" effect that causes the "greater evil" to win. Since third-party candidates have no chance of winning, in this view, votes for such candidates are "wasted." I'm sure most readers are familiar with this reasoning even if they didn't know about its Communist sponsor. Other academics questioned the inevitability of this "Law" given that it is based only on a statistical correlation and that countries that use this system such as the UK and Canada, unlike the US, have multiparty systems with class-based membership parties, some of which claim to be socialist. Few, however, questioned the influence of this system in discouraging successful third parties.[9]

How then, do we explain the fact that the UK and Canada have long-standing multiparty systems despite using the FPTP-SMD plurality method? Some have argued that this is explained by geographic and or ethnic concentrations, such as the Bloc Québécois in Canada or the Scottish National Party (SNP) in the UK. Class, too, however, plays a role in this. Not only do some of these nations unlike the US have labor-based parties created under FPTP-SMD conditions, but some also have long-standing class-based *third* parties: the labor-backed New Democratic Party (NDP) of Canada, which currently holds office in British Columbia, and the middle-class Liberal Democrats in the UK, for example.

A replacement of a first- or second-rank party by an initially third-ranked party in a specific district, therefore, is possible if the *organized* forces of nationalism, regionalism, socialism, or class consciousness or some combination thereof are strong enough, as they were in the UK in 1906 with the founding of the Labour Party, or more recently in Scotland, where the SNP completely displaced Labour as the dominant party in the last several years. After all, Duverger himself had compared the different ballot systems to "that of a brake or an accelerator." And while the FPTP-SMD plurality system acts as a brake, he wrote:

> The multiplication of parties, which arises as a result of other factors, is facilitated by one type of electoral system and hindered by another. Ballot procedure, however, has no driving power. The most decisive influences in this respect are the aspects of the life of the nation such as ideologies and particularly the socio-economic structure.[10]

I take Duverger's reference to "socio-economic structures" as Aesopian academic language for class structure. Thus, the impact of the FPTP-SMD plurality system is not absolute in its power to prevent third-party formations in countries that employ that system of representation. Both "ideologies" and "socio-economic structure" are sufficient to explain the multiparty systems of Canada and the UK. As Duverger notes, while the FPTP-SMD system "tends to the creation of a two-party system inside the individual constituency; the parties opposed may be different in different parts of the country."[11] Is there then something besides the lack of a mass base built into the US electoral system that has prevented a multiparty choice?

What allegedly clinches the two-party district-as-destiny argument in the US is its presidential system. As A&G argue, the presidential system tends to create parties with broad appeals based on coalitions of voters rather than clear ideological appeals in order to win a national majority. Furthermore, since presidential, congressional, state, and even local elections are often held simultaneously every four years, they argue, down-ballot candidates tend to latch on to the presidential candidate's "coattails" during presidential elections.

As traditionally measured by the number of gains in congressional seats by the victor's party in presidential election years, however, the "coattail" effect has declined over the decades. By this measure JFK, Clinton, both Bushes, Trump, and Biden all had negative "coattails" in their initial election. That is, their party actually lost congressional seats in the year they were first elected—the opposite of a "coattail" effect. In any case, this effect collapses in the midterm elections where the president's party typically loses seats.[12] Although it is true that since the late 1980s voters have increasingly voted straight-party tickets in presidential years, this has also increased in midterm elections, sometimes more so than in presidential years.[13] There is more to this than "coattails."

This trend toward straight-ticket party voting—that is, voting for the candidates of the same party up and down the ballot—is more a function of the increased ideological and partisan polarization discussed below in which voters for presidential candidates *and* those down the ballot for Congress, state offices, etc., for each party have been more polarized mainly due to the Republican's relentless rightward movement. In general, this has led to greater partisanship in voting. As an article in *New York* magazine explained the decline of split-ticket voting generally:

> In reality, serious ticket splitting had been declining for decades. The primary reason has been the ideological sorting-out of the two major parties that accelerated with the civil rights revolution, and culminated with the conquest of the Republican Party by the modern conservative movement while left-of-center voters and candidates increasingly voted for Democrats.[14]

A leading text on congressional elections makes the same point, concluding with academic caution that "citizens sort themselves into the appropriate party (given their ideological leanings and positions on issues) a good deal more consistently now than they did in the 1970s."[15]

A more compelling argument for the influence of the presidential system on elections, the two-party system, and the failure of third parties is made by Chris

Maisano.[16] He argues that the New Deal "nationalized" politics through its broad national programs from the National Labor Relations Act to the Works Progress Administration, and the welfare state generally, etc. This undermined the constitutional federalism in which the states played a major role, such as it was, in economic and social programs. This, in turn, rendered state-level third parties such as Minnesota's Farmer-Labor Party and the Progressive Party of Wisconsin untenable as they could not deliver comparable rewards at state or local levels. States became, among other things, more dependent on federal funds. Historically, this is what happened. Both the Minnesota and Wisconsin third parties became essentially New Deal parties and eventually merged into or were absorbed by the Democratic Party.

What allowed the Democratic Party to do this, however, depended on its ability when in national office to deliver material benefits to its mass constituencies. This it did more or less for almost four decades, from the New Deal through the 1960s. Beginning with the stagflation crisis of the 1970s, however, this material largesse began to evaporate. It was precisely at that point that the Democrats began their relentless trek to the center and beyond. The period of recurrent crises, slumping profit rates, and slower growth introduced by the double-dip recession of 1980–82 meant that the party of the New Deal and Great Society was no longer able or willing to play that role. It is this inability on the part of the Democrats to deliver material benefits beyond existing entitlements to working- and middle-class people that has allowed the Republicans to define the partisan polarization largely around so-called cultural or moral issues. One consequence has been the fragmentation of the old New Deal coalition. As a result of these changes in the underlying conditions now almost four decades old—as long as the New Deal/Great Society era itself—the Democrats have been the party of centrist neoliberalism offering less and less to the middle and working classes or to the nation's cities. The absolute "nationalization" of politics has lost most of its force.

It has been the Republicans who took advantage of this relative decline in the material rewards from the federal government to revive a version of federalism in order to overcome their status as the minority party in terms of voter identity, by building strong state-level organizations that helped them hold the Senate for some time and win the Electoral College even with a minority of presidential votes nationally. It is hard to see how they could have done this if "nationalization" had maintained its alleged force. Abandoning traditional Republican fiscal conservatism, they have used this focus on state politics to reward their business and petit bourgeois base via "cost-free" tax breaks, regulatory leniency, and "right-to-work" and other anti-labor laws, supplemented by the culture wars. To hold their positions they have gerrymandered state and congressional districts, disenfranchised poorer voters, created state-level policy think tanks, and built solid organizations in the suburbs, exurbs, and rural areas that regularly win them more state legislative seats than the Democrats. Since the 1960s, furthermore, state parties have become professionalized and well-funded and party caucuses in state legislatures more disciplined.[17]

As a consequence, despite strong straight-ticket voting, there is a disconnect between presidential victories and advances by the candidates' party. Presidents frequently lose congressional support and seats in the midterm elections following their initial election. In 2018 when the Democrats took the House back, there was no presidential candidate. "Coattails" and "nationalization" both failed again in 2020 as the Democrats suffered severe setbacks in House and state-level elections rather than riding the "blue wave" many expected.[18] This is not to say that the popularity or performance of a president doesn't have any influence on how people vote—Trump showed that—but rather that this can be negative as well as positive and is not absolute. In any case, it doesn't have the impact it was once thought to possess. Straight-ticket voting, again, is above all a result of the polarization of politics and increased partisanship between the two major parties discussed below. It is an unusual polarization in that it is one between the right and the center in which an organized left plays no independent role. The American two-party duopoly itself and its apparent stability requires a deeper investigation.

## The US Electoral System Reconsidered: Class Conflict Matters

The explanation of the apparent solidity of the contemporary two-party system in the US lies beyond the static fact of the FPTP-SMD system of representation (the FPTP-SMD as "brake"). This system of representation is, in effect, no more than the passive stage on which the historic drama of class formation and conflict that shaped and reshaped the practice of elections and the uniquely elite parties that would dominate them unfolded in the decades that followed the Civil War. This alternative explanation is rooted first in the relative institutional strength of American capital and its active class in relation to the nineteenth-century American state in comparison to that in other countries beginning in the post–Civil War period. This was the era of the relative decline of the major older capitalist/colonial powers—above all Britain, until then the world's dominant economic power—and the rise of the US as a world economic and imperial power.[19] The rise of the US was characterized by the enormous growth of American capital's wealth, corporate organizational power, national impact, imperial expansion, cultural influence, and ability to intervene politically with few obstacles—including that of a pre-existing, expensive, tax-demanding, bureaucratic state.

Historian Nelson Lichtenstein points to the unique power of American capital in relation to the state that is relevant here:

> In sharp contrast to their counterparts in Britain or Germany, American businessmen had presided over economic institutions that were of both continental scope and vast revenue long before the rise of a powerful state or the emergence of overt class politics.[20]

Business historian Alfred D. Chandler makes a related point in contrast to European capitalism in terms of the growth, training, and influence of administrative and managerial personnel in which he states, "In the United States, the railroad, not government or the military, provided training in modern large-scale administration."[21] He might have added the other giant industrial corporations that emerged toward the end of the nineteenth century. Hence the political and cultural influence of capital not only grew but reached beyond that of the owners through the growing managerial and professional middle class dependent on corporate employment or revenue rather than careers in or largesse from the state, as was often the case in much of Europe, notably in Britain and Germany.

Second in the development of relative class power in the US was the fact that the rising capitalist class faced a working class in formation that was divided by ethnicity and race, largely new to the country, and on the move across the continent. These dimensions of uneven working-class formation limited this new class's ability to organize and intervene independently in elections despite a number of attempts.[22] As a result of this unique balance of power, the rising US bourgeoisie had an advantage over both the legislative and governing processes

that made opposition to the influence and priorities of capital and their two major parties extremely difficult.

While both parties had their merchant and banking business elites even before the Civil War, the end of slavery, and hence the end of the slave-owning class
as such, on the one hand, and the rise of industrial capital, on the other, meant
that both parties became increasingly dominated by various factions of the new
manufacturing, mining, transportation, and communications corporate capital
and their financial allies, particularly in the North and West, and commercial
agricultural and "New South" capitalists in the South.[23]

However, this burgeoning industrial and financial capitalist class, along
with a "respectable" middle class dependent on it, became alarmed by the initial
electoral successes of Populism in the 1892 elections,[24] a series of violent mass
strikes in the 1890s, the rise of socialism in the US as well as internationally, and
the massive influx of immigrants from eastern and southern Europe, whom they
saw as a political and cultural threat. As Walter Dean Burnham put it, in the face
of "the threat of mass political movements" and high levels of political participation "the mood of panic among the 'comfortable classes' . . . was so striking a
feature of the political climate in the 1890s."[25]

To deal with these threats, capital used its growing wealth and power to engage more directly and forcefully with politics through both major parties from
the post-Reconstruction period, culminating in the dominance of capital by the
1890s. Already by the 1880s, financial and industrial capitalists played increasing
roles in both parties, while the US Senate became known as "The Millionaires'
Club."[26] As Piven and Cloward argue, after the "critical realignment" election of
1896, which was driven by the Populist rebellion and deep economic slump, and
in which, as a consequence, big corporate money played a major role in the presidential contest for the first time, "businessmen were prompted by economic expansion to try to assert firmer control of government." Reflecting this effort, the
two major parties, dominated by regional and/or national sections of business,
consolidated their positions with the Republicans dominant and Democrats
subdominant in the electoral system of that period.[27]

To institutionalize this two-party consolidation and head off both internal
and external oppositional political challenges, business elites encouraged a series of electoral "reforms" between the 1890s and 1920s that ended the period
of mass (white male and briefly African American male) participation and high

voter turnout that had typified US elections for decades. The old system of voting had few rules governing party organization or mass participation, and major
as well as minor parties depended on a large activist base. Capital and its "Progressive" allies in both parties proposed rules that favored their interests, along
with those of the two parties they increasingly dominated, and reduced activist
and popular participation in party affairs and elections.

The "Progressives" of the pre–World War I era are often seen as the precur-
sors of the New Deal. In some ways, of course, they or some of them were. They
advocated greater political centralism through the national state, an income tax,
regulation of corporations or "trust busting," women's suffrage, child labor protec-
tions, etc. The Democrats' unsuccessful attempt to court the labor vote in 1908 was
thoroughly top-down and limited to the white skilled workers of the AFL. They
had more success by going around the AFL in 1916, somewhat foreshadowing the
New Deal coalition, but this didn't hold up into the early 1920s.[28] When it came to
politics in general, most Progressives were elitists dedicated to what they saw as efficiency, individualism, American values, the exclusion of immigrant working-class
voters, and racism, which as Burnham argues was at "the height of acceptability
among 'scientific' academic elites, political and business leaders, and the white An-
glo-Saxon component of the mass electorate in this period between the depres-
sions of the 1890s and the 1930s."[29] On the basis of these views, the Progressives
proposed a series of electoral reforms that altered the political system.

Though often presented, sometimes sincerely no doubt, as measures to
reduce corruption, which was indeed widespread, the major target of these reforms was the reduction in voter turnout of various rural and urban, mostly immigrant working-class constituencies which were seen as the source of corruption. "Overt class politics," as Lichtenstein put it, as well as racist politics were
peddled as electoral reforms in the name of "good government." The "legal"
disenfranchisement of African Americans and many poor whites in the South
carried out by Southern reactionaries *and* Southern Progressives between 1890
and 1904 is the best known and most blatant of these, but personal voter registration and lengthened residency requirements introduced by Northern and
Western Progressives in that era diminished working-class and immigrant voter
participation throughout the country.[30]

As Martin Shefter argues, "The central thrust of Progressivism was an attack
on the political party which since the Jacksonian period had been the central

institution of American government—and an effort to create an executive estab-lishment to supplant the party in this pivotal position in the American political system." For all their obvious limitations, the "Jacksonians extended the fran-chise; the Progressives contracted it through registration, literacy, and citizen-ship requirements."[31] Historian Samuel P. Hays put it bluntly when he wrote, "Industrial leaders pioneered in the struggle of economic groups to emancipate themselves from partisanship." For them "political reform was an instrument of political warfare," and to a large extent it was the Progressives who waged the political battles.[32]

The majority of Progressives, who were drawn mainly from Northern up-per-middle-class "old stock (settler-colonial) 'natives,'" it should be noted, did nothing to redress the racist limits of the white male franchise of the Jacksonians or of the two major parties that buried Reconstruction in the notorious "com-promise of 1876." Indeed, in Virginia, at least, they helped to implement African American disenfranchisement in the 1890s and early 1900s. As C. Vann Wood-ward put it in his monumental work on the New South, Progressivism in the South was "For Whites Only."[33] As president, "Progressive" Democrat Woodrow Wilson enabled the segregation of several federal agencies including the Post Of-fice.[34] The main targets of disenfranchisement for Northern Progressives, howev-er, were the immigrant masses and the new industrial working class in general.[35]

Between 1896 and 1924, by which time the "reformed" electoral system was largely in place, voter turnout in presidential elections fell from 79 to 49 percent nationally, while only 31 percent of the electorate voted in midterm congressio-nal elections by 1926. Not even the passage of women's suffrage in 1920 stopped this decline. This marked the end of mass working-class and agrarian partisan participation that had characterized pre-1896 elections.[36] This also meant an electorate in which the rising managerial and professional middle class more sus-ceptible to capital's market-driven "common sense" became a disproportionate part of the voting public. An indication of just how enduring this class distortion of the voting public became is the fact that even today, "better-educated, wealth-ier, and older people are clearly overrepresented in the electorate."[37]

There is nothing in the FPTP-SMD system itself that prevents high voter turnout that would increase the proportion of working-class voters. It was the capitalist-backed "reforms" of that period that produced turnout rates well be-low those of other nations with the FPTP-SMD system and below what they had been in the US. In the UK and Canada voter turnout in national elections averaged around the mid-70 percent range from the early 1920s to the late 1990s, compared to about 60 percent in the US. Since that time, turnout has fallen in most capitalist democracies but still remains above US presidential election participation, despite a larger US turnout of about 66 percent in 2020.

In liberal democracies, political parties are the main way in which citizens participate directly in politics. The introduction of the direct primary for local, state, and congressional elections in most states between 1903 and 1915, however, was specifically "designed to destroy parties as an instrument of governance."[38] (Presidential primaries, which did not become common until the 1970s, were a different matter.) As the late socialist and political scientist Arthur Liplow pointed out, what became most distinctive about the US political system as a result of the primary system was that "only in America is it true that direct membership participation in the parties does not exist except in the sense that individuals register their party preference with an official agency of the state or are habitual voters for one or another party."[39] Duverger noticed this as well. To the question "How do we define a party member?" he replied, "For American parties it even has no meaning."[40] Other countries with the FPTP-SMD system have membership-based parties in which the members select the party's candidates, including the bourgeois parties. Largely because of the primary system for choosing party candidates, *only* the US came to have major parties with no grassroots, branch-level, dues-paying members to influence candidate selection or party program. There was nothing in the FPTP-SMD system to require a party without a grassroots membership. That was accomplished by the direct primary and the actions of party elites.

It is an axiom of socialist politics and analysis that the working class can express its power only through organization, whether unions, community-based groups, workers' councils, or political parties. Liplow argued that direct primaries were established by upper-class reformers precisely to undermine grassroots party organization, such as the activist/member-based Greenback-Labor, Union Labor, Populist or People's, Socialist, and Farmer-Labor parties that stretched from the end of the Civil War through the early twentieth century, and thus to head off what they saw as the danger of a European-style class party system.[41]

Even the two capitalist parties had a mass activist base before the implementation of the electoral reforms. Writing just prior to most of the "Progressive" reforms at the turn of the century, Moisie Ostrogorski estimated that the two major parties and their local organizations and clubs could mobilize as many as 4 million volunteers and activists in presidential elections out of an electorate of about 16 million.[42] This, without the benefit of social media or the internet! Of course, these impressive numbers were split between the two major parties and could at times cancel each other out, while some launched surprisingly success-ful third parties.[43] Nevertheless, not even Obama's short-lived 2008 army of 2 million or so election volunteers could come anywhere near that that proportion of the electorate even if Ostrogorski exaggerated somewhat.[44] In any case, today's "active" party or candidate supporter is more likely to make a small donation via the internet than to knock on doors, while the campaign is typically run by pros, quants, and media buffs along with temporarily mobilized volunteers.[45] Or, as a memo from a coalition of self-styled progressive campaign groups including the Justice Democrats proudly proclaimed, they had *hired* canvassers numbering in the "dozens" in a congressional district.[46]

The congressional, state, and local primaries were also meant to reduce political opposition *inside* the major parties. As mainstream political scientist Walter Dean Burnham put it, the primary was meant to eliminate "party-activist control of nominations and platforms through the convention" at state and local levels. They were, in his words, "in effect devices of political stabilization and control."[47] Through the primary, potential grassroots political activists were dis-placed from internal party participation in candidate nominations and program-matic content to an external, state-run individual act of voting in local, state, and congressional elections.[48]

Here I am speaking of the congressional, state, and local primaries. While the presidential primary was first proposed and used in a few states during the Progressive Era, it did not come into general use until the 1970s, following the post-1968 Democratic Party reforms. Furthermore, it is a very different process in that its object is the selection of convention delegates rather than the can-didates themselves. It is an indirect election of candidates.[49] It also lasts much longer than ordinary congressional, state, or local primaries, and is national in scope and hence highly visible in a way most of those primaries are not. Un-like his high-profile presidential primary runs, Bernie Sanders winning Vermont Democratic primaries for the House and later the Senate, as he has for years, was basically invisible outside of Vermont. Furthermore, while it is unlikely, the final nomination at the Democratic National Convention does not necessarily depend on the primaries. Delegates can switch candidates. Presidential primaries do share one characteristic with the more local primaries in that "primary voters are older, have higher incomes, are more educated, and are more ideological and politically active."[50]

The primary election for congressional, state, and local candidates was presented as a form of direct democracy for the public, when the reality was meant to be the opposite. It is rather the perfect capitalist marketplace of candidates in which passive consumption (voting for your choice) is substituted for participation in the messy reality of party organization, debate, and conflict. The campaign that is necessarily temporary has more the character of advertising than of building permanent class organization even when it raises real issues. Of course, even a primary campaign can be exciting, raise issues, and mobilize some activists—while it lasts. But without its own ongoing party organization, it is nevertheless a plebiscite rather than participatory democracy.

Lipow points out that the primary came in for severe criticism at that time as undermining real democracy. The socialist *Call*, for example, wrote in 1914 that it was a "danger to real democracy" and a "pseudo-democracy that is sweeping the country." A conservative critic noted that the primary tended to displace "discussion of real principles" for "personal contest for power." In 1924, political scientist Henry Jones Ford argued that because the real choices of who can run in primaries were made by small groups with the "time, means, and opportunity" to promote candidates or be candidates themselves, "the practical effect of the primary has been to establish a class rule of a singularly degraded and irresponsible character."[51] Today, in congressional, state, and local primaries these are the national and local party functionaries; the behind-the-scenes business or "interest groups"; and the professional campaigners, fundraisers, etc. While the progressive or socialist primary challengers avoid the functionaries and business interests, the professional campaigners and fundraisers have become standard and money central.

It is odd that those who frequently argue that the Democratic Party is "permeable" are really referring to primaries where successful challenges of incumbents are rare (see below) and which are actually less democratic than even money-corrupted general elections. They are based not on active grassroots participation in a party or even in the election beyond casting a vote or temporarily volunteering or working for a campaign, but on exclusion from internal party affairs and low voter turnout of less than half that in midterm general elections. The voter turnout for the 2018 midterm primary elections, while up from the 2014 midterm, saw just under 20 percent of eligible voters cast a ballot.[52] Thus, as originally intended, in recent years a greater proportion of those who vote in primaries tend to be "older, wealthier, better educated," etc., than even those who vote in midterm congressional general elections.[53]

If anything, this class imbalance has gotten worse even when voter turnout increases somewhat. As Matt Karp points out in his *Jacobin* analysis of the Sanders primary campaigns, in 2020 "wherever Democratic turnout climbed from 2016, it climbed highest in the wealthiest and whitest suburbs." And while the wealthy Democratic vote rose everywhere, "the richer and more conservative the suburb, the more dramatic the increases."[54] Primaries were designed to reduce working-class participation, individualize and fragment the voters, and increase the influence of the well-to-do. With rare exceptions, they have succeeded.

While these early twentieth-century reforms undermined the urban machines' old clientelist methods of voter mobilization, most machines allied themselves with local business interests and in many cases survived into the 1970s. In fact, contrary to much of the conventional story, the party organizations of the late nineteenth and early twentieth centuries had not been the dominant, centralized, patronage-driven "machines" in most cites as budgets were limited, patronage was still slight, and contending factions inside and outside the major parties prevented absolute dominance. Patronage or the "spoils" of politics, such as they were, was more likely to be at the state or federal level. In the pre-reform era, even Tammany Hall in New York never won more than a slight majority from 1865 through 1884 and less than a majority from 1886 to 1897 in a Manhattan election.[55]

As Martin Shefter pointed out concerning the relationship of corruption in the pre-reform era, "it was the very weakness of New York City's Tammany machine that contributed to the massive corruption of the Tweed Ring."[56] Later, Tammany would attempt to centralize authority and develop the club system. An indication of the relative weakness of the Democratic Party's urban organizations prior to most of the reforms was the fact that in city after city the Democratic vote declined significantly from 1892 through 1904. Ironically, it was only during and after the "Progressive Era" that centralized machines, supported by patronage and backed by factions of local or national capital, came to fully dominate Northern cities.[57]

High levels of voter and campaign participation prior to the Progressive reforms were largely a voluntary phenomenon, with many of those involved participating in party affairs and campaigns through "primary assemblies" of party members and committees at the precinct, ward, and county levels that chose members of higher committees, according to Ostrogorski. To be sure, the committees were often dominated by "cliques" or "rings." Party "caucuses" or "primaries" in the pre-reform era, however, were internal party meetings or assemblies attended by members where candidates were selected albeit usually as the local leaders desired, not state-run public elections.[58] While not always democratic, the scale of participation in the party was comparatively large and in general elections very large. In contrast, the twentieth-century urban machines of the post-reform era depended not on mobilization but on low voter turnout in state-run primaries and general elections, usually based in a limited number of ethnic groups of which the Irish were the largest. As one study put it, "machines have preferred a small and controllable electorate over a large and unpredictable one."[59]

In other words, despite anti-machine rhetoric, these "Progressive" reforms did not kill the political machines. Indeed, the major, almost exclusively white urban machines flourished for decades on the basis of low turnout before demographic changes in urban populations undermined them in the post-WWII era.[60] The removal of popular participation and influence in party organization and activities, on the other hand, along with the reduction in voter turnout particularly in primaries, freed capital to influence elections whether through machines that survived, elite party candidate promotion in the primaries, and/or by just spending more money.

The effort to restrict political participation and undermine party organization continued after the Progressive movement collapsed with US entry into World War I. The introduction of laws limiting ballot access began with the "red scare" and the rise of Farmer-Labor parties that followed World War I, further disadvantaging nascent third parties. This was followed by other reforms in the 1920s such as at-large and nonpartisan municipal elections, again directed at "the erosion of party" encouraging the further individualization of voting.[61] By the 1930s, voter turnout would go up somewhat from its all-time low in the 1920s, but never achieve anything like the pre-1896 levels. As a result of the consolidation of the two major parties during the "Progressive Era" and the patently reactionary 1920s, subsequent party realignments of voters, as in the 1930s, did not change the major parties as they had in the 1850s with the collapse of the Whigs and formation of the Republican Party in the midst of the slavery crisis and an "irrepressible" split in the ruling classes of the day. After 1896, dissatisfied voters attempted to challenge the party establishments through the primaries or simply moved from one major party to the other.

All these reforms, of course, did not reduce the electoral dominance of the two major parties, but helped solidify them as elite organizations with no membership, composed instead of embedded layers of elected officials and party functionaries, while at the same time making third-party challenges more difficult. It was the combination of the decline in voter turnout, the rising importance of externally raised (business) money, the primary system and the high levels of incumbency it encourages, restrictive ballot access laws, and the limiting of party decision making to party functionaries and office holders that consolidated the duopoly of the two capitalist parties. Given their business sponsors, ideological proclivities, and class bias in candidate selection and voter turnout, their continued loyalty to the capitalist system was never in doubt.

The FPTP-SMD plurality system was the static background to these far-reaching post-1896 alterations to the US electoral system introduced by the rising US capitalist class and its upper-middle-class "reform" or "Progressive" allies. It was not the fundamental determinant of which parties would dominate the system, how they accomplished this, their elite nature, or of their stability. In other countries with the FPTP-SMD system such as the UK and Canada, political parties are membership organizations with at least rudimentary, if bureaucratized, internal democratic procedures for electing leaders and formulating programs. The membership rebellion in the British Labour Party that propelled Jeremy Corbyn to its leadership in 2015, if only temporarily, could not happen in the Democratic Party.

The failure of third parties in the US since the introduction of these "reforms" lies above all in two realities. On the one hand, over the decades US capital has been able to recover from recurrent economic crises and maintain its effective management of the economy at least up to 2008, while at the same time, avoiding "irrepressible" splits within the ruling class up until recently. This stabilized the "reformed" electoral system. On the other hand, the relative weakness of the working class into the early twentieth century undermined the various attempts at independent political action. Since the implementation of the reforms of 1896–1924, none of the third-party movements have had a large or solid enough mass social base *and* a leadership layer committed to independent political action to break through these barriers permanently even at the state level.[62]

A major guarantor of this situation has been the majority of the American labor bureaucracy with its pro-capitalist "business unionist" ideology, which when it comes to electoral action has been thoroughly integrated into the Democratic Party's field of control and influence (see below) as a junior partner with (little) voice and no vote. Despite some emerging challenges to this ideology and practice in parts of the labor movement, this remains the primary political orientation of most union leaders—even as the unions shrink and they lose members' votes to the Republicans or the "party of nonvoters."

This is why a rank-and-file orientation to socialist union work is essential in order to break the unions from the conscious or unconscious institutional and ideological commitment to capitalism that underlies the *practice* of class collaboration in various forms, from concessions to labor-management cooperation schemes to dependence on Democratic politicians. Rank-and-file movements fight for the *independence* of the unions from capital and, therefore (by implication if not always formal program), from the union leadership's dependence on the Democratic Party.[63]

To summarize: none of the major features of the US electoral system that have evolved since the late nineteenth century—low voter turnout, the primary system, elite-run parties without members, the huge role of business-generated money in party organization and elections, extremely high levels of incumbency, and barriers to ballot access—is required by the FPTP-SMD system of representation or is for the most part found in other nations with this electoral system. Nor is any the result of the separate method of electing the president. The United States' two-party system is primarily the result of an *uneven political class struggle* fought out originally over a hundred years ago, has continued ever since, and is yet to be reversed by the self-organization and actions of a diverse working class experiencing both restructuring and the increased pressures of capital's multiple crises.[64]

The implication of this view is that the weakening of the two-party system depends in part on the decline of the relative power of US capital and its control over the emergent crises as well as its ability to contain the accelerated and exaggerated political/ideological splits in the ranks of capital and its hangers-on. The difficulties with both are in the process of unfolding before our eyes. A hint at the possible implications of this lies paradoxically in capital's attempt to exclude political and social revolt from the electoral arena, whether from inside or outside the two parties, driven by the competitive escalation of money by both major parties in elections at all levels.

I say "paradoxically" because it is this spiraling use of money and intensified but restricted ideological conflict that has once again changed the way elections are conducted and their outcomes in contradictory ways *and* created more anger and frustration among a potential diverse working-class electorate at a time of rising social discontent, deepening multiple crises, and the first appearance of a still relatively small but visible socialist movement.

## Incumbency, Money, and Two Parties in Separate Districts

The ability of incumbent officeholders of the major parties to stay in office for long periods is a major factor in the stability of the two-party system provided by the money-greased primary election system. There are many traditional advantages to incumbency enabled by the primary election system, but the most obvious change in election conduct in the last half century has been the rise of money as a means of scaring off challengers or defeating those who persist. The rising importance of money in elections at all levels since the 1970s has produced a major change in the manner in which elections are won and political offices held onto that has weakened the positive presidential impact on down-ballot elections by strengthening the power of incumbency. As A&G show, over the last four or five decades money has come to dominate the entire election process.

So powerful has the electoral funding arms race become that progressives who shunned Super Political Action Committees, or Super PACs, as undemocratic tools of the rich not so long ago have turned to them in the 2020 election cycle. The former Sanders chief aid Jeff Weaver, the Justice Democrats, and the Working Families Party (WFP) all set up Super PACs in 2020. Weaver's Super PAC supported Biden's campaign, while the WFP and Justice Democrats used theirs to support Jamaal Bowman's primary victory, and WFP's to back DSAer Rashida Tlaib's successful re-election.[65]

Another funder of "progressive" Democratic Party politics is a relatively un-known 501(c)(4) "dark money" dispenser known as the Sixteen Thirty Fund. This liberal version of the Koch brothers' style dark-money operation, which does not have to disclose its donors' identities, dispensed $143 million in 2018 and $137 million in 2019, over half the latter coming from three anonymous donors. Grants go to Super PACs and social issue NGOs, but funds go through some of these to political campaigns, often for attack ads against opponents. Six-teen Thirty played a role in the 2018 congressional elections through another dark-money group, House Majority Forward, and several 2020 Senate contests among others, according to *Politico*. The bulk of its funds come from a handful of anonymous ultrarich Democratic donors. The biggest single donation in 2018 was $57 million, while that in 2019 was $33 million.[66] The process of the su-per-rich corrupting politics and even social action continues and reaches deeper into "progressive" Democratic territory.

As the financial escalation continues, state parties have upped their fund-ing efforts as well, pouring millions into battleground states. As *Politico* recently reported, "Some of the top givers in the Democratic Party—people known for writing six-or-seven-figure super PAC checks—have turned state parties' donor rolls into who's-who lists of mega-givers from New York to California." State-lev-el groups also received money from the Sixteen Thirty Fund.[67] It is not much of an exaggeration to say that the Democratic Party and its candidates from the left, center, and right are, in effect, attempting to buy votes—indirectly to be sure, but at a much higher price than the old urban machines. The net effect is to increase the stability of the party establishment.

This escalation of funding over the years has tended to reinforce the power of incumbency to the point where 91–98 percent or more of sitting members of the House of Representatives who run for re-election and almost 90 percent of state legislators are re-elected over and over. In the US Senate it is slightly lower at about 84–88 percent. In 2018 it was 91 percent for the House and 84 percent for the Senate, down due mainly to the larger number of Republican retirements from the House creating open-seat contests, and the Democratic defeat of some forty Republican representatives in the general elections.[68] Incumbents, howev-er, lose even less often in primaries.

For socialists and progressives trying to permeate the party in order to re-form it, or break in to break away via the Democratic Party ballot line, the most relevant rate of incumbency is that for primary elections.[69] Since its creation in the Progressive Era, however, the primary has never been a democratic opening for dissidents. Outside of the "Solid South," incumbents held office for long periods and saw defeat in only 3.5 percent of House elections in the Progressive Era itself, after which the rate fell to about 2 percent in the 1920s, then plunged during the New Deal and World War II to nearly 1 percent by the 1950s.[70]

Since World War II, on average only 1.6 percent of congressional incumbents have lost their primaries in each election cycle. Since 2006, it has been just 1.3 percent.[71] So far, outfits like Our Revolution and Justice Democrats have failed to break this primary barrier, and in Democratic primary contests where there is an incumbent, they lose more often than not. Despite some high-profile congressional primary contests only two challenges of House Democratic incumbents were successful in 2018 and only three in 2020—both close to the 1.3 percent average over recent years.[72] As political scientist Robert Boatwright put it, "for all but a very small number of unfortunate incumbents, the threat of primary competition is largely a paper tiger."[73]

Open seat Democratic primaries in which there is no incumbent are far fewer in number: eleven in 2020, eighteen in 2018, and seventeen in 2016.[74] While some see these as more accessible to progressive challengers, they can be even more expensive and more difficult to win. Congressional election experts Gary Jacobson and Jamie Carson argue, "Contenders are much more likely to face difficult primary contests because the opportunity offered to ambitious politicians by an open seat attracts more and better-qualified candidates."[75] In particular, open seat primaries attract more previous officeholders who generally have an advantage in name recognition, party support, and fundraising. In addition, average spending in open seat primaries tends to equal that of incumbents defending their seats and far exceeds that of those challenging incumbents.[76] Furthermore, party elites actively recruit and support candidates for primary elections who they believe can go onto win the general election and who best fit their ideological views.[77] In general, open seat primaries are subject to most of the same forces as primaries with incumbent officeholders discussed below.

For many on the left, the Democratic Party is just a state-sponsored ballot line through which candidates compete and party organizations and operatives play little or no role. Hence the idea that entry via the primary faces fewer barriers than the general election. Until recently, political scientists have tended to reinforce this impression by focusing on general elections in their analysis of the outcomes of congressional elections, concluding that elections had become "candidate-centered" since the era of the machines. Until a decade or so ago, "there was no established literature within political science on congressional primaries," writes political scientist Robert Boatwright.[78] This has obscured the role of party organizations and networks in the low rate at which incumbents are defeated in primary elections and hence the difficulty of reforming or influencing the Democratic Party via primary challenges.

More recent research, however, has shown that money is more important and party-generated money and resources are central to primary elections. Both incumbents and challengers have spent more on primaries over the decades, but for incumbents that has increased much faster. The average campaign funds raised by House primary challengers rose from $96,476 in 1980 to $417,796 in 2020, or by 3.3 times. That raised by incumbents, however, soared from about $125,000 in 1980 to $2,725,130 in 2020—by over twenty-one times.[79] In other words, incumbents now spend 6.5 times as much as challengers. Much of this increased money has come from the networks of party insiders and wealthy donors that contribute to both favored candidates and the party's congressional ("Hill") committees, which in turn coordinate campaign funding and resources that have played a significant role in primary election outcomes. As Hans Hassell has shown, "party elites routinely take cues from the Hill Committees." In reality, elections have long been "party-centered."[80]

The major measure of the importance of money in the primary is in early contributions and election expenditures. This holds true despite the different types of primaries (closed, open, semi-open, "top-two"). Put simply, candidates who can raise the most money in the early phase of the election cycle are most likely to win both the primary and the general election—and these are overwhelmingly incumbents. While there may be a number of reasons a candidate wins, by one estimate those who spend the most in a contested House primary will win 79 percent of the time.[81]

To get an idea of the significance of early money, Table I uses Federal Election Commission data to show the growth in and the increased proportion of early money, defined as funds spent by March 31 in the election year. Although the bulk of House primaries go on through August, I have chosen March 31 as the cutoff to maximize the amounts spent solely on primaries (including those later in the schedule) rather than on the general election. If the cutoff is extended to June, the proportion of early spending is much larger, but the proportion going toward the general election will also be greater. Although the importance of early fundraising in primaries is not new, it has nonetheless grown in the recent years.

*Table I: Early Democratic House Election Spending Growth (+) and as % of Total*

| Year | Total (+) | To March 31 (+) | % |
|------|-----------|-----------------|---|
| 2020 | $937,161,275 (+137%) | $283,743,070 (+201%) | 30.3% |
| 2018 | $983,490,936 | $273,141,346 | 27.7% |
| 2016 | $425,084,545 | $124,307,218 | 29.2% |
| 2014 | $422,493,377 | $129,284,520 | 30.6% |
| 2012 | $479,063,510 | $131,832,231 | 27.5% |
| 2010 | $534,651,499 | $145,919,190 | 27.3% |
| 2008 | $495,489,097 | $147,612,383 | 29.8% |
| 2006 | $394,974,819 | $94,213,761 | 24.0% |

Source: Federal Election Commission, House and Senate Financial Activity, Table 1, 2006–2020.

Mainstream incumbents have an easier time raising money at national and even state levels because they can turn to the national and state party committees as well as the party's wealthy and business donors' PACs and Super PACs. This has added to the old incumbency advantages of name recognition, legislative impact, and "bringing home the bacon" to their districts.[82] Thus, with rare exceptions, politicians of both parties hold office for years and decades no matter who is running for president or who sits in the White House or how worthy the challenger. What has often been overlooked in the origin of all this money, however, is the role of the national and/or state Democratic Party as a coordinator of resource allocation. Here "the party" is understood as the network of party officials, officeholders, major donors, and political operatives who are coordinated by one or more of the party's formal committees.

Although the dynamics for Senate and even state legislative elections are similar, in the interest of space and emphasis on the national offices that socialists are more likely to run for, this analysis will focus on primaries and party committees in elections to the House of Representatives. In the case of House elections, it is mainly the Democratic Congressional Campaign Committee (DCCC, pronounced "D Triple C") that plays this role. Although DCCC funds go exclusively to incumbents, party committees seldom publicly endorse primary candidates and most of this coordination is done behind the scenes. The DCCC raises and organizes money via individual and bundled wealthy donor support. It does not run campaigns itself. Rather, the bulk of direct party committee expenditures go to hiring consultants and vendors that provide campaign professionals and staff, computer and other services, and media connections within the party network that are essential to winning campaigns as well as acting as coordinators in the allocation of these party-connected resources.[83] The consultants hired by the DCCC are often run by former DCCC staffers and work in the private corporate sector. A 2021 investigation of DCCC practices in hiring campaign consultants by *The Intercept* found "a structure in which major Democratic Party firms spend part of their time working on behalf of candidates and the party, and the rest of their time working for corporate clients. Firms and operatives who reject that approach continue to be shut out, as the party's position with working-class voters of all races continues to weaken."[84] It is these class-biased, party-connected, consultant-provided resources that are a key element in winning a primary these days.

*Table II: DCCC $ Disbursements as % of Democratic House Elections Total Spending*

| Year | Total | DCCC | % |
|------|-------|------|---|
| 2020 | $937,161,275 | $330,434,544 | 35.3% |
| 2018 | $983,490,936 | $297,489,175 | 30.3% |
| 2016 | $425,084,545 | $216,358,584 | 50.9% |
| 2014 | $422,493,377 | $296,791,993 | 70.2% |
| 2012 | $479,063,510 | $183,160,443 | 38.2% |
| 2010 | $534,651,499 | $163,582,280 | 30.6% |
| 2008 | $495,489,097 | $176,523,631 | 35.6% |
| 2006 | $394,974,819 | $140,806,970 | 35.7% |

Source: Federal Election Commission, House and Senate Financial Activity, Table 1, 2008–2020; Federal Election Commission, Democratic Party Committee's Financial Activity, Table 2a, 2006–2020.

Table II shows that DCCC spending in House elections has grown apace with and remains a significant and sometimes dominant proportion of total spending. While this is a strong indicator of the importance of coordinated party funding, it is actually only part of the funds that the party makes available to favored candidates. A large though unfortunately not measurable additional amount comes from the party's network of wealthy funders. This occurs both from "cues" sent by party leaders and from the "bundling" of donations coordinated by the DCCC or other party centers.[85] Early party support in particular is key to keeping favored candidates in races where several candidates compete, including open seat contests, as well as in securing an eventual victory. Table III indicates the importance of DCCC money in the primary as a significant proportion of early contributions and disbursements. Along with professional assistance and media connections, it is clear that the Democratic Party's formal organization and elite networks play a major role in candidate selection through the primary system.

*Table III: Early DCCC Disbursements as % of Total in Election Year*

| Year | December 31 | March 31 | % |
|---|---|---|---|
| 2020 | $330,434,544 | $119,292,885 | 36.1% |
| 2018 | $297,489,175 | $115,983,539 | 39.0% |
| 2016 | $216,358,584 | $66,762,178 | 30.8% |
| 2014 | $296,791,993 | $75,310,227 | 25.4% |
| 2012 | $183,160,443 | $74,874,972 | 40.9% |
| 2010 | $163,582,280 | $60,428,708 | 36.9% |
| 2008 | $176,523,631 | $55,222,713 | 31.3% |
| 2006 | $140,806,970 | $46,384,764 | 32.9% |

Source: Federal Election Commission, Democratic Party Committee's Federal Financial Activity, Table 2a, 2006–2020.

The distribution of all this money and other resources, however, is not spread equally across primaries. Because of the high rate of secure incumbency and the large proportion of "safe" Democratic districts, much of the party's efforts at coordinating funds and resources have gone to competitive races—that is, those in which the margin of victory or defeat is relatively small.[86] Nothing fits this definition better than the suburban districts that have become the major targets of party strategy to expand its presidential and congressional electorate discussed below. Nevertheless, since a few incumbents have been caught off guard and lost to left or progressive challengers in the last couple of elections, it is to be expected that the DCCC and other parts of the Democratic Party's elite networks will shift resources to prevent future repetitions.

As Hassell notes, "Party leaders are not shy about funneling staff or supporters or donors to particular candidates." Summarizing the political leanings of party elites in primary elections he writes, "In general, parties support more moderate primary election candidates, although the strongest moderating force is the party's defense of its own more moderate incumbents."[87] Among the most important means of support to House incumbents are expenditures specifical- ly for the coordination of Democratic Party–connected campaign resources and activities. The targeting of these resources is in no way politically neutral in terms of internal Democratic Party factions and caucuses. For example, of the thirty-seven House Democrats who received substantial coordination funds from the DCCC in the 2020 election cycle, twenty were members of the centrist New Democrat Coalition, five of the conservative Blue Dog Coalition, while only two were members of the Congressional Progressive Caucus and one of those was also a centrist New Democrat—an indication of the political "bal- ance" pursued by the DCCC. Not surprisingly, the last two chairs of the DCCC, Sean Patrick Maloney (2021–22) and Cheri Bustos (2019–20), are members of the New Democrat Coalition.[88]

Far from being a democratic opening or simply an accessible "ballot line," the congressional primary has increasingly become a cesspool of financial cor- ruption and the party elite's active favoritism. Insofar as left-leaning candidates attempt to imitate party elites by raising huge amounts of money, by whatever means, and relying on campaign professionals and digitally driven campaign techniques such as those offered by the Justice Democrats, the new socialist movement faces the problem of its own adaption to undemocratic practices that are the opposite of mass grassroots organization. Taken together with the older forms of incumbent advantage, it should be clear that the congressional primary is by no means a likely or principled path to political office or power for those seeking radical social change.

On the other side of the coin is the impact of congressional redistricting largely initiated by Republican state administrations in the last two decades, which has meant that a declining number of congressional and state legisla- tive districts are competitive. That is, many congressional districts are in effect "one-party states." In about a hundred congressional districts, Democrats now win by about 67 percent of the vote. In thirty-nine Democratic-dominated con- gressional districts in 2020, there was no Republican candidate at all.[89] More generally, urban districts tend to vote heavily Democratic, and over half of all congressional districts are at least 85 percent urban, though this tendency can include suburban areas. In the 2018 midterm general elections, urban voters favored Democrats by 73 to 25 percent on average, according to a Pew Research Center poll based on actual voters. In urban areas even whites voted 64 percent Democratic.[90] Hence there is virtually no Republican opposition and no "spoiler" effect.

This affects not only congressional districts, but state legislative and city council seats as well, where in most urban-based districts at all levels a Republican presence is marginal or, as Matt Karp put it in *Jacobin*, in "deep-blue areas where Republicans are banished from politics altogether."[91] Judging by the 2016 presidential votes, in Chicago about 11 percent of the electorate is Republican, while in Los Angeles it is 16 percent.[92] In over half of New York's city council and state assembly districts Democrats win by 80–90 percent of the vote—many more by 70 percent or so—and sometimes don't even face a Republican challenger.[93] On average almost 40 percent of all elections for state legislatures go uncontested.[94]

It is this result of redistricting, money, and polarization that has increased the power of incumbency, making primary challenges harder, on the one hand, while paradoxically eliminating the "spoiler" effect in many districts, opening the door to experiments in independent political action, on the other. This represents a major change in the US electoral system—a switch in which the general election has become relatively more open to an independent or third-party challenge, on the one hand, while the primary has become more costly, more subject to intervention by the party elite or DCCC, and more difficult for outsider candidates to contest, on the other. Furthermore, these Democratic districts are virtually all urban, including some dense inner-ring suburbs which tend to be working class, Black, and Latinx, while predominantly Republican districts tend to be rural, exurban or outer suburban, white, and middle to upper class. Many predominately white middle-class suburban districts are among the remaining swing districts in the country. Inner-ring suburbs that have become predominately Black, like Ferguson, Missouri, or Latinx, like parts of Suffolk County, Long Island, of course already vote heavily Democratic. It is the prosperous, mainly white, often older suburbs that have tended to vote Republican that have become the main targets of Democratic electoral strategy.

In other words, there is not only a political polarization of election districts, but a geographic, contradictory class, and often racial one as well. That is why for years now the Democrats' strategy for winning presidential, state, and congressional elections has been to take its urban districts for granted ("They have no place to go") and focus on winning suburban middle-class and wealthy moderates as a means of increasing their national and statewide votes and representation. From a strictly electoral point of view, it is a rational strategy and worked well in 2018. This was so successful that the Democrats came to represent all ten of the nation's wealthiest congressional districts and forty-one of the top fifty, thirty-nine of which they maintained in the 2020 elections, while losing seats in less prosperous districts.[95]

The class contradiction flows from the fact that the Democrats now do better among the well-off than the Republicans. According to the Pew Research Center poll, in the 2018 midterm general election the Democrats outran Republicans among suburban voters 52 to 45 percent, compared to 45 to 47 percent in favor of Trump in 2016. At the same time, voters with family incomes of $150,000 *or more* voted Democratic by 59 to 39 percent in 2018, up from a result of 51 to 44 percent in 2016. (Comparable figures for 2020 are not available.) This latter upper-income group increased from 7 percent of the electorate in 2016 to 12 percent in 2018. In contrast, those making under $30,000 who voted heavily Democratic fell from 28 percent of voters in 2016 to 17 percent in 2018 and 15 percent in 2020. Similarly, those earning $50,000 or less who also favored Democrats fell from 48 percent of voters in 2016 to 35 percent in 2020.[96] Not surprisingly, the suburban strategy has been a major force in keeping the Democrats on the centrist track they have followed for decades. Obviously, the growing weight of well-to-do voters in wealthy districts electing more centrist politicians has shifted the political/ideological balance in Congress and state legislatures, making the possibility of socialists functioning in this party even more difficult than in earlier eras. We will look at this "realignment" in more detail in chapter 3 when discussing the 2020 elections.

## Ideology Matters: Right v. Center

The other major change in US politics is ideological. As political institutions go, the Democratic Party, like its Republican rival, is by every measure a capitalist political organization financially dominated by major sectors of capital, run by professional politicians and operatives mostly drawn from the professional upper and upper-middle reaches of society whose political careers were heavily funded by business and the rich, and ideologically committed to capitalism. It is by any reasonable definition a capitalist party.

A major transformation in global capitalism, however, has pushed both capitalist parties rightward as the post–World War II era of capitalist growth and relative prosperity in the developed nations gave way to one of recurrent deep crises, weak recoveries, the rise of global competition, and massive rises in economic inequality. Overall, declining rates of profit and slower growth have meant the fight over the division of the surplus between factions of capital both domestic and international has intensified, with politics taking on a more open ideological character than has been traditional in US party competition.[97] Around the world political parties attempted to adjust to the new situation within the framework of capitalism as conservatives moved further to the right and centrist and center-left parties followed suit. In various degrees and at different speeds, traditional parties of the left and center-left adopted what became known as neoliberalism in the vain hope of stabilizing the system once again. Intra-capital competition, however, has rendered this impossible and political impasse has become the norm. The United States' political parties, far from being an exception, were leaders of the pack.[98]

Despite the alleged pressures of the FPTP-SMD system, therefore, the Republican Party ceased to be a broad political coalition with a moderate center and even a liberal wing and became a far more disciplined right-wing force. This process goes back to the 1964 Goldwater campaign, accelerated during the Reagan years as the period of crisis took hold, gained ground as the South went Republican, and has solidified ever since, pushed by the "Tea Party" up to the far-right party of Trump.[99] This is primarily the result of sections of capital, small business, and the professional middle classes' fear and sense of declining economic conditions and the loss of a privileged (white) place in American society and the world. It is this trend that has encouraged greater straight party ticket votes in recent years for both parties. But the polarization that has taken form is not one of right versus left in any meaningful sense, but of right versus center, what political scientists call an "asymmetric polarization."[100]

Politically, in the face of the Republicans' move to the right, the Democratic Party as a whole, confined by its (assumed, but often unspoken) commitment to capitalism and further limited by systemic crises, has attempted since the 1970s to defend itself by moving further toward the center or beyond. The theory was that in the new situation to capture the votes of middle-class moderates needed for a national majority, the party had to abandon "tax and spend" liberalism for the political center and austerity. The dividing line between the old liberalism and the Democrats' trend toward neoliberalism was in the mid-1970s with the recession of 1974–75, the crisis of "stagflation" that followed, the "business mobilization" led by the Business Roundtable, the election of the first wave of middle-class suburban congressional Democrats in the "Class of '74," efforts to change the party rules, new rules on campaign finance that allowed businesses to form Political Action Committees, and the nomination of Jimmy Carter as the Democrats' standard-bearer in 1976.[101] All of the party's presidential candidates since the mid-1970s have been ardent centrists and neoliberals.

Legislatively the party not only abandoned New Deal or Great Society–type programs and dropped labor law reform, but actually turned on its core urban base by eliminating virtually all federal urban grants and programs as well as welfare ("as we knew it"). This was a process completed under Clinton with Democratic congressional support and in no way reversed by Obama.[102] The same timetable and Democratic personnel, it should be noted, were present with the 1994 Crime Act that encouraged mass incarceration and the militarization of the police through federal grants of military gear.[103]

Judging by the relative gains of the House Democrats' internal "ideological" caucuses, this centrist direction continued into the 116th Congress elected in 2018, despite the election of two DSAers. While the liberal Congressional Progressive Caucus (CPC)—only 9 of whose "progressive" members endorsed Sanders in 2020, compared to 32 for Biden *before* Bernie withdrew—grew by 24 percent from 78 to 97 members in the House (plus Bernie alone in the Senate), the militantly centrist New Democrat Coalition shot up from 59 members to 103 or by 75 percent, with the conservative Blue Dog Democrats making a comeback from 15 to 27 members or by 80 percent.[104] Furthermore, the "progressivism" of the Progressive Caucus has long been a political joke as anyone, including members of the New Democrat Coalition, can and do join it. In the face of the increase in centrist and conservative organization in the House and the election of Joe Biden, the CPC has recently discussed actually requiring members to adhere to a program and attend some meetings of the caucus.[105] As we will see, however, the 2020 election only reinforced the centrism of the Democrats up and down the ballot.

To be sure, Biden and other party leaders have had to respond to the reality of the Sanders vote and the movements around climate change, #MeToo, and Black Lives Matter. Nevertheless, despite the flirtation with some more progressive policy ideas and a climate change plan that, while substantial, falls far short of the Green New Deal, the draft party platform includes no job guarantees or attacks on the fossil fuel industries, no defunding or even budget reductions for police or the military, no opposition to Israel's occupations on the West Bank, and limits health care reform to fiddling with Obamacare and lowering the Medicare age to sixty. Indeed, the new party platform as it emerged in late July 2020 was by most accounts solidly centrist, particularly when measured against today's multiple crises. There was opposition to the platform to be sure, reflecting Bernie's strength among the delegates. Nevertheless, the 4,700 elected "convention" delegates, the party's most active supporters, passed it by three and a half to one.[106]

While the choice of Kamala Harris for vice president may seem bold, politically she is, as the *New York Times* put it, "a thoroughly establishment-friendly figure" and a centrist like Biden.[107] In other words, for all Bernie has done for Biden and the party, he didn't get any major policy concessions. In terms of electoral strategy, the 2020 Biden campaign is no different in its suburban/centrist voter focus than in previous years. The active support of Bernie, Alexandria Ocasio-Cortez, and other left Democratic officeholders for what became the Biden-Harris ticket and the party slate up and down the ballot line only reinforced this direction since they no longer posed a problem. Reflecting this, Biden's choices of positions in his transition team and cabinet represent not only a rerun of the Obama administration, such as former Obama agriculture secretary and subsequent lobbyist for the dairy industry, Tom Vilsack, for his secretary of agriculture. In addition, there is the return of old Clinton centrists, including those who drafted the 1994 crime bill. Then there is the proposed secretary of defense, General Lloyd Austin III, who sits on the board of directors of defense contractor Raytheon. The major innovation seems to be the absence of Goldman Sachs and the addition of operatives from the alt-finance world, including from the nation's number-one asset management outfit BlackRock.[108]

In organizational terms, this increased polarization and partisanship has forced the Democrats to tighten up their organization from the national committees mentioned above to Congress on down, increasingly professionalizing both national and state parties. At the same time, the legislative party caucuses have become more centralized and disciplined and the leaders more forceful. The rise in disciplined party "unity" votes in Congress that A&G note accelerated precisely during the Reagan administrations and has increased ever since along with the rise in straight-ticket voting. Equally important has been the increase in the percentage of representatives who vote with the party majority in these "unity" votes from 75 percent in the 1970s to around 90 percent in the last decade or so.[109] It is just one of the centralizing oligarchic tendencies in the Democratic Party that A&G describe as making a leftward "realignment" or reform of the party a pretty hopeless endeavor.

The conduct of the elections in the US as well as the two parties that dominate them have changed a great deal since Michael Harrington, Bayard Rustin, and other socialists launched their efforts at realignment and reform of the Democratic Party in the 1960s and 1970s. The parties are more tightly organized, more ideologically distinct, and far more dependent on wealthy donors. The whole electoral process and party organization is now far more dominated by money, professional strategists, digital technology, social media, etc. The political geography has altered dramatically between rural Republicans and urban Democrats with the suburbs a contested terrain. The electoral coalitions have changed as well. The Republicans have picked up a section of working-class votes while losing some in the well-to-do suburbs. The Democrats, on the other hand, have lost some of their working-class base while becoming increasingly dependent on more prosperous voters. The self-styled "Party of the People" has shifted to become increasingly the "Party of the Prosperous."

Since the 1970s the Democrats, sometimes driven by all of these changes, have moved steadily toward the political center and succeeded in repelling or taming various efforts to reform or move the party to the left from the DSOC/DSA-led Democratic Agenda; Jesse Jackson's Rainbow Coalition; the CPC; and, of course, organized labor's persistent but failed fight to win pro-union labor legislation.[110] The Democrats' success in this has stemmed from a combination of resisting external pressure, as well as its ability to absorb and defang internal opposition from the left. We turn now to look at this in more detail.

## Chapter 2

# "Upward" and Rightward

*Although Bernie's campaign engaged in a great deal of on-the-ground organizing, it may have missed the opportunity to engage in more systematic movement-building. Part of this is due to the fact that electoral enterprises necessarily operate according to different sets of principles and imperatives than do movements.*[1]

—Heater Gautney, researcher and organizer for
Bernie Sanders's 2016 presidential campaign

One of the main reasons why individual left-leaning politicians have failed to successfully challenge this centrist direction over the years and why a leftward "realignment" goes nowhere are well described by Abbott & Guastella (A&G). In particular, they argue:

> The decentralized and duopolistic nature of American politics, combined with the oligarchic nature of the party structure and candidates' financial dependence on the superrich and party leadership, compound to effectively induce even the most progressive candidates "upward" and rightward—that is, closer to the party leadership and toward the center politically.[2]

This describes all too well the political career of a self-identified socialist and DSOC/DSA member such as John Conyers of Michigan. Conyers, who was first elected in 1964, was a founding member of the Congressional Progressive Caucus (CPC), and was one of three DSA members to sit in the House in the 1980s and one of four for part of the 1990s and early 2000s.[3] Conyers eventually obtained positions of power in the House by playing by the rules but, caught in the centrist direction of the party as a whole, proved unable to make real changes or get anywhere near winning such long-held personal goals as universal health care. Indeed, Conyers sponsored the original Medicare for All Act in the House in 2003 and ritually reintroduced it in every congressional session until he retired in 2017.[4] When the Democrats had a congressional majority, Medicare for All was sidelined by Obama's Affordable Care Act. This "upward" and rightward process also goes a long way to explain the ineffectiveness of the CPC as a whole.

During her first term and heading into her second, the "upward" and rightward dynamic already appears to be having its impact on Congress's most outspoken socialist, Alexandria Ocasio-Cortez (AOC). After an initial period of open confrontation with party leaders in the House, AOC has replaced some radicals with mainstream advisers on her staff, reduced her support for left primary challengers, supported mainstream Democrats up and down the ballot line, made her peace with Speaker Nancy Pelosi, who she calls the "mama bear of the Democratic Party." She was integrated into the Biden election campaign and supported party candidates up and down the ballot as expected. When it came to the election of House Speaker after the 2020 election, AOC argued that there was no alternative to Pelosi.[5]

The way in which the party leadership in the House Democratic Caucus has dealt with AOC is instructive of how the "upward" and rightward process works. There is both the stick and the carrot. The stick was first applied as the Democratic Caucus leadership sent AOC's Green New Deal House Resolution to no less than eleven committees "for a period to be subsequently determined by the Speaker" (i.e., no deadline) as a sure death sentence. As Oleszek et al. argue, "Multiple referrals augment the power of Speakers by enabling them to delay (by sending a bill to several panels) or expedite (by fixing committee reporting deadlines) action on legislation."[6] This is exactly what Pelosi did. Hence, the Green New Deal sat dead in the water with no action taken by any committee since AOC introduced it in February 2019. Nor has AOC visibly fought to get action on it. At the same time, House Speaker Pelosi got an alternative resolution simply supporting the Paris climate agreement sent to just two committees and passed in a record two months. The Green New Deal resolution expired in January 2021 as the new 117th Congress took office.

In 2019, in the House where representatives are expected to specialize in issues, AOC was assigned to the Financial Services and Oversight Committees instead of Energy or Education and Labor, where she would have been better able to pursue her major policy priorities.[7] In 2020, AOC actively campaigned to get the open seat on the Energy Committee, where she could continue the fight for a more thorough climate policy if not for the Green New Deal in its entirety. She was opposed by fellow New York delegate Representative Kathleen Rice, a leading member of the centrist New Democrat Coalition. This time, Speaker Pelosi threw the decision to the Democratic Caucus Steering and Policy Committee knowing full well this centrist-dominated caucus leadership group would favor Rice. Not surprisingly, this committee rejected AOC 46 to 13.[8]

At the same time, Pelosi and other leaders have not attempted to silence or suppress AOC or other members of "the squad," but to integrate them. This is traditional Democratic "big tent" strategy toward its left and right margins. In a gesture of inclusion, at Sanders's request, AOC was put on Biden's "advisory" task force on climate change for her active support of Biden's campaign and other party candidates. Pelosi even went so far as to endorse the re-election of "squad" members Rashida Tlaib and Ilhan Omar in their contested primaries.[9] As in the case of John Conyers, what is required of AOC and other dissidents is not a surrender of ideas or left identity, but conformity to the norms, protocols, and discipline of the Democratic Caucus which have long been sufficient to incorporate dissidents and preclude radical legislation.

Of course, AOC is a gutsy and savvy activist as her response to a sexist slur from Republican Ted Yoho demonstrated. Her initiative in "inviting" other women representatives to tell their stories of sexual harassment was truly one of a kind. No doubt the party leaders did not appreciate her unconventional action. But they are savvy in their own ways as well. So, thirteen Democratic women and three men, including male House majority leader Stenny Hoyer, spoke up for AOC and against Yoho and sexist abuse, turning this into a partisan confrontation rather than a critique of sexism on both sides of the aisle in Congress. The following morning, Pelosi did the same. As the Associated Press reporter described it, "The lawmakers joining Ocasio-Cortez represented a wide range of the chamber's Democrats, underscoring the party's unity over an issue that is at once core to the party and capable of energizing its voters."[10] In the final analysis, the political framework in which individuals act makes a difference.

## Democrats' Field of Influence and Control

Abbott and Guastella's (A&G's) discussion of the structure of the Democratic Party and the role of money in why it is virtually impossible to reform it is well done and important. I would take it further, however, by pointing to the interlocking hierarchy of the party's organizations that has developed since the 1960s and includes the totality of the party establishment's effective field of internal party influence and control as the political context in which individuals act. The first refers to the professionalization as well as funding of the interlocking structure of the Democratic National Committee (DNC), which integrates state party leaders into the national leadership, and the House, Senate and state legislative campaign committees. This is not just a matter of institutions, but of processes of power and socialization that continue to take shape in response to internal and external challenges and events. One measure of this is the vast growth of money from capital and the wealthy that supports this process.

These official organizations of the party alone raised $770 million in the 2020 election cycle as of August 1. While available figures don't identify all sources, from those for the top industries that do, 54 percent came from corporate capital with other large amounts from well-to-do groups such as lawyers and lobbyists at 7 percent, and an undisclosed amount from wealthy individuals of the sort who write six-figure checks mentioned in chapter 1, compared to 4 percent from labor. This does not include the $2.5 billion raised for Biden, the $632 million for House Democratic campaigns, the $406 million for Senate Democratic campaigns, or the approximately $180 million in "outside" spending for Democrats or against Republicans in this election cycle as of August.[11] While some candidates refuse to take corporate donations, many take large individual donations and nevertheless enter a political milieu in which the organizations they now belong to, the colleagues they must work with, and the leaders who they cannot ignore take both.

The party's field of direct control also includes the party leadership and party caucuses in Congress and state legislatures, discussed below, which control committee assignments, decide who gets to chair these committee and subcommittees, prioritize legislation, impose discipline on floor votes, etc. "The contemporary Congress is largely party-centric," as one study put it, and the party organization is leader-dominated.[12] In other words, in addition to money, it is this extension of elite party organization into the legislative process that is the primary basis of the "upward" and rightward dynamic described by A&G. It is in this context that the process of compromise, negotiations, trade-offs—between members of the same party as well as between parties—inevitably leads to the dilution of most legislation and the absorption and socialization of members into the "rules of the game" if they hope to have any influence.

The total field of control, however, extends even further into the surrounding dense social thicket of interacting *personnel* (not just money) composed of Democratic-friendly lobbyists, donors, corporate executives, executive branch bureaucrats, party notables, and some top union officials. Except for the union officials who are the "poor relatives" in this "family," many of these figures often move from one position to another through a "revolving door" of offices and influence, all relating to the officeholders/politicians who depend on them for legislative as well as electoral help.

The party's tentacles in turn spread deeply into communities, unions, liberal NGOs, and social movements. In this way, the Democratic Party through its operatives, politicians, campaign professionals, the media, sympathetic academics, think tanks, and the labor bureaucracy influences movements, sets the limits to "the art of the possible," defines alternatives, and recruits candidates and voters. As a leading text on congressional process put it in its most innocent form in the limited terms of legislation, "From a party perspective, Democratic and Republican leaders devote considerable attention to the many ways of using the media and the Internet to frame the terms of public debate on substantive and political issues so as to promote the outcomes they want."[13] This is not a conspiracy. It is American "big tent" electoral politics. It's an aspect of what Gramsci called hegemony—American-style.

One of the most famous instances of this process of co-optation was the close relationship between Amalgamated Clothing Workers and Congress of Industrial Organizations leader Sidney Hillman and FDR in the period leading up to and during World War II. In return for "access," Hillman, an erstwhile socialist who was said to have the ear of President Roosevelt, in turn waged war against those union leaders and activists who clung to the CIO's earlier militancy. More than anyone, Hillman solidified the CIO's relationship with the Democratic Party through the formation of the CIO's Political Action Committee (PAC) in 1943. This involved combating the sentiment and movements around various state-level, labor-backed third parties of the time as well as subjecting the industrial unions to war production speed-up and a no-strike pledge. As historian Nelson Lichtenstein writes, "In launching the new Political Action Committee, the CIO leadership specifically rejected any 'ultraliberal political party in the name of the workingman.' Instead, they sought to discipline the unruly rank and file by channeling its energy into a firmly controlled political action group that could function safely within the two-party system."[14] The new PAC was simply the CIO's way of supposedly influencing the Democratic administration in return for mobilizing the union vote for the Democrats. Simultaneously, it was the Democrats' conduit for far more effectively influencing the CIO's behavior.

Two decades later, John F. Kennedy attempted to stop the 1963 March on Washington by courting, flattering, and "consulting" A. Philip Randolph, Martin Luther King Jr., and other civil rights leaders—which fortunately didn't work. A year after that, the effort of the Black-led Mississippi Freedom Democratic Party to replace the all-white Mississippi delegation to the 1964 Democratic Convention was stifled by "sympathetic" liberal Democratic stalwarts at the behest of LBJ—which did work. Then there was Lyndon Johnson's courting Walter Reuther and the leadership of the United Auto Workers by involving them in the design of the famously ineffective War on Poverty—at a time when LBJ was pushing wage restraint. As historian Kevin Boyle summarized the UAW's political experience at that time, "No matter how hard it tried, however, the UAW leadership could not overcome the political and structural forces pulling the Democratic Party away from even piecemeal reform."[15] These, of course, are just some of the most public and visible examples of the intervention of the Democrats in labor and the social movements.

For decades the bulk of the labor bureaucracy has been thoroughly integrated into the Democratic Party field of influence via both formal and informal ties that have long framed and limited how most US union leaders see political possibilities, including the basic practices of bargaining, organizing, and the process of social change itself. It is of a piece with their view of collective bargaining as something that mustn't kill the (capitalist) goose that lays the golden egg. The fact that the Democrats do this in competition with the Republicans who represent the most retrograde sectors of capital provides the cover story and motivation for accepting this hopeless class imbalance. Nevertheless, the limitations imposed by the Democratic apparatus's intervention and field of influence in the labor movement remains a major barrier to winning gains whether in the workplace or politics. It is these limitations, among others, that rank-and-file movements and organizing are meant to overcome and destroy.

A recent display of the results of the Democratic Party's octopus-like reach into the social and labor movements was apparent during Biden's selection of administration personnel and cabinet members in the obsequious response of DC-based liberal advocacy organizations and leaders to Biden's pro-corporate appointments. In their analysis of this process, Sirota and Perez argue that by praising Biden's deeply compromised appointments, these "Beltway" liberals in fields from the environment to labor "are betraying their missions in order to try to gain influence."[16] In fact, of course, this is actually what these liberal groups and leaders have always done—seek "to gain influence." And it is the appearance of influence that Democratic administrations and politicians have offered for decades often in the form of testimony before House or Senate committee hearings, meetings with congressional staffers or even politicians, for a seat on the DNC, the support of well-meaning progressive politicians who are in no position to deliver on the "mission," or even for a few the president's ear. It is a substitute for power, but nonetheless is why, as Sirota and Perez put it, these liberals and progressives "genuflect for access and influence."

This appearance of "access" is why late AFL-CIO president Rich Trumka "lauded" the choice of entitlement-cutter and union-buster Neera Tanden as director of the important Office of Management and Budget, while environmental groups praised the choice of John Kerry as climate czar. This praise for Kerry wasn't limited to the likes of the Sierra Club or the Environmental Defense Fund, the latter of which called Kerry "one of the world's most effective climate champions." Even the "radical" Sunrise Movement's executive director, Varshini Prakash, opined that Kerry was committed to listening to youth and "ensuring we have a seat at the table."[17] It is more likely these liberal advocates will be on the menu than at this mythical "table," as the new administration feeds the appetite of its business sponsors in hopes of reviving the economy. Sirota and Perez hit the nail on the head when they refer to this process as one of "ideological capture."[18] Part of the problem is that for all their "radicalism" or left populism, some groups like the Sunrise Movement are products of this NGO culture. Their proposals are, as Matt T. Huber points out, drawn up far from the daily experience of working-class people. They are, as he puts it, "class focused," but not "class rooted," "for" the working class but not "of" it.[19]

The Democratic Party, of course, is far more than a ballot line. Furthermore, the twenty-first-century Democratic Party is a more professionalized, year-around organization than the party of Roosevelt or even Kennedy. While, as we have seen, it does not have members it does have a well-funded and staffed hierarchical structure that intervenes in candidate selection, funding, and campaigning. In the 2020 election cycle, the DNC, which sits atop the party hierarchy, raised $410.9 million, more than twice its 2000 budget. Of the donations whose sources are specified by OpenSecrets for 2020, over half came directly from business sources with finance, investment, and real estate at $74 million, the largest by far. Lawyers and lobbyists gave $24.6 million, while labor sources contributed a miniscule $3.5 million, or 1 percent of the total.[20] The largest amount specified by OpenSecrets came from "other," which would be mostly from individuals and, as we will see in chapter 3, most of this now comes from wealthy donors. The Democratic Congressional Campaign Committee (DCCC), which helps fund congressional campaigns, received $240.5 million in 2020, compared to $129.8 million in 2000. Of the sources cited for 2020, business contributed $72 million, compared to $3.2 million from labor sources. One difference between 2020 and 2000 for the DCCC was the increase in individual donations.[21] The story is pretty much the same for the Democratic Senatorial Campaign Committee (DSCC), with its total raised increasing to $251.3 million in 2020 from $84.8 million in 2000 with business sources dominating.[22] By 2020, in other words, the Democratic Party's basic visible structure was nearly a billion-dollar business.

As a consequence, those who choose the Democratic ballot line to advance their cause are stepping into a well-established, highly financed network of practical and "ideological capture" and most likely the frustration of their goals. The question arises, then, of just how a party-surrogate or similar organization that sends its members into the Democratic Party's field of control can "shield candidates from their outsize influence" and maintain the independence that A&G claim. The answer to that, it is implied, depends on the organization of a mass social base.

## A Mass Base for a Surrogate?

A&G present a well-developed picture of an electorate that seems susceptible to dissident or left political action. Disaffected working-class people of voting age have ceased to identify strongly with either major party, though most lean toward the Democrats. Many millions simply no longer vote altogether, having seen no improvement in their stagnant or deteriorating living and working conditions. They are, as A&G argue, disproportionately among the poor and racially oppressed. This army of disaffected and nonvoters has been there for a long time. It is largely ignored by most Democratic incumbents because these voters tend to be concentrated in districts where Democrats already have a large majority, and incumbents have no interest in mobilizing the most disaffected constituents.

In addition, A&G list among possible financial and infrastructural supports for a party-surrogate: "organized labor for finances," "well-organized labor and community activists, as well as electorally focused progressive, socialist organizations," the thousands of activists who have been trained in electoral campaigns, and the growing Democratic Socialists of America (DSA) for infrastructural resources.

Third-party advocates have many times pointed to these same disaffected potential voters and sources of support as the basis on which to form a new party.[23] Indeed, with the possible exception of DSA, A&G's list of assets for a party-surrogate are pretty much the same as those named by party realigners and reformers, those proposing an eventual "dirty break," and advocates of independent political action or a third party. There are, after all, only so many working-class, oppressed, and potentially progressive constituencies out there on which to build any sort of movement or strategy for basic social change. Simply identifying them doesn't get a party-surrogate off the ground any more than it does a third party.

A&G's more specific strategy for successfully launching a party-surrogate emphasizes sectional or regional geographic concentration, which is perfectly sensible in terms of resources. Interestingly, however, all the successful examples of regionally based independent working-class electoral efforts they mention are third parties not independent pressure groups: Britain's Labour Party, the Brazilian PT (Workers' Party), and the Canadian New Democratic Party, two of which exist in "first-past-the-post" single-member-district (FPTP-SMD) systems.[24] There is no example of a party-surrogate.

The difficulty of developing a formally independent, ongoing, organized mass base for intervention in the Democratic Party has been demonstrated by the failure of the New Politics movement of the 1960s and '70s,[25] the Democratic Agenda of the 1970s and 1980s, Jesse Jackson's Rainbow Coalition, and Bernie's two campaigns in that regard. Despite the latter two drawing millions of votes and tens of thousands of active supporters or more during the campaigns, neither was able to create an ongoing grassroots organization capable of moving the Democratic Party to the left for more than a moment, stopping the drift to the center once it had started, or shielding activists from the party's "outsized influence."

One of the main problems is that the entry point to the centers of power in this party—the primary election—is itself a well-constructed barrier to outside challenges that discourages mass, ongoing participation, as we saw above in the alternative analysis of the origins of the United States' contemporary two-party system. Seeing the primary ballot line as an easier means to radical electoral success misunderstands its function in the two-party system. Indeed, almost all the recent written arguments for "using" the Democratic ballot line say nothing about the problems and realities of the primary system. The "Progressive" reforms of a hundred years ago were meant to protect the position of the two major parties within the FPTP-SMD system. So far, they have done their job all too well.

## Ballot Line as Border Line

For the average American voter the ballot line *is* simply that—a state-provided lever to be pulled, a hole to be punched, or a box to be checked in favor of your preferred candidate on a single day every couple of years. It is the passive act of an individual regardless of how they are temporarily mobilized or motivated to vote that gains the voter no influence over the victorious candidate much less the party as a whole. Even those active in the election itself have no institutional influence over the candidate once elected. Although an election may reflect mass discontent, as in 1932 or 1936, lacking a democratic membership party, such influence as "the people" have in the outcome of politics—policies, legislation, budgets, wars, etc.—actually comes mainly from organizations removed from the voting process—pressure groups, unions, lobbyists, community organizations, and above all historically in periods of social change, mass social and class-based movements.[26]

For candidates, on the other hand, the ballot is a border. If you win you cross it into the institutional framework and field of control and influence described above with its own institutions, power structure, internal rules, norms of behavior, pressures, rewards and punishments, and with no democratic means for bringing about change. Those who see the ballot line as nothing more than an opportunity to run leftists for office don't grasp its actual place in the process of elite party-based governance that has evolved in the US since the late 1890s. Part of the consequence of this reality beyond the ballot line is what A&G describe as the "upward" and rightward dynamic that absorbs elected progressives into the dominant norms of behavior and views of what is within "the art of the possible" once in office. [27]

In the first instance, the primary is less an opportunity than a process of discouraging or weeding out candidates who lack name recognition, ever-increasing piles of money, party endorsements, the backing of well-known political figures or celebrities, access to mainstream media, etc. That is, it is a process meant by its elite "progressive" founders a hundred years ago to favor the selection of similarly elite or elite-supported candidates over the huddled masses of immigrants, machine politicians, and Populist or Socialist agitators of that era. Today, it is even more of a political filter by virtue of the amount of money needed to get anywhere.

Organizations like Justice Democrats attempt to get around this through crowdfunding, the mobilization of volunteers or *hired* campaign workers, the use of social media, professional campaign strategists and organizers, etc. Sometimes this works, but as we have seen the outcomes of primary elections at almost all down-ballot levels continue to favor party-establishment-backed incumbents by more than 98 percent of the time. In 2020, despite some hype from the left about electoral "earthquakes," only 3 incumbent House Democrats out of 223 incumbent Democrats lost their primaries to progressives or anyone else, once again around the recent average of 1.3 percent.[28]

Even in the case of open-seat primaries where there is no incumbent, as one study of state-level elections put it:

> Primary campaigns are different because, by definition, partisanship plays no role in the race. Therefore, money assumes greater importance, particularly in races without an incumbent. We have found that if one candidate has a very large funding advantage, that candidate usually wins.[29]

Of course, this isn't always the case. AOC was heavily outspent in her 2018 primary and won. While the 2018 primary seemed to defy the general rule, things went back to "normal" in 2020 when AOC, now the incumbent, outspent her primary challenger five-to-one. Altogether, a lot of money was spent in both years and far from being an exercise in mass democracy or working-class rebellion, voter turnout was low as it always is in primaries.[30]

In AOC's 2018 primary, run by the Justice Democrats initially using a volunteer list from Sanders's 2016 campaign, only 29,778 people voted in a mixed-class and mixed-race district with a population of over 700,000 and 214,570 active registered Democrats, a turnout rate of 14 percent of registered Democrats. She won by just over 4,000 votes. Since this was one of those urban districts that are overwhelmingly Democratic, in effect, she won a seat in Congress with a majority of about 4,000 votes, or a total of just under 17,000 votes if you include all those who voted for her in the primary.[31] Taking no chances in her 2020 primary, AOC raised $10.5 million, compared to her primary challenger's $2 million, and handily won by 72.6 percent with just 37,825 people voting out of 225,829 eligible, a turnout of 17 percent up from 2018.[32] Even so, fewer than a fifth of registered Democratic voters bothered to cast a ballot in these primaries, not to mention all those potential Democrats who didn't register in time under New York State's stringent rules, or at all. Or those disaffected eligible citizens who are excluded from the primary by virtue of not identifying as Democrats, or the numerous immigrant residents not eligible under the country's restrictive rules.[33]

Indeed, big-time fundraising has become a feature of AOC's 2020 campaigns. Although few doubted she would win the 2020 general election, as of October 4 she had raised a total of $17.3 million. Most of this was in small donations, over 80 percent of which were from out of state. None of it from business PACs, which play a much smaller role these days. Silicon Valley, however, counted for some big individual donations either from company officers or employees, including Alphabet, Inc. (Google), $71,795; Amazon.com, $42,805; Microsoft Corp., $30,128; Apple Inc., $28,950; and Facebook Inc., $22,733.[34]

The point is not that AOC was doing something any less virtuous than anyone else, but that her campaigns almost inevitably followed the norms of contemporary elections in terms of low turnout; big money; professional consultant–driven campaigning; dependence on a party that has no internal democracy or membership from which to seek support; and a result, win or lose, that leaves behind no independent mass working-class organization. For regular Democrats, whether liberal or moderate, this is not a problem. For democratic socialists it should be. Operations like Justice Democrats are staff-driven organizations of electoral technocrats expert at crowdfunding, social media, digital voter-targeting, and the temporary mobilization of volunteers or hired campaign workers—not the building of permanent grassroots organization. When the exceptional campaign is victorious the candidate's biggest problems begin.

Upon crossing the ballot-line border to Congress or most state legislatures and city councils, the successful *Democratic* candidate becomes a member of the Democratic Party Caucus.[35] The Democratic Caucus along with its leadership and Steering and Policy Committee organizes and guides the legislative activity of its members. The party caucus elects its leaders, who are already people with legislative status, and under the direction of its leaders makes committee assignments, imposes discipline in voting with the help of its "whip" structure, determines the fate of proposed bills and resolutions, and opens or closes doors to money, promotion, and influence. When it is the majority party caucus in the House it also elects the powerful Speaker of the House, who dominates the caucus as Nancy Pelosi does. In extreme cases, it can strip from a member of committee their seniority or leadership.

The caucus operates by consensus in most other matters, a process of compromise that invariably favors the leadership and produces both centrist leaders and centrist policy and legislative positions. Since the 1970s, party leadership in both houses have become more powerful and party operations more centralized.[36] After nearly two years in the House, Alexandria Ocasio-Cortez drew the same conclusion when speaking of the "structural shifts" in leadership power. She named for *The Intercept* 'the structural shifts of power in the House, both in process and rule, to concentrate power in party leadership of both parties, frankly, but in the Democratic Party leadership to such a degree that an individual member has far less power than they did 30, 40, 50 years ago."[37] The same is true in most state legislatures.[38]

In addition to their behavior in the legislature itself, of course, Democratic officeholders and caucus members are expected to contribute to (via the DCCC and DSCC and/or the House and Senate Democratic Super PACs) and support other party candidates up and down the ballot from left to right in the general elections regardless of their own views. In other words, they are expected to increase the power and electoral effectiveness of the Democratic Party.

A&G as well as those calling for a "dirty break," of course, are advocating a membership-based organization that might be able to overcome some of the fundraising problems. But just how successful candidates of a party-surrogate or "dirty break" organization plan to get around the "outsized influence," pressures, and obligations imposed by the party caucus and other aspects of the party's total field of control is by no means clear or even discussed by A&G or various "dirty break" advocates beyond the assumption that an independent organization solves the problem.

## Torn between Two Classes

What this would mean in practice is that party-surrogate or "dirty break" candidates who are elected would become "accountable" to two distinct political organizations representing different and opposing class interests—the party-surrogate that elected them and the Democratic Party organization they are now part of. To put it more bluntly, they would be "accountable" to a relatively small organization that hopes to represent the working class, on the one hand, and a much larger one that is, in the composition of its real "members," the officeholders and functionaries of its various levels, almost entirely upper-middle-class and funded mainly by and accountable to capital and the wealthy. The imbalance is enormous.

The idea that an electorally oriented organization that runs candidates on the Democratic ballot line and thus implants its elected members and, therefore, the organization they represent, in internal Democratic Party affairs is "independent" in any real sense is an illusion. Power does not respect such nice distinctions. As soon as it becomes electorally successful, the party-surrogate or similar organization becomes in effect another faction in the Democratic Party's field of control if not in its official structure. Given the track record of its various left factions in altering the centrist direction of the party—New Politics of the 1970s, Democratic Agenda of the 1970s and 1980s, Rainbow Coalition of the 1980s, Our Revolution, and the long-standing CPC, or for that matter organized labor's various efforts at "independent" Democratic Party pressure groups like CIO-PAC, the AFL-CIO COPE, and innumerable individual union PACs—this is not a promising proposition. While sometimes mentioned, the lack of analysis of these prior efforts at "independent" organization in the Democratic framework in most arguments for "using" the Democratic ballot line is glaring.

Those advocating a "dirty break" differ from the realigners and from A&G in seeking a workers' party—a goal I share. Indeed, I agree with much of what they say about why we need such an independent class-based party and many of their arguments about the capitalist nature of the Democratic Party. In particular, the need for socialist-led mass organization they argue for is crucial to any working-class political perspective.[39] But I find a disconnect between the two arguments when it comes to neutral sounding phases about "using the Democratic Party ballot line" or that socialists shouldn't "always avoid the Democratic Party ballot line," as though this ballot line were simply one of many tools in our political tool box.[40] As they make clear, they are talking about running candidates as Democrats over an extended period, which raises questions that require more than a passing mention or that simply having an "independent" organization like a party-surrogate, as Eric Banc suggests, is supposed to address.[41]

There is also the problem that the nature, timing, or mechanics of the "break" are not really discussed in any of the works I have seen so far. What has been presented by Eric Blanc are arguments by precedent rather than analysis. In particular, he points to the Minnesota Farmer-Labor Party's (MFLP's) brief excursion in major-party primaries in 1920 before founding the MFLP in 1922 and the Labour Representation Committee (LRC), founded in 1900, that formally became the Labour Party in 1906, though ties forged by some of its candidates to the Liberals lasted somewhat longer.[42] The LRC was a delegated body of union and socialist leaders, not a mass organization.

In a deal made between LRC leaders and the Liberal Party, the Liberals agreed to let the LRC run its own candidates in some constituencies, while the Liberals ran in others so as not to divide the anti-Tory vote. The LRC won 5 seats in 1903, at which time there were 670 members of the House of Commons representing seven different parties. The deal brought significant opposition from the ranks of the Independent Labour Party that played a major role in launching the LRC. When it became the Labour Party in 1906, it won 29 seats. It would only grow significantly after it became an independent party distinct from the Liberals. In 1910 Labour elected 42 members of Parliament, which increased to 57 in 1918. By 1922 the Labour Party surpassed the Liberals as the major opposition party, electing 142 members in the House of Commons.[43] The same was true of the Minnesota Farmer-Labor Party (MFLP), which did not do particularly well in the 1920 major-party primaries as the Working People's

Nonpartisan League, but elected two senators and a representative in 1922 and 1923 as the MFLP, eventually electing more representatives and the governor of Minnesota as an independent party until it merged with the Democrats in 1944.

If we are to draw lessons from the British experience of this period, I would draw two that have very little to do with the Lib-Lab phase that Blanc emphasizes. First, Labour did better contesting elections as an independent party from 1906 onward than inside or in alliance with the Liberals as the figures above show. The second is, as George Dangerfield showed in *The Strange Death of Liberal England*, it was mainly the uncontrollable multiple social upsurges of militant women's suffrage, the fight for and resistance to Irish independence, and the rise of union militancy of the pre–World War I period known as The Great Unrest that made the crisis of the Liberal Party unavoidable and opened the door to the Labour Party.[44] Another mass workers' upsurge following the Russian Revolution and World War I swept the industrial world, and in Britain propelled the Labour Party to further electoral victories in the 1922 elections in the wake of a defeated miners' strike in 1921.[45] The same sequence of mass upsurge from 1918 through 1922 and growth was true for the MFLP as well. So why the emphasis on the Lib-Lab and primary election phases rather than the independent self-activity of the working class?

In any case, can anyone imagine the Democratic Party agreeing to separate workers' or labor party candidates to run in any districts the Democrats controlled or thought they could win—or any districts at all? Can anyone even imagine a group of US union leaders asking for such a deal? After all, the US labor leadership has been mired in the Democratic Party's field of control for generations with its own political organizations (PACs, COPE, etc.) and no sign of a break or even an experiment in running independent union candidates is visible in the upper strata of most unions.

The only attempt in the last half century to raise the idea of an independent party in the labor movement was the Labor Party initiated by Tony Mazzocchi of the Oil, Chemical and Atomic Workers in the 1990s. Mazzocchi, however, ran up against the unwillingness of almost any of the union leaders, including most of those whose unions paid their $25,000 Labor Party affiliation fee, to make a break—dirty, clean, partial, or otherwise—with the Democrats despite their frustration with the Clinton administration. Hence, the Labor Party defined itself in oxymoronic manner as a "nonelectoral party" and unfortunately went nowhere.

Even assuming changes in the labor movement in the coming period, which I do, a delegated body of union leaders is not the sort of mass democratic political organization that will be needed to break the grip of the Democratic Party over labor, much less undermine the impasse of US politics. Even Blanc argues that is what is needed. The fight for a political break in the unions will have to come from the ranks as part of both a broader struggle to transform and expand the existing unions and create new ones, and as a major component of the broader social movements of the period. Hopefully, socialists will play a role in that by actually arguing and organizing for a break rather than an indefinite future of more of the same, digging the left deeper into the Democratic Party.

Fundamentally, the case for using the Democratic ballot line for a "dirty break" somewhere down the road rests on the same arguments about the FPTP-SMD plurality as those used for the party-surrogate and realignment. It also shares the assumption that the Democratic ballot line is no more than a passive ballot line. Its advocates call for some sort of "independent" organization to run candidates on the Democratic line that does not sound all that different from the party-surrogate and, therefore, shares its class contradictions. Furthermore, some "dirty breaksters" point to elected socialist Democrats who explicitly reject the idea of a break as somehow aiding their strategy.[46]

In short, their proposed *practice* for the foreseeable future is not noticeably different from that of either reformers or party-surrogate advocates. Insofar as one's practice influences one's politics, this is not a hopeful sign. So, all of what has been argued above about the two-party system and the institutional realities that lie beyond the ballot-line border apply with equal force to those who advocate using the Democratic ballot line in pursuit of a "dirty break."

One of the biggest problems with the "dirty break" perspective as developed so far, however, is that there is nothing in it to break to. If there is not a workers' party in formation, a serious effort in that direction, or at least a substantial number of successful independent candidates to show it is possible to run as an independent and win sometimes, what is there in real life to convince a sufficient number of Democratic voters or officeholders needed to make the break successful to actually take this step? History as well as the reality of the Democratic Party and its field of control tells us that the negative experience of frustration with this party is not sufficient to motivate a break into the unknown.

To a greater extent than those calling for a party-surrogate, some "dirty break" advocates point to the dynamics set in motion by Bernie Sanders's two runs for the presidency in the Democratic primaries as a major cause of the popularity of socialism.[47] This dynamic, it seems, is meant to be the wind behind the sails of those socialists who run on the Democratic ballot line in the future. Possibly it also is this dynamic that is supposed to keep socialists elected as Democrats on track for an independent workers' party later on. There is no doubt that the Sanders campaigns shook things up, mobilized tens (or hundreds?) of thousands of campaign volunteers, highlighted crucial reforms such as the Green New Deal and Medicare for All, encouraged other democratic socialists to run for office and in some cases win, helped make the idea of democratic socialism more legitimate and popular, and contributed to the growth of DSA.

As DSAer Natalia Tylim points out, however, most of these ideas and trends were already in circulation before Bernie announced his candidacy and almost certainly played a role in Sanders's decision to run in 2016 and the campaign's initial dynamism.[48] Aside even from the popularity of his particular policy themes, the approval of socialism sometimes attributed to Bernie was already on the rise well before his campaigns; that is, before most people had even heard of him. Two Gallup polls in 2010 and 2012 showed favorable views of socialism rising from an already historic high of 36 to 39 percent, years before the 2019 poll that put this at 43 percent. In 2010, already 54 percent of young people approved of socialism before it rose to 58 percent in 2019. Self-identified Democrats and those leaning toward the Democrats already favored socialism over capitalism by 53 percent in 2010 and 2012.[49]

Sanders was certainly aware of this shift in public opinion before he ran. Writing in her 2018 account of Bernie's 2016 campaign, Sanders aid Heather Gautney reports that before deciding to run Bernie toured the country and solicited opinions from a wide variety of progressives to see if a Democratic primary run was feasible with his identity and politics. Gautney specifically refers to the earlier polls showing favorable attitudes toward socialism, particularly among a majority of Democratic voters.[50]

The biggest problem for the Bernie-as-cause-or-prophylactic argument is that, as far as presidential politics are concerned, this phase of electoral development is over. As Bernie himself has said, it is "very, very unlikely" he will run again. In any case, it seems clear that after what seemed like a promising start the 2020 campaign saw a decline in momentum in relation to 2016. This time around Bernie took 27 percent of the total primary vote and seven states, compared to 43 percent and twenty-two states in 2016.[51] He understood this, which is why he withdrew. The relative gains of Congress's ideological caucuses described above also reveal that in the 2018 midterm elections the center and right groups did better than the "progressives," even broadly and generously defined. Nor, as we will see in chapter 3, did the outcomes of the 2020 congressional elections point to a major shift to the left due to Bernie's faltering campaign or the election of only a handful of progressives.

The overwhelming electoral dynamic for the foreseeable future for those involved in Democratic Party politics has been to defeat Trump and the Republicans and elect Democrats up and down the ballot no matter who they were in 2020 or will be in 2022 and beyond. If anything, the virtual spectacle of the 2020 Democratic National Convention with its "big tent" of "circus-size proportions," as one *New York Times* commentator put it, with Bernie's blessing and ranging all the way to anti-abortion Republican John Kasich, demonstrated more clearly its centrist direction for the campaign.[52] If there was any doubt, Biden's concluding convention speech was "careful to appeal to voters in the center ground," as *The Hill* reported.[53] On top of that Biden appointed arch neoliberals and Obama leftovers to his economic advisory group and assured his financial backers the reforms he suggested were window dressing.[54] As we will see in chapter 3, his cabinet appointments reflected the same centrist orientation. The party will struggle to hold on to the congressional centrists it gained in 2018 or those it held onto or won in 2020. In summarizing the dilemma of the Democrats in the 117th Congress, Charlie Cook of the *Cook Political Report* appropriately headlined his article "Centrism or Bust in the 117th Congress."[55] This is not a source of opportunity for socialists. In this dynamic, Bernie and the socialist Democrats are, for all practical purposes, captives, albeit restive ones.

Furthermore, Bernie's campaigns, as inspiring as they were, have not left behind the kinds of organizations required to build the working-class movement needed to create momentum and power—even for a rerun. Our Revolution, never a democratic membership organization, has been declared a failure by its own former director and, like Bernie's campaign organization, splintered with many of its leaders and operatives going into the Biden campaign.[56]

Part of the reason for the failure to develop permanent mass organizations lies in the differences in electoral campaigns and the building of mass movements and ongoing organizations. Heather Gautney described this well when she explained why Bernie's 2016 campaign did not build a broader movement:

> Although Bernie's campaign engaged in a great deal of on-the-ground organizing, it may have missed the opportunity to engage in more systematic movement-building. Part of this is due to the fact that electoral enterprises necessarily operate according to different sets of principles and imperatives than do movements. It is the job of political consultants and staffers to concern themselves with optics, staging, and their own "punch lists," rather than constructing lasting democratic organizations and grassroots networks.[57]

The top-down campaigning methods she describes employed by Bernie, including their crowdfunding, volunteers, and mobilizations, are by now the norms for many conventional as well as left Democratic Party campaigns. It seems clear that a working class/socialist politics and political party must be able to build on organized grassroots movements and not simply on a series of temporary mobilizations and inspiring campaigns no matter how good the message or the candidate. It is not enough to attach a more permanent organization of socialists to this type of campaigning; the norms of electoral action themselves need to be challenged. Given the actual outcome of Sanders's two campaigns, one has to ask: if Bernie's huge, high-profile campaigns couldn't produce something like a party-surrogate, how and from what current developments do the advocates of such a mass organization propose to create one?

Finally, given the depth of the multiple crises faced by capitalism, the deep changes likely to be wrought by them in the next few years, and the certainty of mass resistance to their consequences, it is astounding that proponents of remaining in the Democratic Party or "using" its ballot line talk about years of patient work to achieve a social democratic current in the Democratic Party large enough to either influence the party or break from it. There is a linear projection in this view that is out of step with today's unfolding turbulence and even with some of their own analysis. The alternative, to be discussed further in the concluding chapter, is rooted in rising class and social struggle outside of and against a Democratic administration that will once again prove inadequate to the tasks posed by today's multiple crises, on the one hand, and experiments in independent political action in the "one party" urban districts where Duverger's Law has been repealed.

To summarize, the analytical focus of much of left electoral theorizing on the barriers to third-party success inherent in the static FPTP-SMD representation system has blinded many to the more active barriers to *socialist* political success in mainstream party politics wrought through top-down class struggle and imposed by the primary system, the Democratic Party's living internal institutional field of influence and control and its dependence on donations from the rich and super-rich, as well as its increasing active voter base among the well-to-do and wealthy.[58] There is no inevitable triumph for the new US socialist movement through the primary money pit. Far from opening this channel of electoral action, the "victory" of Joe Biden and Kamala Harris illustrates the problems of functioning in the Democratic Party as this party has become ever more dependent on wealthy voters and super-wealthy donors.

CHAPTER 3

# The History and Future of the 2020 Elections

*For those of us who focus on government and economics and so-cial justice, this election is a dismal rubber stamp of the unaccept-able status quo. Black, brown, and white working Americans see their hopes of real reform evaporate for now, even while cheering the victory over Trump.*[1]

—Larry Cohen, chair, Our Revolution, former president, Communications Workers of America

American politics have been at a political impasse for years. This political grid-lock has been characterized by the Republicans' relentless journey to the right, the Democrats' attempt to counter this by moving to the political center, and the "asymmetric polarization" this has produced. Serious reform legislation to the extent of the New Deal or Great Society has proved impossible under these circumstances even as politicians are forced to take on new issues from climate change to police reform. While the Democrats will control a majority in Congress as well as the presidency, the 2020 election in no way changed this fact. Despite the triple crises facing the US and the world, as Mike Davis put it, "the election results are a virtual photocopy of 2016: all the disasters of the last four years appear to have barely moved the needle."[2]

Biden beat Trump, to be sure, though by dangerously narrow margins in the battleground states that won him the Electoral College vote, as well as in the

Georgia elections that won the Democrats the Senate. His popular majority was based in the same two or three solidly blue states that gave Hilary Clinton her popular majority in 2016. Furthermore, his cabinet is composed overwhelmingly of centrist Obama and Clinton veterans and business-linked habitués of the revolving door. Biden's new ethics policy meant to limit the role of lobbyists is full of loopholes and doesn't cover "consultants," hence allowing the appointment of former strategic consultants such as Tony Blinken of WestExec Advisors as secretary of state.[3]

The impasse will remain not only because of Biden's razor-thin margins in those battleground states, Democratic losses in the House, and Republican victories down ballot, but because the Democratic Party is internally stuck in the center where no serious reforms are likely. Furthermore, whatever the turmoil among Republicans, Trumpism, as Samuel Farber has argued and Trump militants demonstrated at the Capitol in January 2021, will not go away.[4] Here I will examine the outcome of the 2020 election from the vantage point of the Democrats changing class base over the last two decades or so. In addition, I will attempt to explain in class terms why the Democrats are stuck in the political center even beyond their basic commitment to capitalism, unable to adequately confront the crises that face them. The roots of this problem lie in part in the changing class structure of the Democratic Party's funding sources *and* its evolving electorate that are major factors in keeping this erstwhile "party of the people" smack dab in the middle. We start with changes in the master's voice: capital itself.

## Billionaires and Bottom-Feeders

The turbulent dynamics that have characterized capitalism for most of its life— its recurring crises, winners and losers, relentless expansion—have changed not only its industrial and financial structures over time, but the very class that bears its name. The neoliberal period has accelerated this process. A perusal of the Fortune 500 list of top companies for the years 2000 and 2020 reveals major changes not only in the rankings of familiar corporate giants of the twentieth century, but the presence of a host of new players. Such current familiar giants as Alphabet (Google), Amazon, and Facebook did not appear on the 2000 list, while Microsoft was number 83 and Apple ranked a mere 285th. By 2020 such older giants as General Motors, General Electric, Ford, etc., had moved down the list to be replaced by significant numbers of newcomers. Just to get an idea of this change, Table IV shows the ranking of the top 10 Fortune 500 companies by profitability.[5]

These shifts were for the most part a product of the neoliberal period that began in the late 1970s with its recurring recessions, leveraged buyouts, huge merger movements, and the rise of new, high-tech outfits and alt–Wall Street bottom-feeders—those who used other people's money to make fortunes through arbitrage and speculation. By the 1990s, under the influence of Harvard management guru Michael Jensen and his colleagues, the behavior of corporate executives switched from being mere administrators to owners via huge stock option compensation packages. This not only made such managers capitalists, at least millionaires, but shifted their focus from long-term profit management to short-term quarterly returns that made them and many shareholders very rich even if it harmed their firm. With stocks themselves the target of activity, the era of leveraged buyouts contributed to shifting ownership.[6] The big shift in the capitalist class itself, however, was in the rise of a new breed of billionaires.

*Table IV: Fortune 500: 10 Most Profitable Companies, 2000 and 2020 (in millions)*

| Rank | 2000 | Profits | 2020 | Profits |
|------|------|---------|------|---------|
| 1 | General Electric | $10,717 | Berkshire Hathaway | $81,417 |
| 2 | Citigroup | $9,867 | Apple | $55,256 |
| 3 | Exxon Mobile | $7,910 | Microsoft | $38,240 |
| 4 | IBM | $7,712 | JPMorgan Chase | $36,431 |
| 5 | Altria Group* | $7,675 | Alphabet (Google) | $34,240 |
| 6 | Ford Motor | $7,237 | Bank of America | $27,430 |
| 7 | General Motors | $6,002 | Intel | $21,048 |
| 8 | Wal-Mart | $5,377 | Wells Fargo | $19,549 |
| 9 | AT&T | $3,428 | Citigroup | $19,401 |
| 10 | Boeing | $2,309 | Verizon | $19,265 |

Source: Fortune 500, Most Profitable, 2020, https://fortune.com/fortune500/2020/search/?f500_profits=desc; Fortune 500 Archive, Company, Profit, https://archive.fortune.com/magazine/fortune.fortune500_archive/full/2000.

*Formerly Philip Morris Companies, Inc.

As Doug Henwood has pointed out, beginning in the 1980s there was the rise of a new class fraction of billionaires "made up of owners of private companies as opposed to public ones, disproportionately in dirty industries."[7] This includes "alternative investments," hedge funds, and private equity outfits. Henwood emphasizes the role of such capitalists in the rise of Trump and the right and, indeed, as Mike Davis pointed out more recently:

> Trump's key allies are post-industrial robber barons from hinterland places like Grand Rapids, Wichita, Little Rock and Tulsa, whose fortunes derive from real estate, private equity, casinos, and services ranging from private armies to chain usury.[8]

As we will see, however, many of these new, more urban "entrepreneurs," notably the Silicon Valley crew, hedge funders, and asset managers of alt-finance, support Democrats in disproportionate numbers.

Indeed, the rise of billionaires is one of the most striking characteristics of the changes in the US capitalist class in the neoliberal era. In 1987 there were a mere 41 billionaires in the US. By 2020 there were 623 by *Forbes* count, a leap of 1,420 percent in twenty-three years, a far greater increase than can be accounted for by inflation.[9] There were, of course, ups and downs as some of these bottom-feeders lost their shirts and many Silicon Valley start-ups failed. Not only are these new billionaires associated with private companies as opposed to publicly traded corporations, but their fortunes have originated outside the traditional twentieth-century corporate sector as Table IV suggests.

A look at the 2018 "Billionaires List," which includes brief descriptions of where they made or inherited their money, reveals very few of the corporate giants that dominated the Fortune 500 even as recently as 2000. There is Sanford Weill from Citigroup and a Rockefeller representing the old corporate giants on this list of 585 billionaires, but, unless I missed some, none of these billionaires got superrich from GM, Ford, or even that perennial Democratic favorite Goldman Sachs, and many were associated with "alt-finance," high-tech, real estate, and retail.[10] These billionaires would engage more directly in politics than their older corporate predecessors.

Twenty-twenty was the most expensive election in US history. According to OpenSecrets, it cost about $14 billion up and down the ballot, which was over twice what was spent in 2016. For their narrow victory, Democrats outspent Republicans $6.9 billion to $3.8 billion. "Outside" donations mostly from wealthy individuals not including those to party committees came to $3 billion, of which two-thirds were via Super PACs. The two major parties themselves raised another $3.6 billion, much of it from wealthy donors as well. In contrast, combined spending from union and "social welfare" groups such as Our Revolution scarcely passed the $100 million mark.[11] There is not much doubt about where all this money comes from.

This billionaire fraction of the ruling class has been key in bringing about a change in the way capital funds political parties and candidates. Back in the days of the twentieth-century corporate giants, business money came mostly from corporate PACs, which frequently contributed to candidates of both parties, often slightly more to the party in control of Congress in order to influence legislation. Since the early 1990s, individual contributions have outweighed those from all traditional PACs. By 2016 PAC donations accounted for only 9 percent of all election spending. By 2020 it was down to just 5 percent. For Democratic House candidates the percentage of PAC money, including labor and social issue PACs, fell from 47 percent in 1992 to 23 percent in 2020.[12] Of course, corporations continue to make political donations through their PACs, and you can be sure the suspension of this following the Trump-inspired storming of the Capitol by far right-wingers is temporary. But the bulk of political money is now coming in different forms.

Part of this came initially from the rise of small donors individually and through crowdfunding outfits like ActBlue for Democrats or WinRed for Republicans that hold your credit card information and forward your donation to the candidate of your choice. In the 2008 presidential election, small donations of $200 or less outstripped large donations of $100,000 or more. By 2016 and 2018, however, the small-donor boom was eclipsed by large donations of $100,000 or more that composed a much larger portion of total individual contributions, about 40 percent for 2018 midterms and over 50 percent for the 2016 presidential cycle.[13] And, of course, those millions of small donations are essentially anonymous, while big ones are more easily recognized by their grateful recipients.[14] The billionaires were spending big and were also highly partisan in how they contributed.

According to OpenSecrets' listing, 58 of the top 100 individual political donors in the 2020 election cycle gave to Democrats. The smallest Democratic donor in the top 100 gave just over $3 million, compared to the smallest Republican funder who gave just under $3 million, while the largest Democratic contribution came to $107 million—that being, of course, Michael Bloomberg's.[15] Comparing these Democratic donors to the "Billionaires List," of those that could be identified by source of wealth, twenty-two of the fifty-eight were in alt-finance, not traditional banking, much less any sphere of the real economy. It is perhaps not surprising that so many superrich donors should be Democrats since it was the Clinton administration that abolished financial regulation, opening the door to these alt-finance bottom-feeders. Others were from Silicon Valley and the media. None derived their billions from the big twentieth-century corporations.[16]

The story of the Democrats' absorption of the new billionaires and of capital in general would not be complete without a look at how they won Silicon Valley. There is more here than the humble suburban-garage origins or (designer) T-shirt-and-jeans style of these high-tech entrepreneurs. Bill Clinton gave them what such innovators always want: patent and copyright protection for their income along with the completion of financial deregulation that played no small part in the rise of high-tech venture capitalists. Despite the resistance of some Democrats, Bill Clinton, Obama, and Hillary Clinton as secretary of state gave them free trade deals. In return, the newly rich helped fund this party.[17]

By 2020 OpenSecrets calculated that only about 22 percent of funds raised by candidates came from small donations of $200 or less. In fact, at the congressional level, of the 537 candidates OpenSecrets reported on in 2020, only 12 got half or more of their contributions from small donors, while a total of only 37 got a third or more from that source.[18] So, the well-to-do and the super-rich have given generously to both parties. This was really a culmination of trends in which wealthy individuals play a bigger role in politics and, due to changes in just who the rich are, in the Democratic Party in particular.

The Democratic Party and its candidates are, with few exceptions, increasingly dependent on donations from twenty-first-century capitalist bottom-feeders and high-tech entrepreneurs. It hardly needs to be stressed that dependence on such individuals and their money is a significant factor in the Democrat's persistent centrism. The presence of Biden cabinet appointees from BackRock, the largest asset management firm in the world, is an indication of the dependence on such alt-financial newcomers.[19] It is worth mentioning as well Biden's pick for secretary of the treasury, Janet Yellen. Praised by many liberals, Yellen took at least $7 million in speaker's fees from financial institutions, ranging from a mere $67,500 from Democratic old-timer Goldman Sachs to $292,500 from hedge fund Citadel, whose boss Ken Griffin is a top Republican funder.[20] Yellen appears to be a friend to all financiers. The secretary of the treasury, of course, has enormous influence on economic policy.

The pressures on the party apparatus and its officeholders up and down the ballot to keep within what the wealthy and well-to-do consider the acceptable center have also increased as the party has also become increasingly dependent on well-to-do voters, while losing some of its traditional working-class electoral base.

## Realignment by Stealth and Wealth

In mainstream political science, political realignment, or the shift of groups of voters from one party to another, is generally seen as something that emerges more or less suddenly, often in a "critical election," such as 1896 or 1936.[21] While there have been elections that seemed to indicate a realignment, such as 1964 where Republicans voted Democratic to defeat Goldwater, or 1968 where significant numbers of white working-class voters cast a ballot for George Wallace, what has actually occurred in the US over the last few decades is more of a stealth realignment in which voters of different social classes have switched from one party to another. Two trends in particular affect the Democratic Party and its electoral prospects: the relative decline in the working-class and union household votes that began long ago, on the one hand, and the increased dependence on middle- and upper-middle-class, well-to-do urban and suburban voters that is more recent.

Most pundits and polls provide two ways of identifying working-class voters: by education and by income. The most common blue-collar identifier is the lack of a college degree or a "high school or less" formal education. Looking at this measure in the AP VoteCast survey, we see that Trump won 52 percent of these voters to Biden's 46 percent in 2020. Even more starkly in the Edison exit poll, Trump took the "White noncollege graduate" cohort by a huge 64 percent.[22] This amounts to 34,498,533 voters—a lot.[23] From this we are supposed to conclude that Trump and the Republicans have taken a majority of blue-collar votes. The class picture, however, is more complex.

There are approximately 22 million white small business proprietors in the US; about 60 percent don't have a college degree and estimates of their average income ranges from $62,000 a year to $70,000. Some 60 percent of all small business owners said they approved of President Trump, and Republican small business owners outnumber Democrats by about two-to-one. Those in the $50,000-to-$100,000 voters cohort in 2020 in which these small business owners are located voted by 50 percent for Trump in 2020, according to the AP survey. If we could adjust those figures for white owners only, the Republican and Trump approval and voting rates would be significantly higher. So, we can estimate that there are about 13 million white small business owners (about three-fourth male) who lack a college degree, make more than the $50,000 limit often used to identify workers, who tend to approve of Trump, about 8 million of whom are Republicans.[24] Most of these petty capitalists have spouses who are likely to share their opinions more often than not, so we can estimate that there were about 16 million petty bourgeois Republicans in Trump's $50,000–$100,000 column. There are also millions of white managers, police, and other non-working-class people without college degrees more likely to be Republicans than Democrats. Though an exact estimate is impossible, this reduces Trump's actual working-class voter support among the 43.5 million "less educated" who voted for Trump by as much as half.

In geographic terms, Trump carried the nation's exurban counties by huge margins. This prosperous new frontier of reaction, comprising 34 million people whom the American Community Project described as "relatively wealthy" and "among the most educated," voted 54.9 percent to 43.3 percent for Trump in 2020. Interestingly, Trump's 2020 margin of victory with this segment was slightly less than the 55.5 percent to 38.0 percent Trump vote in 2016, indicating that the Democrats made some gains even in this most Republican of well-to-do territory.[25]

None of this is necessarily good news for those who seem to believe, as a fund appeal from "Team AOC" put it, that the Democrats are "a multi-racial working-class party."[26] The Democrats do consistently win majorities among voters in the less-than-$50,000 household income cohort, which is disproportionately Black and Latinx. But this working-class cohort has shrunk as both a percentage of the total vote and that of the Democrats as this cohort has declined in the population. In 2000 these lower-income voters composed 47 percent of the voting electorate and of the Democratic vote. By 2020 this had shrunk to 34 percent of all voters and 40 percent of those voting Democratic. More of the Democratic vote necessarily moved into the $50,000–$100,000 range, which would include not only better-paid workers such as nurses, skilled workers, and many teachers, though proportionately fewer Blacks and Latinxs, on the one hand, and many of the small business owners and managers discussed above as well as middle-class professionals, on the other. While about two-thirds of these petty bourgeois voters went to Trump, some would go to Biden as well. Clearly, the Democrats' working-class vote was getting watered down.

The other stalwart of the Democrats' working-class electoral base is the union household vote. In 1948 fully 80 percent of union household members voted Democratic in the presidential election. This proved to be the last gasp of the New Deal Coalition. With the sole exception of 1964, when confronted with blatantly anti-union Berry Goldwater, the union household vote rose to 83 percent but never reached that level again. This collapsed to 56 percent in 1968 as George Wallace took some of the union vote in the wake of the white "backlash." Since then, for most years it has gone Democratic in the mid-to-high 50 percent level. In other words, the drift of union voters to the Republicans began a long time ago, well before Trump, as the Democrats moved toward the political and programmatic center. Trump did reduce the Democratic union household vote to 51 percent in 2016, but it returned to 57 percent in 2020. While the numbers of union household voters have held up in more years than not since 2000, as a proportion of the electorate they have fallen from 26 percent in 2000 to 19 percent in 2020, and as a percentage of the Democratic vote from 32 percent in 2000 to 21 percent over those years.[27] If it is fair to say that the working-class vote is most dependably represented by the overlapping union household vote and those in the $50,000-or-less income cohort, then the Democrats' New Deal working-class base has shrunk and its electoral coalition altered.

*Table V: Union Household Vote, 2000–2020*

| Year | % all voters | Dem % of Vote | # Democratic | % Dem Vote |
|---|---|---|---|---|
| 2020 | 19% | 57% | 17,169,640 | 21% |
| 2016 | 18% | 51% | 12,589,747 | 19% |
| 2012 | 18% | 58% | 13,492,410 | 20% |
| 2008 | 21% | 59% | 16,289,592 | 23% |
| 2004 | 24% | 59% | 17,318,188 | 29% |
| 2000 | 26% | 59% | 16,172,346 | 32% |

Source: Edison Research, "National Exit Polls: How Different Groups Voted," *New York Times*, November 3, 2020, https://www.nytimes.com/interactive/2020/11/03/us/elections/exit-polls-president.html; Roper Center for Public Opinion, "How Groups Voted in 2016," https://ropercenter.cornell.edu/how-groups-voted-3016; Roper Center for Public Opinion, "How Groups Voted in 2012," https://ropercenter.cornell.edu/how-groups-voted-2012; Roper Center for Public Opinion, "How Groups Voted in 2008," https://ropercenter.cornell.edu/how-groups-voted-2008; Roper Center for Public Opinion, "How Groups Voted in 2004," https://ropercenter.cornell.edu/how-groups-voted-2004; Roper Center for Public Opinion, "How Groups Voted on 2000," https://ropercenter.cornell.edu/how-groups-voted-2000.

The disdain that leading Democrats have for these working-class voters was all too well expressed by Democratic Senate leader Charles Schumer when he stated, "For every blue-collar Democrat we lose in western Pennsylvania, we will pick up two moderate Republicans in the suburbs in Philadelphia, and you can repeat that in Ohio and Illinois and Wisconsin."[28]

Furthermore, while the lack of a college degree does not necessarily point to working-class status, the possession of that degree *is* to a certain extent an indicator of both relatively higher income and middle- or higher-class status. And it is in this large cohort that accounted for 37 percent of all voters in 2016 and 38 percent in 2020 that the Democrats outstripped the Republicans. The Democrats carried this educated group by 57 percent in both years, a fact that has been noted by virtually every commentator. The Democrats also won in the $100,000-plus level, where the education level is very high.

In general, the Democrats have captured more of the upper-income groups over the last few decades. Using the top income levels reported in the major exit polls and adjusting them roughly for the impact of inflation, in 1980 the Democrats won only 26 percent of voters at the $50,000-plus level, the highest reported at the time. By 2000, the Democrat Al Gore took 43 percent of the $100,000-plus top cohort. In 2008, Obama tied McCain for 49 percent of the $100,000-plus level. In 2016, however, Clinton won 51 percent of the $150,000-plus cohort and in the 2018 midterm, when the upper-income group always plays a disproportionate role, the Democratic candidates for the House took 59 percent of that top income level.

The most astounding aspect of this stealth realignment, however, is the turn of the very wealthiest to the Democrats. The first exit poll to record this was in the 2008 election when Obama beat McCain in the $200,000-plus income cohort by 52 to 46 percent—well before the Trump phenomenon encouraged Republicans to flip to the Democrats. In 2016, Clinton beat Trump in this income range by a narrower 47 to 46 percent, and in 2020, Biden beat Trump by 47 to 43 percent, bringing in 5.2 million relatively rich Democratic voters. It is not simply that these rich people have turned to the Democrats in the last two decades, but that they have been courted and pursued by the Democratic Party, its operatives, and politicians.

This trend is not limited to presidential elections. It carries over into congressional and state elections as well. The Democrats pursued and won forty-one of the fifty wealthiest congressional districts in the country in 2018 and held onto thirty-nine of these in 2020. Of the forty-three House seats the Democrats took from Republicans in 2018, eighteen were among the richest 15 percent of wealthiest congressional districts. Those richest 15 percent of districts are now represented by fifty-six Democrats and only ten Republicans, according to a conservative source.[29] As Matt Karp described the trend from 2016 to 2020 in *Jacobin*, "Though the Democratic turnout rose everywhere in the wealthy suburbs, from Silicon Valley to Metro Boston, a clear pattern was visible: the richer and more conservative the suburb, the more dramatic the increases."[30]

The growth of the wealthy Democratic vote, however, is not limited to suburbs. One recent study of the alleged urban-rural voter polarization demonstrates that the denser the urban area the more Democratic it is—even in small metro areas where Democrats lose elections. While this is typically the result of Black, Latinx, and white working-class voters, the author states, "First of all many of these dense places that vote for Democrats today are not poor. Many of their voters are in high tax brackets, relatively few make use of means-tested antipoverty programs, and public sector union members represent only a small portion of their voters."[31] This study mentions San Francisco, Philadelphia, Boston, and Seattle in particular as sites of newer high-tech industries where highly paid and educated "knowledge" professionals live in the city center. In a facetious expression of the Democratic strength among these upscale urbanites, the *Cook Political Report* noted that "Biden carried 85 percent of the counties with a Whole Foods Market."[32]

A look at Manhattan in New York City reveals the same high and growing proportion of well-to-do voters. The median household income in Manhattan (New York County) grew from $48,000 in 1999 to $94,000 in 2019, nearly doubling as inflation grew by only half. By 2019 those households earning $100,000 or more composed 48 percent of the total, while those making $200,000-plus alone accounted for a quarter of all households. In this borough the Democratic presidential vote rose from 73 percent in 2000 to 81 percent in 2004, then to 86 percent in 2016 and 2020.[33] Very few counties in the US vote Democratic to that extent. While Manhattan is not typical of most urban countries, it is not the only city where this trend has occurred. Rodden, for example, notes that "wealthy, educated, largely white professionals have taken over the urban core of Philadelphia."[34] The rise of the well-to-do Democratic vote is by no means limited to wealthy suburbs.

Despite suburban gains in 2018, the Democrats obviously did less well in 2020 congressional contests. Whereas in 2018 their average share of the total vote was 56.1 percent, in 2020 it fell to 50.6 percent.[35] Furthermore, they lost twelve House seats to Republicans in 2020. Only two of them, however, were in the top 50 income districts. Indeed, with a couple of exceptions, most of those lost were in districts where the median household income was below the national median of $68,703. Not surprisingly, it was the conservative and more rural Blue Dog Democrats who lost the most House members in this election. Moreover, 2020 saw the Democrats make further gains in the suburbs. While Trump did better in the more solidly white exurbs, according to a *New York Times* analysis of results in the nation's 373 suburban counties, Biden did better than Hillary Clinton. As the authors summarized the 2020 results,

> Suburban counties that were already Democratic-leaning before 2020 tilted more so. And many that were deeply Republican nudged several points away from the president.[36]

In other words, if anything, the average income and class status of voters in Democratic congressional districts most certainly rose somewhat in 2020.

Nor did the 2020 election alter the ideological balance in the 117th Congress significantly. All three caucuses in the House lost some members. The Congressional Progressive Caucus slipped from 97 House members to 94, while the centrist New Democrat Coalition fell from 103 to 93. The conservative Blue Dogs, who represent more Southern and rural districts rather than prosperous suburbs, fell from 27 to 18. The numbers, however, hide the pull of the center. Despite some tightening up of the CPC rules, fully 15 of the 94 House members of the CPC also belonged to the New Democrats, indicating how porous the term "progressive" is and that the CPC's real strength was closer to 79 members. The New Democrats, in turn, contributed 18 of the 25 Democrats, one of whom was also a member of the CPC, to the even more conservative bipartisan, 50-member "Problem Solvers Caucus." This outfit was founded in 2017 with 36 members in order to break the legislative gridlock by proposing compromises acceptable to "moderates" in both parties; i.e., in reality to the Republicans.[37]

A further sign of the centrist direction comes from one of the first efforts to assess the party's losses in 2020 by a group of Democratic advocacy groups that include the centrist think tank Third Way. They are particularly concerned about the loss of Black and Latinx votes in 2020. They have hired the Chicago-based consultancy 270 Strategies, founded and led by veterans of Obama's 2008 and 2012 campaigns. It will consult with the Black and Latinx caucuses in the House, but the only ideological caucus it plans to work with is the New Democrat Coalition.[38]

The Senate, too, saw a shift to the right as newly elected centrists John Hickenlooper (CO) and Mark Kelly (AZ) filled two of the Democrats fifty seats, adding their voices and votes to the likes of self-proclaimed moderates Joe Manchin (WV), Jon Tester (MT), Kyrsten Sinema (AZ), and others. Their increased leverage due to the 50-50 split in the Senate showed up almost immediately in opposition to the $15 minimum wage, while eight Democratic centrists voted against including stimulus payments for undocumented immigrants in the COVID-19 relief package. It is expected the centrists will oppose significant cuts to the military in the 2022 budget resolution and resist even some of Biden's climate proposals. Eight of these centrist Democrats joined with eight Republicans to form a Senate counterpart to the Problem Solvers Caucus initially called the "Common Sense Caucus."[39]

State-level elections were just as disappointing for the Democrats in 2020. They failed to flip any state legislatures, while the Republicans turned Montana and New Hampshire from divided government to Republican trifectas (governor and both state houses). The Republicans now completely control twenty-four state governments compared to the Democrats' fifteen.[40] Like congressional districts, those for state legislatures favor rural areas where the Democrats have failed to make any breakthroughs, despite the existence of working-class people throughout these areas. This is particularly problematic because the states will redraw the already distorted election districts in 2021.

It is simply no longer tenable, if it ever was, to consider the Democrats as a party representing the working class, much less as a "working-class party." While it has always been a cross-class party, today the Democratic Party is also the party of the majority of wealthy voters, funded by a majority of the new billionaire class fraction, as well as a good deal of the old corporate elite, for example, defense contractors.[41]

Not surprisingly, it was possible for a group of academics who studied the impact of money on policy outcomes to write in 2013 that not only donations impact politicians:

More broadly, there does seem to be evidence that members of Congress represent the views of their high-income constituents much more than those of low-income ones. Gilens (2012) presents considerable evidence showing that the policy outputs of the US government are far more responsive to preferences of high-income voters, especially policy domains where the opinions of the rich and poor diverge.[42]

While this policy preference is hardly new to US politics or government, the stealth realignment of funders and wealthy voters has increased the pressure for this policy bias and for the persistent centrism of the Democratic Party. Looking at the policy outcomes as measured by how representatives vote in House floor votes over a long period, this same study concluded that "Democrats as a whole have not moved much to the left. Overall, entering and exiting Democrats have looked much like those that have continued to serve."[43] This is particularly significant because floor votes, being the result of compromise, disguise the politics of individuals.

So, self-described democratic socialists and DSA members like Representatives John Conyers, Major Owens, or Ron Dellums in the 1980s, 1990s, and early 2000s regularly proposed bills to the left of the party as a whole, which like the vast majority of bills submitted in the House went nowhere for all the reasons argued earlier in chapters 1 and 2.[44] In the end they mostly voted with the party caucus for far more moderate programs like Obamacare rather than Medicare for All. Or they watched progressive labor legislation like the Employee Free Choice Act go down to defeat. The process is further rigged against the so-called progressives by preferences of superrich funders and well-to-do voters who elect enough representatives to give the Democrats their national majority. The impasse holds.

Few things point to this aspect of the impasse more clearly than the Democrats' abandonment in policy terms of the lower-income population of the cities, their largest single source of voters. Beginning in the 1990s the Clinton administration not only "reformed" welfare, but closed down all but one of the urban grant programs, and that was for "downtown development." In particular, "four programs of special interest to city governments, General Revenue Sharing, Urban Development Action Grants, Local Public Works, and Antirecession Fiscal Assistance, were zeroed out—were eliminated entirely."[45] Henceforth urban issues relating to the poor and working class disappeared from the national

Democratic agenda. While the Obama appointed an "urban czar," as Judd and Swanstrom summarized this gesture in *City Politics*, "as time passed little was heard from the urban czar, and there was no prospect that urban issues would be able to compete in a crowded political agenda any time soon." The Obama administration allocated some of its Recovery and Reinvestment Act money to city schools for buildings, but nothing for social issues.[46] Biden's COVID relief package was to include $350 billion for both states and cities to cover lost revenue from the pandemic. But this will be divided between states and hundreds of cities.[47] As yet, there is no urban revitalization policy.

Biden's cabinet choices, his rejection of Medicare for All, the Green New Deal, free college tuition, reduction of police funding, etc., and, despite the election of a handful of "progressives," the political composition of the 117th Congress and its multimillionaire Speaker, Nancy Pelosi, all point to the inability of the Democrats to address the needs of the working class, deal with the country's racial crisis, and attract nonvoters in 2022, much less become the platform for building the new socialist movement in the United States.

The resolute centrism of Biden, Harris, party operatives, campaign consultants, and the increasing majority of officeholders stems in part from the objective need to expand beyond the concentrations of Democrats in the nation's urban cores. The modern method of campaigning via polling, digital targeting, and messaging is based on the assumption that it is the party or the candidate that must adapt to the sought-after voting constituency, mostly suburban as the party already has a majority of the urban vote. That means seeking centrist candidates to match the political preferences of the prosperous suburbanites whose votes they seek. After all, the Democrats do not conduct education to raise people's consciousness. They, like the Republicans, appeal to the voters existing instincts, prejudices, and preferences—in this case a combination of moderate social liberalism and reforms that avoid economic redistribution, higher taxes, or implied threats to private property, property values, and privileged school districts. They are the party of alt-finance, Wall Street, the media, and Silicon Valley not only because of the funds they get from these businesses, but because so many of the voters they pander to earn much of their well-above-average incomes from these and related sources.

None of this, of course, means that Biden and the Congress will do nothing. Nor is the argument in this book that the Democrats and Republicans are the same. Nor does the willingness or reluctance to spend government money necessarily divide Republicans and Democrats, moderates or liberals anymore. These days, just about everyone is willing to rack up high deficits if it will keep them in office. The impasse I have analyzed depends precisely on their differences: right versus center, extreme versus moderate. The issues that confront the new administration are different from those that confronted Obama, much less Clinton, and with real long-term interest rates around zero, they will spend. They will deploy a sizable stimulus plan of $1.9 trillion, even tax business a bit to pay for all of this, insert the federal government into dealing with the pandemic, reverse many of Trump's more outrageous policies, take some action on climate change, extend Obamacare, and readjust US imperial status.

The first couple of weeks of the Biden administration's top-down attack on Trump's authoritarianism might have been seen as a step back toward a more vigorous reformism. On the one hand, the flurry of forty-five executive orders contained a number of good things such as the halts on eviction, student loan payments, and oil drilling licenses, although Biden later signed some thirty permits for oil drilling. Many of the forty-five orders were directed at reversing Trump's most outrageous orders such as those on immigration. On the other hand, most contained little more than temporary measures, pauses, and guidelines meant to "address" rather than resolve the multiple crises facing the nation and the world. As Branko Marcetic put it in *Jacobin*, for many of these orders, "the devil is in the details." So while we can't predict exactly what Biden and the Congress will do, "two things are for sure: his first weeks of the job are closer to a third Obama term than a path-breaking economic populism; and pretending otherwise isn't going to make him get there."[48] Biden's climate policies are, of course, far from Trump's. But as Kate Aronoff, author of a new book on climate change politics, put it, Biden's approach is "the equivalent of maybe a center-right European country."[49] As for health policy, the appointment of Obama veteran and managing director of the private health consultancy Manatt Health, Chiquita Brooks-LaSure, as boss of Medicare and Medicaid pretty much clinches the limits to reform on that front.[50] To be sure, by spring as the first one hundred days neared their end, liberal pundits were speculating whether Biden was the next FDR. It was the triumph of lowered expectations over the heightened problems facing the country.

Lacking a mass upheaval from below *and* from the left, the social and economic solutions the Biden-Harris administration propose will not go beyond the kinds of centrist policies seen in many developed capitalist countries. Nor will they engage in a significant redistribution of wealth or income, much less in any way challenge private property. The Biden administration will not bite the well-to-do hands that fed it and put it in power.

## Culture Wars and the Urban-Rural Divide

While some commentators and academics have noticed the rising income and wealth of Democratic voters, the most common framework of analysis for explaining the Democrats' difficulty in winning congressional and state-level elections in particular has been that of the urban-rural culture wars. The Democrats, it is often said, are too left-wing for many Americans, particularly those in rural areas. The underlying assumption is that urban and rural people have fundamentally different social values and that these polarized forms of consciousness are immutable. Put crudely, urban people are said to be more secular, modern, and tolerant, while rural people tend to hold more traditional and conservative values and opinions, including by implication racism. Before questioning the universal validity of these assumptions, it is worth sorting out just what the rural United States actually looks like these days.

The most obvious problem with the urban-rural polarization thesis is that if it really was a matter of urban people voting mostly Democratic and rural folks Republican, the Democrats would win almost all elections almost all the time since only a tiny minority of eligible voters are rural at least by the Census Bureau's definition, which deems residents "rural" if they live outside a census block with a density of 2,500 people or more.[51] Looking more closely at this in terms of US counties, 1,889 counties or about 60 percent of all counties are either mostly or completely rural. Yet only 13.6 percent of the population of the United States is rural at all by the Census's measure.[52] Clearly, this actually existing rural population could not dominate US politics no matter how clever Republican gerrymanders or demagogues might be.

Furthermore, the US countryside is not populated by peasants or pitchfork-wielding agrarians subjected to what Marx called "the idiocy of rural life."[53] Only about 5 percent of those employed in rural counties make their living by farming, which is increasingly large-scale and pretty capital-intensive these days. As of 2019, 75 percent of farms had internet access.[54] In fact, the country's 391 "farming-dependent" counties are mostly concentrated in the sparsely populated Great Plains states, which do indeed go Republican most of the time, but which clearly could not carry a presidential election or dominate Congress.

In contrast to what one might assume, about 10 percent of those employed in rural counties work in manufacturing, more than the 8 percent average of the US as a whole. This rural manufacturing accounts for 15 percent of rural earnings, compared to 9 percent of all urban earnings. In fact, there are more factory workers than farmers in rural America. And many of these rural factories employ a racially diverse workforce. Furthermore, producer services, which account for about 12 percent of rural jobs, are less managerial and professional than those in urban areas and their employees more likely to be working class. "Other" services account for the biggest share of jobs and earnings, as they do in cities, and are composed of things like health care, retail, telecommunications, trucking, rail, warehousing, and other working-class occupations. And get this, public sector jobs account for a larger share of employment in rural counties than in urban ones.[55] Clearly there are more workers on the town and county payrolls than Deputy Dawg or Barney Fife. Furthermore, incomes are significantly lower than urban ones for most workers. Rural America is looking surprisingly proletarian.

Part of the confusion stems from the fact that much of rural America isn't all that rural anymore. Of those 1,889 counties with rural populations, only 704 are "completely" rural and only 1.7 percent of the US population lives in them—and 20 percent of those people live in a metro area. The rest are "mostly" rural. This means they contain small and larger towns and even small cities and about a third of their population are, on average, urban, according to the US Census Bureau.[56] The fact is that the rural United States has been shrinking for decades as towns and small cities grow and some are absorbed into metropolitan areas. While these small cities and large towns still vote mostly Republican, Jonathan Rodden has shown that their inner urban core votes Democratic just like their big-city cousins.[57] So, while there is something like an urban-rural political divide it is one that occurs all across the country, even *within* most of what is classified as rural by the Census Bureau.

Furthermore, the rural United States is about 25 percent non-white, of which Latinx people make up the largest group followed by African Americans—not that different from the country as a whole. They are not, however, spread evenly around the country. Their numbers are not enough to swing most of these counties outside the Southwest and the old "Black Belt" counties of the Deep South. This is particularly true in the whiter Great Plains and Mountain states, but these "rural" Black and Latinx voters form a base for a left-leaning electorate across much of the country and for the organization of much of rural manufacturing. The Democrats, however, are now so dependent on suburban and urban well-to-do voters that they ignore these "rural" working-class voters as a potential part of a majority even in swing states.

The biggest fallacy in the urban-rural division analysis, however, is the emphasis on the so-called culture wars. It is, of course, true that the Republicans effectively exploit religious and other cultural differences to promote right-wing ideas. And surveys show that, indeed, really "rural" people tend to have more conservative or traditional ideas on matters like abortion, gay marriage, women's rights, race, etc. But once again, these commentors often see these average cultural differences as applied to all rural people and to be a matter of unchanging values. They overlook the ways that most rural, small city, or town people's ideas on these subjects have evolved over time.

In *Why Cities Lose*, Jonathan Rodden, who also focuses on the culture wars, nonetheless does us a big favor by presenting a picture not only of how different rural and urban opinions can be, but how they have actually converged toward more "liberal" views since the 1970s precisely on these "moral" or cultural issues. A graph he produces using statistics from the General Social Survey since the early 1970s shows this convergence among all kinds of small city, large town, and suburban people and even to some extent the most rural residents on matters such as abortion, women's rights, gay marriage, etc. Of course, these are averages and there are enough people in the US who hold strong conservative religious and white-supremacist views to fill the growing far right. Nevertheless, as Rodden comments, "in fact, there has been an interesting convergence over time, such that residents of smaller cities as well as suburbs have come to resemble residents of large central cities on this dimension."[58] This ongoing convergence helps to explain why in the spring and summer of 2020, according to various polls, between 15 and 26 million people took part in 4,700 mostly multiracial pro-Black Lives Matter demonstrations in 2,500 towns and cities. These demonstrations occurred in 40 percent of all US counties, 95 percent of which are majority white.[59]

While Rodden does not draw the obvious conclusion that the timing of this convergence screams out to announce, it is clear that the social movements of the 1960s, 1970s, and since have had a lasting effect on how more and more people in the US view these so-called cultural or moral issues no matter where they live. It is the social movements and the left that put hundreds of thousands of people in the streets over these issues for decades and it has made a difference. Yet, the real left has very little presence in these communities today, and even the Democrats are underrepresented because they have built their electoral majority on the wealthy suburban and urban voters with high turnout ratios. This, in turn, blocks the party from developing the sort of progressive "populist" policies that can appeal to more rural people. The outstanding exception, of course, is Bernie Sanders, who wins elections as an independent and in Democratic primaries over and over in one of the two most rural states in the US with his version of left populism. And no, not everyone in Vermont is an urban refugee like Ben and Jerry or, for that matter, Bernie himself, while that state's median household income is well below the US median.

The convergence of "values" in the US has been toward the left, not toward Donald Trump, evangelical preachers, or the Proud Boys. Trump wins the votes of those blue-collar workers who voted twice for Obama as much or more on economic issues as on these "values" or even racism per se from a population experiencing economic insecurity and decline in part because the Democrats have for decades failed to deliver on jobs, education, health care, trade, etc.[60] Another look at history tells us that even those with conservative religious beliefs have been swept up in progressive movements, from the original rural populism of the 1890s and the "social gospel" movement of the early 1900s to the CIO upsurge, the civil rights movement of the 1950s and 1960s, and the immigrants' rights and Black Lives Matter movements of recent times. No doubt many "rural" town and small city residents are caught up in what Gramsci would call the conservative "common sense" or hegemony of their region. And, indeed, those the American Community Project calls "Working Class Country" voters went for Trump by huge margins in 2020.[61] But like any Marxist, Gramsci would be the last to see this as permanent or immutable. It is the theme of this book that it will take a mass social upsurge to break the political impasse because, for one thing, it is such movements that alter consciousness. The actual shifts in public opinion since the 1970s and the massive Black Lives Matter demonstrations of 2020 are proof of that.

The real urban-rural problem, which Rodden points to, is that by and large Democratic voters are packed into large cities where they carry elections by 70–

80 percent. Republicans, on the other hand, maintain safe districts with about 55 percent, a safe 10 percent spread, and are more widely distributed in congressional and state legislative districts. So, for example, in 2016 Republicans won less than 51 percent of the two-party congressional vote but won 55 percent of seats. The Democrats, on the other hand, got 49.4 percent of the votes and only 44.6 percent of seats. Political scientists call this the "efficiency gap." As Rodden points out, if parts of the urban core were combined with parts of the suburbs, there could easily be more districts with 55 or 60 percent Democratic majorities rather than a single urban district with a 70 or 80 percent majority.[62] They have chosen to recruit voters in the wealthier suburbs to do this and as we have seen had considerable success in those areas. So, in 2020 they got 51.6 percent of the two-party vote and 51.0 percent of the seats, closer to "efficiency."[63] But also, a wealthier, more conservative electoral base.

## 2022 and Beyond

Despite the sizable Democratic victory in the 2020 popular vote, all the signs point toward difficulties in the 2022 midterm elections. For one thing, of course, the working-class turnout of all races will be proportionately smaller in relation to the well-to-do and wealthy in both cities and suburbs as it always is in midterm elections, increasing the incentive for centrist policies. There is no reason to doubt that this will be the case in 2022. Indeed, the increase in the 2018 turnout appears to have been primarily among wealthier voters. The Democrats captured forty-three Republican seats, beating incumbents in thirty and winning the rest in open-seat contests. Most of these were in high-income districts. In 2020, the Democratic apparatus focused on holding these seats. Similarly, the 2022 midterms will no doubt focus on saving these seats, this time after an inevitably disappointing two years of the Biden administration. Whichever way they go, the effort to keep and expand the numbers of these prosperous voters will be one more barrier to any left direction in Congress or the Biden administration.

Another major problem for the Democrats in all future elections, however, is the relative decline of the Black vote, both as a proportion of those voting and of those voting Democratic. That the overwhelming majority of African Americans who do vote in 2022 or beyond will vote Democratic as they have for decades is not really in doubt. Yet, the percentage that do so and their rate of turnout are in doubt. As Table VI reveals, since the increase in turnout during Obama's campaigns, the percentage of African Americans in the total vote has fallen back somewhat despite the Democrats' vice-presidential candidate being a woman of color. Equally important is the decline in the proportion of Blacks voting for Democrats. The combination of a 1 percent drop in the proportion of the total vote and a 6 percent drop in the proportion voting Democratic is significant. In most urban districts in which Blacks are a majority this might not matter, but together these falling proportions could make the difference in some of the more diverse inner-ring suburbs. In either case, it does not bode well for the Democrats in future congressional or presidential races.

*Table VI: The Black and Latinx Democratic Vote, 2000-2020*

**The Black Vote**

| Year | Black % of Total Vote | Black % of Democratic Vote |
|------|----------------------|----------------------------|
| 2020 | 12% | 87% |
| 2016 | 12% | 89% |
| 2012 | 13% | 93% |
| 2008 | 13% | 95% |
| 2004 | 11% | 88% |
| 2000 | 10% | 90% |

**The Latinx Vote**

| Year | Latinx % of Total Vote | Latinx % of Democratic Vote |
|------|------------------------|-----------------------------|
| 2020 | 13% | 66% |
| 2016 | 11% | 66% |
| 2012 | 10% | 71% |
| 2008 | 9% | 67% |
| 2004 | 8% | 53% |
| 2000 | 7% | 62% |

Source: Edison Research, "National Exit Polls: How Different Groups Voted," *New York Times*, November 3, 2020, https://www.nytimes.com/interactive/2020/11/03/us/elections/exit-polls-president.html; Roper Center for Public Opinion, "How Groups Voted in 2016," https://ropercenter.cornell.edu/how-groups-voted-3016; Roper Center for Public Opinion, "How Groups Voted in 2012," https://ropercenter.cornell.edu/how-groups-voted-2012; Roper Center for Public Opinion, "How Groups Voted in 2008," https://ropercenter.cornell.edu/how-groups-voted-2008; Roper Center for Public Opinion, "How Groups Voted in 2004," https://ropercenter.cornell.edu/how-groups-voted-2004; Roper Center for Public Opinion, "How Groups Voted on 2000," https://ropercenter.cornell.edu/how-groups-voted-2000.

The Latinx vote presents a more complex problem. First of all, as many com-
mentors have argued, there really is no such thing as the "Latino vote."[64] Latin
Americans in the US are divided by nationality, culture, immigration status, etc.
Despite some generational changes, there are groups of Spanish speakers who
are heavily conservative and strongly anti-left such as Cubans, Venezuelans, and
Nicaraguans. There is a sizable small business–owning population among those of
Mexican heritage, and so on. Some 8 million small businesses are minority-owned,
while Latinx small business owners employ about 14 percent of those working for
small firms.[65]

Nevertheless, the majority of this broad demographic is composed of immigrants or former immigrants from Mexico and Central America and their chil-
dren are growing into voting age in huge numbers. The party that wins a high
proportion of this vote will have an enormous advantage. So long as there are
only two choices, this is most likely to be the Democrats. But this is by no means
certain to be the salvation of the Democratic Party in 2022 or beyond given the
centrist policies and genuflecting to business and the rich that is the dominant
direction of this party. The exception on this is, of course, immigration policy,
which is important to many Latinx people.

For one thing, although Latinx voter turnout was way up in 2020 and tipped
the balance for the Democrats in several battleground states, Trump actually
captured a larger share in 2020 than in 2016, about 32 percent compared to
28 percent. For another, the vast majority of these new Latinx voters are working-class and their needs and ambitions will not be addressed by this administration or the 117th Congress. The motivation to turn out in large numbers in
the 2022 midterm for a party that has produced little for any of the components
of this broad demographic whose votes have been taken for granted like those of
African Americans is not likely to be strong.

The biggest missing working-class vote is unquestionably that of the "party
of nonvoters." Despite the highest turnout in over a hundred years—that is, since
the "reforms" of the early twentieth century discussed in chapter 1—nearly 77
million citizens eligible to vote did not do so in 2020. These are mostly lower-
income working-class people, many single parents, younger, more urban, and
more racially diverse than the population. Their numbers exceed the margins
of victory or defeat in the major battleground states and their numbers surpass
Trump's entire 2020 vote.[66]

In nostalgic New Deal–style thinking, these are natural Democrats. They, however, obviously don't see things that way. Only about 29–31 percent of non-voters consider themselves Democrats, according to two leading polls, while 45 percent identify as independents. Many of these nonvoting independents are said to "lean" toward the Democrats, but obviously not enough to vote for them.[67] Nor do Democratic Party strategists and administrators of the party's internal fundraising committees, notably and famously the Democratic Congressional Campaign Committee (DCCC) which focuses on suburbs, see these nonvoters as their potential electoral salvation. The very success of the Democrats in courting the well-to-do suburban and urban vote as well has made it extremely difficult to attract working-class nonvoters precisely by limiting their policy options to the moderate economic preferences of these more prosperous voters—and, of course, their super-wealthy funders.

## Conclusion

The 2020 election failed to change any of this and, hence, to alter or even reduce the political impasse of American mainstream politics. As former Communications Workers of America president and Our Revolution chair Larry Cohen summarized the outcome of the 2020 election, "For those of us who focus on government and economics and social justice, this election is a dismal rubber stamp of the unacceptable status quo. Black, brown, and white working Americans see their hopes of real reform evaporate for now, even while cheering the victory over Trump."[68] As the co-chairs of the Poor People's Campaign recently pointed out, polls show that almost two-thirds of Americans believe that "the government has a responsibility to provide health care for all."[69] Yet, this has been specifically rejected by the Biden-Harris team, along with other redistributive reforms. And so it goes on and on.

Despite the radically altered crisis-ridden context, this state of American politics is in many ways an old one in which the Democrats, as the only alternative to a rightward-moving Republican Party, are the major administrator of US capitalism and the imperial framework in which the Democrats from Roosevelt to Obama have helped to develop and fund generously.[70] Since the crisis-driven emergence of the neoliberal era, however, this has meant putting the brakes on even their older, limited reformism, in hopes of stabilizing the system they embrace.

The step back is more toward the neoliberalism of the Obama era than the New Deal. The Biden-Harris cabinet and staff appointments who will "execute" these forty-five orders, the COVID relief bill, and any future legislation can be summarized in three words: Clinton, Obama, and corporate. The legislative agenda for actually dealing with the deeper crises, not to mention soaring inequality or persistent racial segregation and hierarchy in our cities and workplaces, is far more modest, in fact, criminally inadequate given the depths of the crises it is supposed to deal with. Such as it is, furthermore, this agenda of tweaking older policies without antagonizing the prosperous voters who provide their margin of electoral victory depends on a Congress still in the willing hands of those masters of moderation: the Representative of Silicon Valley, Nancy Pelosi, and the Senator from Wall Street, Chuck Schumer.

It needs to be borne in mind that the most basic reason for the existence of America's two major parties is first and foremost the winning of office and state power. For at least the last two decades, however, the Democrats' efforts to maintain or win a majority in government have fostered a gradual and then accelerating political realignment that has sought with considerable success to bring a larger proportion of well-to-do voters into the party's electoral coalition. To finance this shift in voter base they have, in turn, linked themselves with the newer "entrepreneurs" of capital in alt-finance, high-tech, and other emerging sectors, while clinging to old friends in military hardware, classic investment houses, and fossil fuels among others.

In this context, the ideas drawn by many today from past socialist practice in the United States—that this party or its ballot line can somehow be a pathway or an instrument for the types of redistributive, health, environmental, educational, or employment programs that benefit working-class people—is clearly a fantasy. To continue to argue that a political institution disproportionately supported by the wealthy and funded by the super-wealthy can combat inequality of any sort, much less actually increase the social and political power of working-class and oppressed people is to stand political reality on its head.

And yet, a major current in this new socialist movement has turned to a sort of social democratic nostalgia for a failed "coalition politics" and "universal" liberal economic program from the 1960s that demotes race and racism as factors in US politics. While this is done in the name of class, it is in reality a rerun of efforts to reform or use the Democratic Party and its ballot line. As in the

1960s, this approach to electoral politics is almost certainly a consequence of the pressures inherent in this very orientation toward the Democrats that limits the vision of this wing of the new socialist movement to being "the left wing of the possible," at a time when the possible in that party is very limited and discourages more radical approaches based on the independent self-organization of workers and the oppressed. The next chapter will examine one of the major forms of this social democratic nostalgia and argue why the self-organization of oppressed people must be an important part of any upsurge and, therefore, of socialist politics.

## CHAPTER 4

# The New Social Democratic Nostalgia: Class, Race, and "Coalition Politics"

*On to Washington, ten thousand black Americans. . . . We will not
call on our white friends to march with us. There are some things
Negroes must do alone. This is our fight and we must see it through.*[1]
—A. Philip Randolph, 1941
March on Washington Movement statement

*Under present conditions—i.e., general segregation and discrim-
ination, and the unreliability of today's organized (or disorganized) liberalism—the Negro will find it necessary in many instances to organize independently.*[2]
—Bayard Rustin, 1961, in response to George Meany's attack
on the Negro American Labor Council as "reverse racism"

The acceptance of the immutability of the two-party system as it is, along with
the proposition that "politics" means electoral politics, has given rise to a revival
of a backward-looking social democratic trend within the new socialist movement in the United States. The historical reference points of this social democratic revival are found above all in Bayard Rustin's 1965 *Commentary* article, "From

Protest to Politics," and the 1966 *Freedom Budget* drafted by former New Dealer and leading Keynesian economist Leon Keyserling and endorsed by A. Philip Randolph, Rustin, and a hundred other liberals and social activists.[3] Instances of this new social democratic nostalgia for "coalition politics" and Keynesian economic programs that refer to these works in particular can be found in a growing number of articles dealing with such different topics as mass incarceration and the revival of labor's strike weapon.[4] While this social democratic current argues that it is *class* that matters most, the "coalition" politics they propose were and are always cross-class in nature and social content.

What these articles share in common is a tendency to demote, though not necessarily deny, race and racism as a factor in socialist analysis of American society, its working class, and today's politics. The solutions to the problems of African American or Latinx poverty and oppression are sought not in particular demands or policies relating specifically to Black or other people of color and their own self-activity, but in "universal" economic policies similar to that proposed in 1966 that are thought to simultaneously resolve the continuing problems of racism in the United States. This despite or because of the resurgence of such self-activity in the form of the Black Lives Matter movement in particular. And despite the open racism of the Trump-led Republican Party, the growth of armed white-supremacist groups, the continued disproportionate murder of Black men by the police, and the persistent segregation and discrimination in housing, education, and employment for a majority of people of color.

Throughout American history, African Americans have taken the lead in the fight against such conditions through various forms of self-organization, from the slave rebellions of the eighteenth and early nineteenth centuries, to what W. E. B. Du Bois called the United States' first general strike as slaves left the plantation to join the Union army during the Civil War, the Montgomery Bus Boycott that launched the civil rights movement, and the Black Power tendency of the late 1960s and 1970s, through today's Black Lives Matter movement.[5] The history of the Black freedom struggle has always seen a pattern in which African Americans act first and white liberals follow later—some enthusiastically, some reluctantly. To dismiss this history in the name of a failed effort at reform through the Democratic Party is not only to demean the legacy of African American struggle and important leaders such as Rustin and Randolph, but to call up the ghost of a failed political strategy.

This chapter will look at the real history and role of Bayard Rustin and A. Philip Randolph as leading Black American socialists *and* advocates of Black self-organization and mass direct action for most of their lives, before their political shift to the right in the mid-1960s. The purpose of this is not only to recover their radical heritage, but to demonstrate the centrality of Black self-organization and initiative in the fight against racism and its consequences in their lifetime. This is important because in all of the articles cited above, it is *only* the post-1963 phase of Rustin's and Randolph's political careers that is proposed as a model for today.

The arguments for demoting race as a factor in mass incarceration, which is the basis for rejecting specifically Black organization as well as "identity politics," are essentially the same in all these articles despite the addition of other contextual analyses. Some are more sophisticated than others and point to the class divisions within the Black population—a point few would deny. This is a problem that follows any political strategy for combating inequality in any form including coalition reform politics. All the advocates of this perspective to Rustin's post-1963 "coalition politics" and programmatic proposals as a social democratic solution. Because of the recent focus on police murders and incarceration, an appendix at the end of the book serves as discussion of the origins and dynamics of racist policing in the US, without attempting to resolve the debate on incarceration itself. Finally, because "class" is often used in a vague or economistic manner, it is crucial to understand the US working class as a relational product of the evolving conflictual social relations of capital and of the specifics of US history and that it is itself inherently diverse and internally unequal in terms of race, gender, and personnel, not a *thing* to be defined by average income, education, wealth, etc.[6]

What Rustin proposed in his mid-1960s articles was anything but a version of "working-class left politics," as Cedric Johnson called them in his *Catalyst* contribution.[7] Rather, it was a top-down alliance of liberals, labor officials, and African American leaders inside the thoroughly cross-class, middle class–led, bourgeois-funded, business-friendly Democratic Party of the time—the essence of mainstream multiclass liberal politics. This is the reality of the political coalition on which this New Social Democratic Nostalgia draws. This was a politics that downplayed the significance of race as a dividing line in working-class life and American society precisely in order to hold together a contradictory alliance in which many of the key actors did not see race or racism as a priority, feared alienating the white vote, accommodated racism in their own constituency, or believed simple economic improvements would deal with the problem. Simultaneously, this view of coalition politics substituted the trade union bureaucracy for the working class in the practice of "building alliances." Altogether missing from this version of the elements of the Democratic Party coalition are the important sections of US business that have long been funders, advisers, and participants in this party and its leadership even before the "realignment" described in chapter 3.

One of the most peculiar aspects of the New Social Democratic Nostalgia's insistence on demoting race and racism as a factor in mass incarceration, the disproportionate police murder of unarmed people of color,[8] and the deteriorating conditions of life in the country's inner city and increasingly suburban ghettos and barrios is its timing. Overt racism, after all, is on the rise. The capture of the Republican Party by stridently right-wing forces in the last couple of decades bent on deepening the disenfranchisement of African Americans in unapologetic terms, ending affirmative action, and cutting any remaining programs that might aid Black and Latinx people ought to give pause to the notion that such developments are simply economic and racially blind—even if they are part of a class offensive from above. The mass, international upsurge of anti-racist protest in the wake of the killing of George Floyd has blown away the idea that race is somehow secondary or can be fought simply by economic means or "universal" programs. To shift our attention to the failed social democratic electoral strategies of the 1960s and 1970s is surely more self-defeating than whatever limitations a renewed cross-class racial consciousness which confronts the racism of the criminal justice system and other forms of inequality today may embody.

The numerous appeals to Randolph and Rustin's post-1963 political orientation as somehow a "class" alternative to the self-activity and self-organization of African Americans by whatever name then and now involves a misrepresentation of these two key historic actors. For as we will see below, both took a political turn at some point in the early-to-mid 1960s that led away from the grassroots organizing, including that of Blacks-only organizations, and mass confrontation of their earlier years to a politics that assumed a top-down character in the name of coalition-building. One theory was that the fight for economic justice which had characterized the labor movement during its period of upsurge and militancy in the 1930s would be sufficient to advance African Americans now that the era of Jim Crow was over. At the core of this was what Rustin called the "liberal-labor-civil rights alliance."

Cedric Johnson, for example, drawing on Touré Reed, writes that "during the interwar period, through World War II, and well after, organizing based on class was widely accepted as an effective way for blacks to amass power and secure economic gains—specifically participation in the dynamic labor movement of the era."[9] While it is true that Blacks played an important role in a number of key CIO industrial unions in the 1930s and after, and made economic gains as a result, and that much of the Black leadership of the time accepted this view, the picture of labor is far too rosy. The first problem is that the rise of the CIO, as important as it was, did not significantly modify the racial inequality that made the vast majority of Blacks miss out on the post-war prosperity—a condition that led to the civil rights movement of the 1950s and 1960s.

In addition, by the early 1960s the labor movement was significantly less "dynamic" and still not the reliable ally in the fight for Black equality, economic or social, that the coalitionists argued it was. Even its liberal wing proved unwilling to go beyond Lyndon Johnson's weak War on Poverty with its studied avoidance of any significant redistribution of income or wealth, not to mention the hierarchical racial division of labor that is fundamental to American capitalism. Even less were most union leaders willing to confront the racism and discrimination within their own ranks and workplace practices that limited the opportunities for Blacks to advance into skilled occupations. Indeed, it was the reluctance to take on racism in the South that led to the failure of the CIO's 1946–47 "Operation Dixie."[10]

The AFL successfully opposed amendments to the National Labor Relations Act in 1935, put forth by the NAACP, the Urban League, and other Black leaders, that would preclude discrimination by unions on the basis of color. Even as Blacks joined the new CIO unions in growing numbers, the leaderships of almost all these unions remained entirely white, the major exception being the United Packinghouse Workers. When Blacks entered industry on a mass scale during World War II they were confined to the worst jobs and confronted with "hate strikes" in the North when some tried to advance into better-paying jobs. Some CIO unions tolerated segregation within the local unions in the South.[11] Indeed, discrimination in the unions would be a problem well into the civil rights era. And that is where the A. Philip Randolph who advocated separate Black organization to deal with internal union racism comes into the picture.

## Randolph and Black Worker Self-Organization

As a socialist, Randolph naturally believed in working-class organization and emancipation through class solidarity. But he also believed in Black self-organization as an essential means of advancement and of achieving solidarity on the basis of equality. Though Randolph had cooperated with and appeared in rallies together with Black nationalist Marcus Garvey in 1918–19, he came to oppose the separatist nationalism of Garvey and his Back-to-Africa movement in the 1920s and 1930s. Nevertheless, Randolph continued to advocate and practice Black self-organization even when it excluded whites.[12] In organizing the Pullman sleeping car porters he was confronted with the exclusionary practices of many craft unions and the railroad unions in particular. As a result, the Brotherhood of Sleeping Car Porters and Maids that Randolph helped organize and lead was an all-Black union that fought its way into the labor movement of the day. In 1936, Randolph participated in the formation of the National Negro Congress (NNC), an organization that included hundreds of Black groups and leaders and would play a role in helping the new CIO unions recruit Black workers and organizers.[13]

Randolph came into conflict with the NNC's Communist leaders in 1941 when Hitler's invasion of Poland, breaking the Hitler-Stalin Pact, led the Communist Party to turn away from "race" demands and actions in support of war preparations. As a result, Randolph resigned as president of the NNC. In 1941, as US entrance to the Second World War became inevitable and jobs in defense-related industries opened, Randolph broke with the NNC and created a new, exclusively Black organization as he called for a mass march of African Americans on Washington, DC, to demand that these jobs be open to Blacks. His aid was a young Bayard Rustin.[14] In his call for the planned March on Washington set for July 1, 1941, Randolph wrote:

> On to Washington, ten thousand black Americans. . . . We will not call on our white friends to march with us. There are some things Negroes must do alone. This is our fight and we must see it through.[15]

Was this "identity politics"? Or perhaps an exercise in Black power? While, to the disappointment of many and the anger of some, the march was called off when Roosevelt issued Executive Order 8802 establishing a "fair employment practices committee" to prevent discrimination in defense hiring, this was certainly a case of exclusive Black self-organization.

The March on Washington Movement (MOWM), as it soon became known, was more than an event-based coalition. Though the initial march was canceled, during the war it organized mass rallies of twenty thousand or so Black working-class people in New York, Chicago, and St. Louis, with smaller rallies and marches held elsewhere. Some fifty thousand Black working-class people paid a dollar or more to become members and the MOWM went on to act as a watchdog on the hiring of Blacks throughout the war.[16] Randolph's advocacy of Black self-organization didn't end there.

During and after the war Blacks organized caucuses and pressure groups within various unions, including two of the most "progressive": the United Auto Workers and the United Steelworkers. As the merger of the AFL and the CIO approached in 1955, Randolph, writing in the pages of the *Black Worker*, the Brotherhood of Sleeping Car Porters' official ("identarian"?) publication, demanded anti-discrimination clauses in the new federation's constitution. To win this he formed yet another all-Black organization, the Negro Trade Union Committee (NTUC), as a caucus of Black union leaders to fight for anti-discrimination clauses in the AFL-CIO's new constitution and for Black representation on the merged federation's executive board. The NTUC succeeded in winning some general language in the AFL-CIO merger agreement and in winning two Black vice-presidents out of twenty-seven, of which Randolph was one.[17]

Nevertheless, as NAACP labor director Herbert Hill documented in the late 1950s and early 1960s, many unions in the merged AFL-CIO continued to discriminate against Blacks, sometimes even excluding them, often relegating them to the worst jobs in the industry or craft or simply remaining silent as management did so and tolerating segregated local unions in the South. The building trades and railroad unions were the worst and most blatant, but even the social democratic–led International Ladies' Garment Workers' Union and the liberal Steelworkers, as well as the Seafarers International Union and the Hotel Restaurant and Bartenders Union in San Francisco, came under fire for racial bias.[18]

Nor could the liberal United Auto Workers (UAW) under Walter Reuther claim a good record when it came to helping Blacks to upgrade to the skilled trades jobs in auto plants. In the 1950s and 1960s only 2 percent of skill trade workers were Black in an industry that was 13 percent Black by that time, 20 percent in Michigan, and rapidly becoming more so. In the South, Black autoworkers were still restricted to janitorial positions. It was also the case that this most liberal of unions had no Blacks on its International Executive Board until 1962. After years of pressure from the union's Black caucus, the Trade Union Leadership Council (TULC) formed in 1957, and Nelson Jack Edwards was elevated to the executive board by the Reuther leadership in preference to the more militant Horace Sheffield, the leader of the TULC.[19]

By 1960, the TULC had gone beyond union officers and staffers to have two thousand members in Detroit and become one of the most active affiliates of Randolph's Negro American Labor Council (NALC—see below). Most of these members were drawn from the UAW, but included activists from the Steelworkers, Hotel and Restaurant Workers, the Laborers, and others who often socialized at its clubhouse headquarters in Detroit. By 1962 TULC claimed some ten thousand members and had successfully intervened in Detroit city politics to elect a more liberal mayor than the mainstream Democrat endorsed by the UAW leadership. In the late 1950s, organizations of Black unionists similar to the TULC spread to Youngtown, St. Louis, Philadelphia, Buffalo, Milwaukee, Cleveland, Chicago, Gary, and New York.[20]

Thus, long before the emergence of the more famous radical Black workers' groups, such as the Dodge Revolutionary Union Movement (DRUM) in Detroit or the Black Panther caucus at GM's Fremont, California plant, the late 1950s and early 1960s saw the rise of Black caucuses in a number of unions as more Blacks entered industry and encountered discrimination on the job and even in the union. The person who tied these together into a national organization of Black trade unionists was none other than A. Philip Randolph, who founded the NALC in 1960—once again a Black-only organization. Echoing the call to the 1941 March on Washington, the NALC declared, "We ourselves must seek the cure." It rapidly grew to about ten thousand members in 1960 in affiliated caucuses in Chicago, Pittsburgh, and Youngstown, indicating strong support among Black steelworkers, as well as the TULC in Detroit and similar groups in New York and elsewhere.

During this period, Randolph confronted AFL-CIO president George Meany about labor's poor record of racial discrimination in a number of unions. In addition, he blamed the federation's continued toleration of Jim Crow practices in the Southern local unions for the failure of organized labor in that region. This earned Randolph Meany's famous attack: "Who appointed you as the guardian of the Negro members in America?"[21]

In 1961 Randolph was actually censured by the AFL-CIO Executive Council for his ongoing attacks on the racist practices of several of the federation's affiliates. It was Randolph and the NALC at its 1962 convention that first proposed a march on Washington for 1963. Under Meany's leadership, the AFL-CIO would refuse to endorse the 1963 March on Washington. It was mostly the industrial unions that endorsed and sent delegations to Washington on August 28.[22] Randolph remained a self-described socialist all his life and even rejoined the Socialist Party in 1969. Until 1964 he had never voted for a major-party presidential candidate. In that year, at the age of seventy-five, he was convinced to vote for Johnson in order to stop Barry Goldwater.[23] Tragically, it was around then that Randolph, who had spent a lifetime building grassroots Black organizations, campaigns, and actions, turned toward a politics that would lead him to an alliance with Meany himself—in an as yet unreformed AFL-CIO. It was, however, mainly Rustin, then an aid to Randolph, who provided the analytical basis for the shift from direct action, civil disobedience, and Black self-organization to electoral coalition politics. So, a brief look at Bayard Rustin's career as a fighter for equality and peace prior to this shift is called for.

## Rustin as a Radical Organizer and Agitator

Already a convinced pacifist and field secretary for A. J. Muste's Fellowship of Reconciliation, as well as a founder of the Congress of Racial Equality (CORE), Bayard Rustin left the Young Communist League when it turned away from racial issues in 1941 and went to work for Randolph on the March on Washington. Twenty years later in 1961, working with Randolph at the NALC, he continued to defend the right to Black self-organization when Randolph and the NALC were attacked by Meany and other union leaders for "dual unionism" and "racism in reverse." In response Rustin stated, "Under present conditions—i.e., general segregation and discrimination, and the unreliability of today's organized (or disorganized) liberalism—the Negro will find it necessary in many instances to organize independently."[24]

Between these two events, Rustin accumulated a massive track record in organizing Black and civil rights actions and organizations by leading one of the first "Freedom Rides" in the South in 1947 called the Journey of Reconciliation, in 1955–56 as an organizer of the Montgomery Bus Boycott, as an adviser in the founding of the Southern Cristian Leadership Conference, as an assistant to Martin Luther King Jr., and as an organizer of mass civil rights marches that brought thousands to Washington in the late 1950s. Tragically, because he was gay, Rustin was often forced to work behind the scenes and failed to get the recognition he deserved.[25] It was after these achievements that Rustin became an assistant to Randolph at the NALC.

When a new generation of young activists launched the student sit-ins in Greensboro, North Carolina, in February 1960, introducing a new wave of civil rights militancy, Rustin along with experienced organizer Ella Baker helped organize the Student Nonviolent Coordinating Committee (SNCC). SNCC was to be the "vanguard" of the new direct-action phase of the movement. Rustin was also influential in the early development of the Howard University–based Nonviolent Action Group (NAG), whose leader at the time was Stokely Carmichael.[26] Carmichael and SNCC would, of course, become among the first movement activists to oppose Rustin's post-1963 political direction.

## From Confrontation to Coalition

It is difficult to pinpoint the moment at which Rustin took the political turn that led him away from direct action, mass mobilization, and confrontation to the coalition politics directed at "realigning" the Democratic Party he proposed in his famous February 1965 *Commentary* essay, "From Protest to Politics." The decisive event that pushed him to fully embrace this approach appears to have been the 1964 Democratic National Convention and the conflict with the Mississippi Freedom Democratic Party (MFDP) delegation's attempt to displace the all-white official delegation. He later wrote that if the March on Washington had been the high point of "the era of protest," "the 1964 Democratic National Convention marked its symbolic conclusion" and hence the necessity to move from protest to politics.[27] This conclusion is all the more mystifying as the Democratic Party leadership rejected the MFDP's demands.

The introduction of the strategy of Democratic Party realignment and the "coalition politics" that were to achieve it into socialist circles, however, is generally attributed to his connection with the political current around erstwhile revolutionary Marxist Max Shachtman that included Socialist Party (SP) and Young People's Socialist League (YPSL) members Michael Harrington, Tom Kahn, and Rachelle Horowitz. Since the late 1950s, Shachtman and his followers had been "moving steadily to the right," as Maurice Isserman put it rather mildly.[28] For the "Marxist" Shachtman, developing the working-class part of the coalition that was to transform the Democratic Party meant redefining the role of the working class. To fit the necessarily top-down practice of Democratic Party coalitionist politics, Shachtman substituted the interests of the labor bureaucracy for those of the working class and the union rank and file and came, as Isserman put it, to "define those interests solely in terms of what the official leadership of the AFL-CIO said they were."[29]

Rustin had met Shachtman during the Montgomery Bus Boycott when Shachtman and his group, the Independent Socialist League (ISL), had raised money in the North for the Montgomery struggle. Shachtman had been moving away from revolutionary socialism for a number of years, and led the ISL into the Socialist Party in the late 1950s, where by 1961 he adopted the strategy of realignment in the Democratic Party—the strategy Rustin called for, though not by name, several years later in "From Protest to Politics." Though Rustin didn't join the SP, he became part of the group around Shachtman, Harrington, Kahn, and Horowitz.[30]

When the SP split three ways in 1972, Rustin's association with Shachtman, Harrington, Kahn, and Horowitz led him to join the United States' most right-wing, Cold War social democratic organization, Social Democrats USA (SDUSA). This tiny sect supported the war in Vietnam and was friendly to the likes of George Meany and hawk Democrat Henry "Scoop" Jackson. Some of its members soon became neoconservatives around the by then rightward-moving journal *Commentary*. Shachtman died just before SDUSA was officially formed. Harrington to his credit opposed the war in Vietnam and resigned from SDUSA in 1973 to found the Democratic Socialist Organizing Committee (DSOC), the forerunner of DSA. Rustin, however, remained a member of SDUSA.[31]

The concept of realignment, as this strategy of coalition politics came to be known, originated in mainstream (classless) political science in the 1950s as academics such as V. O. Key tried to explain changes in voting patterns and constituencies in the two major parties.[32] Shachtman and others saw organized labor as central to realignment by driving the Dixiecrats from the Democratic Party and defeating the urban machines in order to create what they argued would amount to an American labor party. Jarvis Anderson, one of Rustin's biographers, said that Tom Kahn told him that Shachtman "was critical to the analysis in 'From Protest to Politics.'"[33] While the Southern Democrats would eventually become Republicans and the old urban machines faded by the mid-1970s, it hardly needs to be stressed that nothing remotely like a labor or social democratic party came out of this strategy.

Despite the social democratic wishful thinking, this coalition was always a top-down, cross-class coalition in which capitalism was taken for granted. Indeed, the presence of important sections of capital in the Democratic coalition went unspoken and unacknowledged in this "class" analysis. It was Rustin's close association with the pinnacle of the labor bureaucracy, including George Meany in particular, however, that would eventually pull him far to the right of the politics he held at least through 1961. In fact, at the invitation of Meany, Rustin had gone to work as director of the new AFL-CIO-funded A. Philip Randolph Institute in 1964 before writing "From Protest to Politics."[34] An indication of Rustin's journey from confrontation to accommodation was the shift in how he approached the 1960 Democratic National Convention and that in 1964.

In 1960, he and Randolph worked with Martin Luther King Jr. to organize demonstrations outside the conventions of both parties demanding civil rights legislation. In 1964, however, Randolph, who up to that year had always voted socialist and never for a major-party presidential candidate, attempted to work with and through Rustin behind the scenes inside the Democratic National Convention. Of his experience as an "insider" at that Democratic convention (see below), Rustin wrote, "We hoped to begin the long and difficult process of securing a leadership role within the political system."[35] As to his efforts to build a coalition capable of transforming the Democratic Party and his hope to gain influence "within the political system," as Randall Kennedy put it cautiously in *The Nation*, "it seems the party moved him considerably more than he moved it."[36]

Before analyzing the context in which "From Protest to Politics" and "'Black Power' and Coalition Politics" were written, a summary of Rustin's post-1963 March on Washington actions will give us an idea of just how far coalition politics took him from his earlier political and moral positions:

- Almost exactly one year after the March on Washington the all-Black delegation to the 1964 Democratic National Convention from the Mississippi Freedom Democratic Party (MFDP), a grassroots political organization SNCC had helped to launch, demanded that they replace the all-white "official" Mississippi Democratic delegation. Lyndon Johnson objected and Walter Reuther of the United Auto Workers, one of the more liberal labor leaders along with (Mr. Liberal) Hubert Humphrey, offered a "compromise" that left the racist delegation in place but would have sat two "at large" MFDP delegates. Led by Fannie Lou Hammer, the MFDP delegates rejected what they saw as a "back of the bus" offer.[37] Rustin not only supported the compromise, but in "From Protest to Politics" proclaimed it a "political revolution!" MFDP, SNCC, CORE, Students for a Democratic Society, and other movement groups and activists saw this more as a counterrevolution, and the tensions with Rustin increased.

- As the 1964 election contest between Lyndon Johnson and Barry Goldwater approached, and movement activity was joined by riots in Harlem and other cities, Rustin persuaded Randolph and some other leaders to call on the movement "to observe a broad curtailment, if not a total moratorium on all marches, mass picketing, and mass demonstrations until after Election Day, November 3."[38] Again, politics constrained by the limits of liberalism were to be a substitute for protest, mass action, and independent organization.

- After the passage of the Civil Rights Act of 1964 and the Voting Rights Act of 1965, movement activists looked in different directions for how to fight the deeper conditions racism still inflicted on the majority of African Americans. When in 1968 Martin Luther King, Jr. proposed the "Poor People's Campaign" as the closest thing to an orientation toward the ranks of the working class, Rustin opposed the idea on the grounds that Black people were too volatile. He was overruled by King.[39]

- His support for Meany and the AFL-CIO leadership led Rustin to oppose "preferential hiring," as affirmative action was called then, in the building trades unions even though most of them still discriminated

against Black workers.[40] Some years later the A., Philip Randolph Institute issued a statement saying that while they supported affirmative
action, they didn't believe it should "occupy a pivotal role in a strategy
for racial progress" and were "unalterably opposed to the imposition of
quotas or any other form of ratio hiring."[41] This would seem to render
the whole concept moot.

- Rustin not only abandoned the sort of direct action he had long advocated
  and organized, but shattered the principles of his lifelong pacifist convic-
  tions by his tacit support of Johnson's escalation of the War in Vietnam
  just as the anti-war movement gained strength. He had initially supported the moderate, pro-negotiations wing of the anti-war movement, but
  shied away from the notion of pulling US troops "Out Now!" as the movement increasingly demanded. His criticisms of the Johnson administration's foreign policy "dramatically softened," wrote Randall Kennedy in
  *The Nation*. This was at least in part the result of his embrace of the hawkish leadership of AFL-CIO president George Meany and his dependence
  on a Democratic administration, despite its commitment to war, winning
  in the 1968 elections. As one of Rustin's biographers put it, "Search the
  anti-war movement's great moments and Rustin's absence is glaring."[42]

This listing of Rustin's accommodation to the worst of the labor bureaucracy and the liberal establishment is not meant to be a catalogue of personal
weaknesses, for Rustin was anything but a weak person. Rather it is a chronology
of his political trajectory from radical pacifism, socialism, and mass direct action
to subordination to the liberals he had seen as "unreliable" not so long before.
It was a process in which the forces he hoped would create an American social
democracy instead shaped Rustin's rejection of what he had stood for up to the
very event in 1963 that gained him the recognition he had long been denied. In
fairness, it has to be said, the fact that he never totally lost his radical instincts
can be seen in his later life when he lent his active support to the militant, direct
action gay liberation group ACT UP.[43]

In introducing Bayard Rustin as an exemplar of coalition politics and social
democratic demands in the form of the 1966 *Freedom Budget*, Cedric Johnson
writes critically that Rustin "would increasingly embrace a politics of insider
negotiation during the sixties."[44] In fact, as we just saw, "insider negotiations,"
to put it politely, were a feature of his approach at least from the 1964 MFDP
"compromise" and the "broad curtailment" of demonstrations made to accom-

modate the liberals he had seen as unreliable only three years earlier. Nor was it just a matter of "insider negotiations," but of accommodation to the Johnson administration and its priorities. All before he wrote "From Protest to Politics."

This accommodation or "broad curtailment" of direct action in support of Lyndon Johnson's re-election is all the more inexplicable in strategic terms because it was not accommodation of any sort that had previously induced President Kennedy to finally announce on June 11, 1963, his intention to introduce a civil rights bill and the actual forwarding of the bill to Congress on June 19. Even more than the threat of the March on Washington set for August, it was the explosion of over nine hundred civil rights actions in 115 cities involving the arrest of some twenty thousand demonstrators, set off by the explosion and first "riot" of the era in Birmingham, Alabama. Most of these actions took place in May and early June of that year just prior to Kennedy's about-face in favor of legislation.[45] Later in June, according to historian Arthur Schlesinger, Kennedy himself told civil rights leaders "that the demonstrations in the streets had brought results, they had made the executive branch act faster and were now forcing Congress to entertain legislation which a few weeks before would have had no chance."[46] Somehow, Rustin drew the wrong conclusion from these events and opted, as one writer put it, "to *substitute* politics *for* protest."[47] And did so at the very moment when "protest"—that is, mass disruptive action—had brought the movement's first major national *political* success.

Nor did accommodation produce the political support for the 1966 *Freedom Budget* that Rustin had hoped for once Johnson had been re-elected. According to Anderson, Rustin "envisioned its endorsement and implementation by the Johnson Administration." Not surprisingly, this was not forthcoming. As Rustin himself put it, the *Freedom Budget* "didn't sell."[48] Once again accommodation and "insider negotiations" had failed. It seems strange that so many should see the *Freedom Budget* and "coalitionism" as a precedent for today, given that they had no real impact on events, let alone the eventual direction of liberalism and the Democratic Party.

Accommodation, not only to liberalism, but to the most conservative and hawkish elements of the American labor leadership represented by George Meany, was the formative context in which Rustin's coalition politics evolved at a time when the Black Freedom Movement was moving to a new, more militant stage symbolized by the slogan "Freedom Now!" well before anyone spoke of Black Power.

Indeed, more than any single event, it was the rejection of the MFDP's demands by the liberal establishment and the "compromise" it offered that angered the SNCC, CORE, and SDS activists as well as MFDP delegates and pushed SNCC toward Stokely Carmichael's famous "Black Power" chant at the June 1966 James Meredith March Against Fear that introduced this term into the nation's political lexicon.[49]

The central idea of coalition politics originally presented in "From Protest to Politics" stated:

> The future of the Negro struggle depends on whether the contradictions of this society can be resolved by a coalition of progressive forces which becomes the *effective* political majority in the United States. I speak of the coalition which staged the March on Washington, passed the Civil Rights Act, and laid the basis for the Johnson landslide—Negros, trade unionists, liberals, and religious groups.[50]

This was a somewhat disingenuous presentation of the progressiveness of the coalition partners of the time. First of all, the conservative building trades and other AFL unions which represented well over half the nation's union members did not support the March on Washington. While the AFL-CIO did support the Civil Rights Act, the Democratic liberals in Congress were unable to pass the Act by themselves despite their compromises and Lyndon Johnson's arm-twisting. It took a significant number of Republican votes to get it through Congress.[51] Similarly, while Johnson's landslide was aided by a significant switch of African American voters from Republican to Democrat, it was also in part due to Northern Republican moderates repulsed by Goldwater's extremism who shifted temporarily to vote Democratic that year. In other words, it was not actually the ideal coalition Rustin described that, by itself, passed the Civil Rights Act of 1964 and put Johnson back in the White House.

Furthermore, the central arguments presented in the two articles Rustin wrote for *Commentary* advocating this electoral coalition to realign the Democratic Party were essentially negative. The first was that the direct action methods of the civil rights movement were insufficient to address the deeper economic inequality and conditions faced by most African Americans. The second was that Black people alone could not win the sort of social democratic program represented by the *Freedom Budget* or eliminate the underlying economic inequality they faced. As he put it in the 1966 essay, "one-tenth of the population cannot accomplish much itself."[52] Both, in the largely legislative terms in which he saw things at that time, are, of course, negative truisms—although one doubts he would have said this about a labor movement that around 1960 composed just about "one-tenth" of the population. In any case, neither of these negative arguments by themselves justifies the particular electoral "coalition" orientation Rustin proposed.

Aside from hard-core separatists, most of those who organized around the idea of Black Power in the 1960s and 1970s did so in order to build a power base from which to influence events whether that was by election to local office, seeking a level of community control over poverty programs or schools, self-defense, and breakfast programs à la the Panthers, organizing a Black caucus in one's union, and so on. That the rhetoric often exceeded the accumulation of power in the face of white resistance or moderation or the Black leaders' own opportunism or ultraleftism was often the case. But the urge toward self-organization by oppressed groups, as by the working class as a whole, is a politically rational one. One that is propelled not so much by abstract ideology, as by the conditions of oppression and exploitation. And one that informed a major aspect of Randolph's and Rustin's political lives. Dependence on elite coalitions because they are the norm of American electoral politics even in times of upsurge, it turns out, was not as sensible as it seemed to them by 1964. More generally, the whole coalition/realignment strategy overlooked not only the shadowy presence of big business in the Democratic coalition, but the contradictions and changes occurring in the economy and within the proposed liberal-labor-civil rights coalition itself.

For one thing, alongside their gross failures to deal with internal racism, the trade union bureaucracy, the central partner in Rustin's proposed coalition, was facing a rising rebellion among their members against union leaders who had grown complacent and conceded authority in the workplace to capital. This had allowed an enormous speed-up in industry after industry in what Mike Davis calls "The Management Offensive of 1958–63."[53] As a result, soon the industrial unions that were supposed to be the engine of progress saw many of their members, both Black and white, engage in wildcat strikes, reject contract offers the leaders deemed reasonable, and form opposition rank-and-file-based caucuses both Black and interracial in union after union.[54] All this working-class self-activity was ignored by advocates of realignment and coalition politics even as it exploded in their faces.

Not only that, but even as the *Freedom Budget* was being formulated with the help of Keynesian economist Leon Keyserling, the underpinnings of the era of relative prosperity that most African Americans had missed out on were being undermined by a secular fall in the rate of profit for American industry. This, in turn, would lead to a decade of crisis in the form of "stagflation" in the 1970s and periodic slumps in the following decades.[55] The dramatic change in the US and global economy would be one force in turning the Democratic Party to the center and right beginning in the mid-1970s, as the analytical and organizational underpinnings of New Deal liberalism collapsed and big business organized aggressively for deregulation and market liberalization. Another would be the flooding of the entire political process with corporate and wealthy donor money. The real realignment that took place from the mid-1970s into the twenty-first century saw the Democratic Party move to the center and right in an embrace of what became known as neoliberalism.[56] What about today?

## Class, Race, and the Left This Time

The strong showing of Bernie Sanders in the 2016 presidential primaries, the rapid growth of the Democratic Socialists of America, the election of open socialists to office and the rise of social activism all point toward a revival of radical politics in the US. The context, to be sure, is still dominated by right-wing advance and liberal caution. Nevertheless, for some this renewed hope has brought a demotion of race as a subject of socio-economic analysis and political organization in the name of class that is, in reality, a return to America's quintessential business-funded, neoliberal-dominated, undemocratic, cross-class social construction: the Democratic Party.

As a Marxist who has put class at the center of my analyses over the years, I naturally believe it will take more than the efforts of Black Americans or even Black and Latinx people combined to end economic and racial inequality. It will take a class-based movement with socialist politics at its center. But I have also seen both firsthand through involvement in the civil rights and labor movements as well as through study and research that fighting embedded racism and sexism requires the self-organization of the oppressed to shape or supplement the broader programs in such a way that that they do not simply reproduce racial inequality in new, sometimes less visible forms as they often have in the past; e.g., in the New Deal and the post-WWII GI Bill.

Among other things, the geographic reality of the de facto segregation of the majority of Black and Latinx people means substandard education, housing, food, and services, along with punitive welfare and racist policing operations discussed in the appendix.[57] Medicare for All, a Federal Jobs Guarantee, a decent minimum or living wage, and a Green New Deal are all things worth fighting for that would improve the lives of everyone. But as they fail to alter the geography of race and leave the delivery of services, the content of jobs, and the quality of housing and health care in private/capitalist hands, racial and gender discrimination, harassment, and violence, along with unequal implementation, delivery, and administration, will remain embedded if not specifically rooted out.

These "universal" programs also leave the harassment, bullying, and violence that Black, Latinx, female, and LGBTQ workers experience in the workplace in the hands of managers who tolerate these attacks even when they don't actually participate in them. Hence the ninety thousand EEOC charges every year, about half for race, color, or national origin, a number that doesn't include similar charges made to state and local Fair Employment Practices Agencies and countless lawsuits filed each year.[58] Nor do these "universal" programs deal directly with police racism and violence.

There is, of course, another side to the problem of the sort of coalition politics Cedric Johnson advocates when he speaks of "building alliances not on identity as such, but on shared values and demonstrated commitments" in the context of mainstream electoral politics. Namely, as Mia White points out in her contribution to the *New Politics* forum on Johnson's essays, Black women, followed in numbers by Black men, are already "the most predictable Democratic voters in the United States, and they already and loyally vote with a diverse, white-led political party" and have been for generations. "In other words, there is little evidence that Black voters are not already doing what Johnson asks they do."[59] Without much in the way of success, it must be added—a fact that cost the Democrats Black and Latinx votes in 2020.

The same can be said of almost all union leaders and a majority of working-class voters of various races, despite the shift of some working-class whites to the Republicans. What's new in this proposal for a rerun of "coalition politics"? Ever since the vote was won by Black Americans, the "machines" collapsed, and the Dixiecrats became Republicans, all the coalition partners have been present and accounted for in the Democratic Party as Rustin and others prescribed to precious little effect. The asymmetry of power in this most cross-class of electoral coalitions dictates that this sort of alliance-building in such a highly institutionalized context is a repetitious path to failed hopes, programs, demands, and even reasonable proposals. The idea that the role of socialists is to tell people to stick it out in this centrist party of capital in the belief this will produce anything like what is needed or even in hopes of a break from it in some distant future has it backward.

The hope for political success lies, now as then, in oppositional power based on independent organizations, be they democratized unions, union rank-and-file caucuses, civil rights groups, specifically Black, Latinx, women's, or LGBTQ organizations, the interracial upsurge against police violence, or the rising movement around climate change. By the mid-1970s, after a brief "seizure" of the party's presidential candidacy by the electorally respectable anti-war forces led by George McGovern, virtually all the social movements, including many politicians claiming the Black Power mantle, ended up in this grand multiclass coalition party just at the very moment the leaders, officeholders, and funders began their movement to the political center and beyond in response to capital's new phase of falling profit rates and repeated crises. The master's voice, not the voters in coalition, called the shots.

The fundamental problem that the coalition politics of the 1960s and 1970s and the New Social Democratic Nostalgia share with some versions of "identity" politics is a blindness to the realities of capitalism and its structural needs to dominate, exploit, oppress, fragment, and disarm the working class and its constituent human elements by the dialectics of exclusion and the simulation of inclusion. Self-organization, not permeation, must be the watchword of socialist politics today as in the past, even if the forms are different.

The 1960s failed to produce the sort of class-based politics and political organizations capable of bringing serious social change. Nostalgia for that era cannot be a guide to the tasks of the present and future. As one who supported (and supports) the right of Black self-organization and worked in coalition with the Panthers in Brooklyn in 1968 and has great respect for what they tried to do then, I don't mind saying that this goes for the hope that something like the Black Panther Party will "Save Us Now" as well. They couldn't then, and in any case history doesn't repeat itself. A much broader and more powerful movement was needed then as now. But this goes even more so for the more active contemporary fantasy and alternative bit of nostalgia that coalescing in the Democratic Party will be the salvation for a left long in the wilderness but now growing again.

If there is a lesson to be drawn from the 1960s and 1970s, it is that social movements based in class, race, and gender tended to inspire and encourage one another, not cancel each other out. In the context of the conditions of the time, the civil rights movement inspired rank-and-file rebellion on the "old" unions, the rise of public employee unionism, the women's and gay liberation movements, and so on. They were all too often ideologically limited, too easily torn apart by the system's centrifugal forces of competition and undermined by more than a little state repression. The effort to coalesce them on a lowest common denominator basis in the Democratic Party was a disastrous failure precisely to the degree that this became or remained their political home. This time, we need to take both class and race seriously and to understand that power derives from the independent organization and actions of the exploited and oppressed themselves.

## CHAPTER 5

# The Politics of Winning:
# How Mass Action Brought Victory

*Come senators, congressmen, please heed the call*
*Don't stand in the doorway, don't block up the hall*
*For he that gets hurt will be he who has stalled*
*The battle outside ragin'*
*Will soon shake your windows and rattle your walls*
*For the times they are a-changin'*
        —Bob Dylan, "The Times They Are A-Changin'"

That climate change has moved up the global political agenda, particularly since the 2014 UN report's alarming conclusions have challenged climate deniers and footdraggers alike, seems beyond doubt. In this context, the idea of a Green New Deal has become a programmatic centerpiece of left politics and even a matter of congressional attention in the US. While the idea and the label have been around for a number of years, it is only in the last couple of years that a comprehensive version of the Green New Deal gained any traction in the halls of power. What makes it unique is its attention to and proposals to "create millions of good, high-wage jobs," "invest in infrastructure and industry," provide "high-quality education, including higher education," and other important social aspects of a transition to achieving "net-zero greenhouse gases" and a sustainable economy.[1] It had the backing of many organizations, was visibly promoted by a sit-in of Sunrise Movement activists in House Democratic

Speaker Nancy Pelosi's office, and endorsed by nearly one hundred members of Congress. In the form of a general resolution (H.R. 109) it has been discussed in both chambers of Congress. And that, of course, is where the trouble began.

In the Senate, the Republicans, sure many Democrats would be embarrassed by voting on so "socialistic" a measure, forced a vote on the resolution to put Democrats "on the spot," and, sure enough, four Democrats voted against along with the Republicans. Most Democrats, however, voted "present"—i.e., abstained—on the resolution to prevent an open split or reveal how much or little support the measure really had, a tactic the resolution's House democratic socialist sponsor Alexandria Ocasio-Cortez (AOC) approved, as did activists from the Sunrise Movement.[2] Clever it may have been, but this is only a preview of the flak a real Green New Deal faced in Congress—from Democrats as well as Republicans.

For starters, even though it was only at the stage of a general resolution, the House version was assigned to no less than eleven of the House's twenty standing committees "for a period to be subsequently determined by the Speaker," where it could be torn to pieces, amended beyond recognition, delayed indefinitely, buried, etc.[3] At the time it was introduced, instead of the select committee on the Green New Deal requested by AOC, House Speaker Nancy Pelosi resurrected a general select committee on the climate crisis which includes some of the resolution's sponsors, but not AOC. Again, as a select committee on the climate crisis, it is vague on jobs, etc. and is not meant to deal with the social goals of the Green New Deal.[4]

Contrast this treatment with the unusually swift passage of the "Climate Action Now Act" (bill H.R. 9) introduced in the House on March 27, 2019, "to direct the President" to meet US obligations under the 2015 Paris Agreement. This bill from the party officialdom was sponsored by mainstream Democrat Kathy Castor and cosponsored by House Speaker Nancy Pelosi and House Majority Leader Steny Hoyer among others, but not AOC. As originally introduced, it contained no language on social matters such as jobs, education, etc. It was referred to only two committees, where vague language about taking "into consideration . . . American jobs, wages, pay" was amended. It passed the House in only a little more than a month on May 2 by 231 to 190.[5] While the Republicans, of course, opposed all of this, the initial dodge and subsequent vagueness on the social aspects gives us a clue as to where some of the problems among the

Democrats are likely to appear even with the Democratic victory of 2020. H.R. 109 saw no action in the 116th Congress and expired with the new Congress in 2021. AOC reintroduced the Green New Deal as H.R. 332 in April 2021. It was again sent to eleven committees "for a period to be subsequently determined by the Speaker."[6]

If anything like the Green New Deal is to become a bill and eventually law, what we saw at these early stages of introduction and subsequent treatment is only the starting point of the complex process by which legislation is traditionally crafted, referred to committee(s), opened to hearings, "marked up," split up, lobbied, logrolled, watered down, compromised, frequently buried, and only very rarely passed by both houses of Congress.[7] To paraphrase a then-not-so-famous Representative Bernie Sanders (I-VT) speaking to the opening session of the 1993 *Labor Notes* conference, "I quickly learned that Congress is not a place where you get things done."[8] Or as a leading textbook on congressional politics puts it, "In short, the legislative process favors opponents of legislation and hinders proponents."[9] Especially when the leadership of your own party is not committed to success.

Given the historical realities of congressional politics, and that House Speaker Nancy Pelosi, Senate Majority Leader Charles Schumer, and President Joe Biden oppose it, the Green New Deal has a long and perilous journey ahead. Neither does it help that AFL-CIO Energy Committee members criticized the proposed Green New Deal in a letter to sponsors Senator Ed Markey and Ocasio-Cortez, nor that AFL-CIO president Rich Trumka complained that labor was not consulted prior to the resolution's introduction—despite the resolution's call for "high-quality union jobs."[10] Labor is, in fact, divided on this. Fortunately, other union leaders and members do call for urgent action on climate change.[11]

While we won't dwell on it here, it should also be obvious that capital—and not only fossil fuel capital, which permeates the halls of Congress at all times—will lobby, pressure, propagandize, consult, and organize against a Green New Deal with all its might and money. The gas and oil industry alone spent $2.2 billion in direct lobbying over the last twenty years, $125,197,199 of it in 2018. As a focus of lobbying money in general, the energy and natural resources sector attracted over $6 billion in lobbying money in those two decades, $325,205,586 in 2018. As we have seen, capital is also the major contributor supporting the institutional structures of the Democratic Party as well as the campaign funds of most of its politicians.[12] So, the external and internal hurtles to winning are high indeed.

How, then, can a real Green New Deal be won? The conventional answer, of course, is to elect the right politicians. The 2020 election, however, once again demonstrated that electing the lesser-evil Democrats does not solve the problem as moderate and centrist officeholders increase their domination of the party's elected representatives up and down the ballot. The impasse that prevents legislation anywhere near the likes of a Green New Deal, Medicare for All, etc. remains, and is indeed reinforced by, an administration staffed with creatures from the swamp of alt-finance, defense contractors, etc.

The answer that will be offered here is, in a nutshell, massive disruptive social movements from below that reach deeply into society to include the various sections of the working class. Even when the best that mainstream American politics has to offer sit in Congress in sufficient numbers to matter, which is hardly the case today, getting anything that comes close to what is sought has always required the disruption of business as usual: "the battle outside ragin'" in the streets, workplaces, and public spaces.

It has always been the case that working-class and socially excluded groups in the US have had to fight for change outside the formal political and legislative processes to a greater degree than in other capitalist nations. This rhythm of social upheaval preceding legislative and political change has long been an integral part of the American political system at least since the time of the anti-slavery movements and the Civil War. To make the case for this, we will look at two of the most important, if still very modest, progressive legislative achievements of the twentieth century (sorry, there aren't really any yet in the twenty-first): the original New Deal of the 1930s and the civil rights legislation of the 1960s.

## Winning an Imperfect New Deal

One reason the Green New Deal has been so named is that the original New Deal is still seen as one of the major victories for the majority of people, an advance for organized labor, and the foundation of the modern though minimal American welfare state. When most people think of the New Deal of the 1930s, they usually think of the Social Security Act (SSA, 1935) that brought millions—though not everyone at the time—a guaranteed pension, unemployment insurance, what became known as "welfare" for dependent mothers, and disability benefits; the National Labor Relations Act (NLRA, 1935) that supposedly gave workers a guaranteed right to join a union and bargain collectively; the Works Progress Administration (WPA, 1935) which employed millions to build schools, roads, and even art and theater programs; and the Fair Labor Standards Act (FLSA, 1938) which gave us the forty-hour work week (for a while), to mention some of the major programs. These were the gains from Roosevelt's "Second New Deal."[13]

One thing stands out with this list of achievements: they all became law and policy after Franklin D. Roosevelt (FDR) and a Democratic majority in Congress had been in office for over two years. Was FDR, his famous "brain trust," and the heavily Democratic Congress sitting on their collective hands for two years? No, in fact, what some historians call the First New Deal (1933–35) was enacted in a flurry of legislation known as the First Hundred Days from March, when FDR took office and the new Congress convened, through mid-July 1933. This First New Deal bore little resemblance to the better known Second New Deal (1935–38) that we associate with the welfare state. The legislation and policy-making of the Roosevelt administration's first two years might rather be described as state welfare for big business, along with the continuation and modest expansion of the limited "relief"—as the minimal, temporary unemployed benefits of the time were known—begun under Republican Herbert Hoover. It should be borne in mind that the electoral coalition of the Democratic Party at that time was composed of the segregationist "Solid South," the Northern urban white-dominated machines, and most of the as yet weak AFL unions, as well as the even less well-organized liberals and older "Progressives." This was not a promising assemblage from the point of view of those workers attempting to organize against the massive distress the Depression had thrown them into.

In the depths of the Depression, FDR's first act was to do what had already been done: declare his famous "bank holiday" for the nation's beleaguered banks which had, in fact, already been closed by the states or on their own initiative.[14] The first bill to pass Congress in the spring of 1933 was the "Economy Act," which balanced the government's budget, just as FDR had promised. It did this in part by cutting federal employee pay by 15 percent, reducing veteran's benefits, and authorizing agencies to fire married women if their husbands also worked for the federal government. It was so conservative it took Republican votes to pass.[15] In the spring of 1933, Congress also passed a number of regulatory measures such as the Securities Act and the Banking Act (Glass-Steagall), "popular with investors" and backed by some large banks and most smaller ones, meant to curb the excessive speculation and dishonest representation of securities. In other words, to protect investors.[16]

Most of the "relief" was in the form of direct payments to the unemployed by the individual states or cities—the federal government at that time made no direct "welfare" or "relief" payments, only grants and loans to the states which then passed on money to the cities. The first federal relief bill during the Depression included $500 million in loans to the states and another $300 million for direct hiring on federal public works that had been signed by the Republican Hoover administration in 1932.[17] Roosevelt's first Emergency Relief Act also sent $500 million to the states via the new Federal Emergency Relief Administration (FERA). Other funds came though FERA or the Reconstruction Finance Corporation set up by FDR's Republican predecessor.[18]

There were, however, some new relief programs. Some unemployed workers got jobs at minimal wages through the new Civilian Conservation Corps (CCC, about 300,000) and the Civil Works Administration (CWA; 4 million, about a third of the unemployed), the latter spending about $1 billion on projects. The CWA, however, was closed down in less than a year in April 1934, as FDR considered it too expensive. The workers were transferred to other forms of relief or work where their weekly wage was cut from $15.04 to $6.50. Altogether, during the first two years of FDR's administration, the federal government spent just over $2 billion on relief—a large amount for the time, but small in comparison with what was to come in the Second New Deal. None of these programs were meant to be more than emergency measures since FDR disapproved of relief in general. He later told Congress, "The Federal Government must and shall quit this business of relief."[19] In fact, it couldn't.

Unemployment had hit 25 percent of the workforce by 1932, hundreds of thousands of jobless workers roamed the nation in search of work, while others lived in makeshift "Hooverville" shantytowns. Most remained stuck in their old neighborhood where many lost their homes for failure to meet rent or mortgage payments. The humanitarian crisis itself called out for bold action by the time Roosevelt was swept into office by 22.8 million to 15.8 million votes—though with a surprisingly low turnout of 56.9 percent.[20] As historian Irving Bernstein put it, "Hence mass unemployment stirred the impulse to reform."[21] But this impulse came not only from concerned liberals, bewildered economists, and alarmed politicians. The victims of this crisis had been neither silent nor passive.

From almost the beginning of the Great Depression, as unemployed workers began to recover from the shock and the sense of personal failure many felt, they started to take collective action. Among the first was a direct form of what we might call today "crowdfunding" but authorities then called "mob lootings," where crowds would enter a grocery store and politely, but firmly, take what they needed to survive. More organized were the Unemployed Councils formed by the Communists, the Unemployed Leagues organized by A. J. Muste's Conference for Progressive Political Action (later American Workers Party), and similar groups led by members of the Socialist Party. These engaged in both mass demonstrations for "relief" and anti-eviction "riots" where large crowds prevented eviction. About 350,000–400,000 people belonged to one of these mostly interracial unemployed organizations by the end of 1932. A study in that year concluded that local relief payments were proportional to the strength and struggles of the unemployed organizations in the area. As a result of this movement of the unemployed, total direct relief payments rose by $71 million from 1931 to $315 million by 1932 before FDR took office. Anti-eviction actions were also often successful, with 77,000 families saved from eviction in New York City, according to one source, while such actions were so intense and disruptive in Chicago that Mayor Anton Cermak declared a moratorium on evictions.[22]

As the Depression deepened, actions became larger. In January 1932, twelve thousand unemployed workers paraded in Pittsburgh demanding relief or jobs led by a priest named James Cox, known as "the Mayor of Shantytown." This was followed by a rally of sixty thousand in Pitt Stadium. The Communist-led Ford Hunger March in March 1932 saw three thousand unemployed people march on Ford's giant River Rouge complex just outside Detroit demanding jobs. Police attacked the protesters, killing four. This was in turn followed by a mass funeral procession of ten thousand through the streets of Detroit. One of the most high-profile protests was the march on Washington of the veterans' Bonus Army in the spring and summer of 1932. With no central organization or leaders (or Facebook), this movement by veterans to demand payment of bonuses owed them for service in World War I began in Oregon in mid-May and simply spread across the nation, bringing twenty-two thousand or more veterans to Washington. It would eventually be dispersed by the military led by General Douglas McArthur.[23]

As socialist labor historian Sidney Lens summarized the situation in 1932, "Hundreds of thousands of men were picketing and demonstrating in bonus marches, unemployed meetings, sharecropper and farmer revolts. The temper of the nation became increasingly bitter: a few more provocations and no one knew what would happen."[24] As actions and disruption grew and cities and states went broke, relief from the federal government, via the states, became unavoidable first for Hoover and then for Roosevelt.

The heart of the First New Deal, however, was the National Industrial Recovery Act (NIRA) of 1933 and the National Recovery Administration (NRA) with its Blue Eagle logo, set up in June 1933 to assemble the leaders of business and labor (in the few industries where unions had a foothold) to draft codes of conduct for each industry. This act, too, took Republican votes to pass. The NRA's "code authorities" would set prices, wages, and hours of each industry in hope of reducing competition and stabilizing the economy. The government simply acted as a "broker" for the process. As one labor historian put it, "The code authorities, completely dominated by employers, assumed the function of fixing hours and wages, frequently—with the acquiescence of the federal government—without even consulting the employees." A 1934 review panel headed by Clarence Darrow also concluded that the process was overwhelmingly employer-dominated. Indeed, virtually every account of the NRA notes the powerlessness of the NRA and the dominance of the business leaders. The same held for the Agricultural Adjustment Act (AAA), which mainly benefited the "big boys" of agriculture— commercial and corporate farmers, insurance companies, and banks.[25]

James MacGregor Burns, in his sympathetic biography of Roosevelt, summarized the impact of these programs on most Americans:

> The New Deal benefits had not reached these people. . . . Sharecroppers, old people, hired hands, young jobless college graduates, steel puddlers working three months a year, migratory farm laborers—millions of these were hardly touched by NRA or AAA.[26]

The First New Deal as a whole was a disaster for many African Americans in particular. It drove Black tenant farmers from the land in the South. AAA benefits went to white plantation owners, and Blacks were banned from "model" towns set up under the new Tennessee Valley Authority. An article in the *New Republic* suggested NRA stood for "Negroes Ruined Again."[27] Indeed, while many African Americans made gains under New Deal programs, they also faced discrimination, segregation, and sometimes exclusion in both relief and public works programs particularly in the South.[28]

Workers, more generally, referred to the NRA as the "National Run Around." In any case, even before the NRA was declared unconstitutional by the Supreme Court in the spring of 1935, by early 1934, Burns says, "it was near administrative and political collapse."[29] Up to the time that the main programs of the First New Deal were passed during the First Hundred Days in 1933, even the mass actions of the unemployed and those workers still on the job who were beginning to strike in greater numbers, as we will see below, had not been enough to force the government to go beyond pro-business efforts at recovery and expansion of temporary relief. Things would change as class conflict intensified and took center stage in bringing forth what would become the Second New Deal, the one we know best.

The feature that usually gets much of the credit for the working-class upheaval that accelerated in 1933 was the NIRA's Section 7a, which stated that "employees shall have the right to organize and bargain collectively through representatives of their own choosing," and that employers cannot require employees to "join any organization or to refrain from joining a labor organization of his own choosing."[30] This language and the mere existence of this section of the NIRA in June 1933, and the National Labor Board (NLB) set up in July to administer it, are often credited with the sudden upsurge in both union membership and strikes in the second half of 1933. We will look at the rise of strikes in more detail below, but first a closer look at what 7a and the new NLB actually accomplished.

As with the rest of the NRA setup, the NLB proved to be ineffective from labor's point of view. It had no enforcement powers. As Burns describes the NLB's short life, "Successful at first, the board collapsed in the face of employer intransigence in late 1933 and early 1934."[31] Piven and Cloward concurred, "Despite some initial successes, the NLB lacked legal authority and could do nothing when employers simply defied it, as happened in several major cases in late 1933."[32] Worse still, in terms of union membership, the NLB became the means for the employers not only to avoid unions, but to impose "employee representation plans"; i.e., company unions. Indeed, Roosevelt himself endorsed the legitimacy of company unions under Section 7a in the March 25, 1934, auto industry settlement he personally oversaw.[33] By the time the NRA expired, despite an initial upsurge in union membership, the AFL unions had made a net gain of only 500,000 members while company unions had grown by 1,237,000 "members" to a total of 2,500,000.[34]

The most widely mentioned impact of 7a was on the level of strike activity. As the table below shows, strikes had been increasing since 1930, but it was in 1933 that they took off. While the news of the passage of NIRA Section 7a in June 1933 probably had a strong psychological impact in legitimizing the strike, strike activity was already on the rise not only before 1933, but in the first half of 1933 before 7a became "law."

*Table VII: Strikes, Strikers, and Days on Strike, 1930–1935*

| Year | Strikes | Strikers | Days on Strike |
|------|---------|----------|----------------|
| 1930 | 637 | 183,000 | 3,320,000 |
| 1931 | 810 | 342,000 | 6,890,000 |
| 1932 | 840 | 324,000 | 10,500,000 |
| 1933 | 1,695 | 1,170,000 | 16,900,000 |
| 1934 | 1,856 | 1,470,000 | 19,600,000 |
| 1935 | 2,014 | 1,120,000 | 15,500,000 |

Source: Bureau of the Census, *Historical Statistics of the United States: Colonial Times to 1970*, part 1 (Washington, DC: Bureau of the Census, 1975), 179.

For one thing, almost identical language had been inscribed in the Norris-LaGuardia (Anti-Injunction) Act passed in 1932 before Roosevelt took office.[35] As Sidney Lens put it concerning the impact of 7a, "Actually, of course, labor was already taking that right in increasing measure. Spontaneous strikes were breaking out everywhere."[36] Indeed, in the summer of 1932, twelve thousand "unorganized" hosiery workers in North Carolina struck against wage cuts, as was typical of strikes elsewhere, including coal miners in Harlan County, Kentucky, whose strike produced the famous labor song "Which Side Are You On?" Well before 7a appeared in June 1933, mass strikes began in auto, the industry that would play a central role in the success of the new industrial unions from 1936 on. In January 1933 six thousand autoworkers struck four Briggs Manufacturing Company plants in Detroit. These were followed by four thousand strikers at Murray Body, and three thousand at Hudson in February.[37] There were additional strikes at Willys-Overland (Jeep) in Toledo, Chevrolet in California, and White Motor in Cleveland, all between January and the passage of NIRA and 7a. Labor historian Nelson Lichtenstein described the Briggs strike, where future autoworkers' union leader Walter Reuther and his brothers Victor and Roy were active, as "one of the first mass strikes of the Depression-era auto insurgency."[38] At the same time, the IWW (Industrial Workers of the World) led strikes of coal miners in Kentucky and construction workers building the Boulder Dam in Nevada.[39] As A. J. Muste wrote at the time, "Early in 1933 hell began to pop. Strike followed strike with bewildering rapidity."[40]

Burns offers an additional reason for the upswing in union activity prior to 7a, writing, "As business improved during 1933, workers flocked into unions."[41] John L. Lewis, head of the United Mine Workers of America (UMWA), actually launched his campaign to reorganize the coal industry before 7a passed, putting one hundred organizers in the field. In fact, as Michael Goldfield and Cody Melcher has shown, coal miners mounted massive strikes and had mostly organized themselves before 7a became law, much less before any attempt to enforce it was put in place. These authors concluded that "rank and file miners, often led by radicals and unassisted by the UMWA itself, organized virtually every mine before the passage of the NIRA" in 1933.[42] The same was true of steelworkers, 150,000 of whom flooded the old Amalgamated Iron and Steel Workers on their own for a time in 1933, 37,000 of whom went on strike, many before 7a was passed and three years before Lewis set up the Steel Workers Organizing Committee (SWOC) in 1936.[43]

This rising militancy in turn led to the belated addition of the National Labor Board to mediate disputes after 7a had passed, as "the government feared that these stoppages would impede the recovery of business," according to Bernstein.[44] In other words, even if 7a encouraged workers to join unions and strike once it had passed, the momentum was already there given previous acceleration of large-scale strike activity and a (short-lived) boost by improved economic conditions. The government was responding to this momentum. Even after the economy resumed its slump in late 1933, the momentum continued and the number of strikes, strikers, and days on strike would remain high or grow, as the table above shows.

Not only were there more strikes and strikers, but by 1934 the struggles themselves became more intense, better organized, drawing in other groups, reaching more deeply into the communities affected, *and*, to the alarm of some of those in power, led by political radicals and revolutionaries. These strikes confronted not only employers, but city and state governments. They were in the best sense *political*. The three strikes usually emphasized in left accounts are the Minneapolis Teamsters led by Trotskyists, the San Francisco longshore workers led by Communists, and the Toledo Auto-Lite workers led by A. J. Muste's American Workers Party. The classic Trotskyist account is Art Preis's *Labor's Giant Step*. Jeremy Brecher's *Strike!* looks at these strikes from an independent radical perspective, while a more recent telling can be found in John Newsinger's *Fighting Back*.[45]

What is important in all three is the highly organized involvement of broader sections of the working class and the community, the unemployed, the backing and leadership of well-organized radicals, and the fact that all three won. A fourth mass strike of 350,000 members of the United Textile Workers in September 1934, geographically dispersed "from Alabama to Maine," as Bernstein put it, was unable to organize the sort of mass mobilizations the other strikes had, lacked effective leadership despite the leaders' Socialist Party affiliation, and went down to defeat.[46] Unlike the strikes of the early 1930s, some of which were led by the dual unions organized by the Communist Party in its "Third Period" ultraleft phase, all of these strikes in 1934 began within the "official" AFL "House of Labor." This sent a message of warning to both the Roosevelt administration and the incumbent AFL bureaucracy. This was a foreshadowing of the growth of industrial unions and the formation of the Committee (later Congress) of Industrial Organizations (CIO) in 1935 that would transform the labor movement.

The worker upsurge would continue into 1935 even as the institutions of the First New Deal collapsed one after another—the NRA and its "codes," the NLB, the CWA, and the makeshift "relief" efforts—while the economy slumped once again. Capitalism was in danger and working-class rebellion, sometimes led by radicals or revolutionaries, was on the rise. While the likelihood of revolution was actually remote, some in ruling circles, with the revolutionary upheaval of 1917 to 1923 in Europe still a live memory, were not so sure. Roosevelt told a biographer in 1938 that his motive for passing the Second New Deal "was my desire to obviate revolution.... I wanted to save capital."[47] Nevertheless, many in his class didn't appreciate the effort.

The story of the debates and legislative efforts that would create the Second New Deal, the one most of us recognize, is, of course, complicated and beyond the scope of this chapter. What is important is that the Great Depression, from its onset in 1929 through early 1935, had not brought any major concessions

by the Democratic administration that took office in March 1933 to the working class itself beyond the expansion of the temporary relief, much of it already
begun under the Republican administration. The NRA and AAA were clearly
designed to give business the upper hand—even if much of the capitalist class
complained at first. The public works programs employed only a fraction of the
unemployed. The "right" to unionize in Section 7a of the NIRA had already appeared in the Norris-LaGuardia Act of 1932 and was, in any case, ineffective.
Even union leaders like John L. Lewis of the miners and Sidney Hillman of the
Clothing Workers, both of whom would play major roles in the formation of
the CIO and who welcomed 7a, soon became disillusioned with its results and
demanded more.

The rising rebellion of the working class could no longer be ignored by the
powers that be. As a result of the 1934 strikes, in particular, and the continuation of high levels of strike activity in 1935, some in the Roosevelt administration and in Congress began to propose and push for more solid reforms by early
1935. After months of conflicting pressures and internal debate, by June 1935
the Second Hundred Days began and much of the Second New Deal took its
familiar shape and was passed into law.[48] From a socialist perspective, it should
be clearly understood that while the programs of the Second New Deal would
help millions, they were far from universal for African Americans or women, far
from limiting the power of capital over labor in the workplace, and far from guar-
anteeing "social security" in unemployment, retirement, or social reproduction
in general. Nor did they end the Great Depression. It would take World War II
and the rise of the United States to dominant imperial status during the war to
do that. Nevertheless, without the upsurge of class struggle, it is doubtful even
the limited reforms of the Second New Deal would have seen the light of day.

## Defeating Jim Crow with Mass Action

If the social upheaval of the 1930s was born in the depths of economic depression, the mass upsurge that became the civil rights movement of the 1950s
and 1960s emerged in the midst of an era of economic growth and relative
prosperity in the US and much of the developed capitalist world.[49] It was, however, a prosperity from which the vast majority of African Americans were
excluded in large part by the institutional barriers of Jim Crow in the South

and its spillover in the North and throughout the country. The contradiction between the prosperity and the Jim Crow system of segregation that denied Blacks social and economic equality and advancement was highly visible to the nation's Black population. Furthermore, African Americans in the South had seen profound changes as more and more of them moved (or were forced) off the land to the North and into the growing cities of the South. The Black urban population in the South had grown from 2.3 million in 1920 to 5 million in 1950. By 1960, 58 percent of Southern Blacks lived in cities, while the farm population had fallen to 11 percent.[50]

Beginning in World War II, urbanization combined with Jim Crow brought concentrations of Blacks in large numbers in growing ghettos of the cities of the South and inadvertently helped create some of the Black-controlled institutions and organizations that gave new strength to African American communities. This was particularly true of Black urban churches with large congregations and independent finances that provided much of the institutional support of the movement and a new generation of leaders drawn from the younger Black clergy. World War II and the war in Korea in the early 1950s also contributed a layer of Black veterans disinclined to accept the insults and humiliation that accompanied the Jim Crow system and who would play a key role in early resistance and the movement to come.[51]

The increased concentration of Blacks in the cities of the South provided spaces for resistance as well as targets of police victimization and repression. As Robin D. G. Kelley writes of the urban situation of working-class Blacks in the South, "For black workers, public spaces both embodied the most repressive, violent aspects of race and gender oppression and, ironically, afforded more opportunities than the workplace itself to engage in acts of resistance."[52] While he is speaking mostly of unorganized or "spontaneous" acts of resistance, this holds true for organized protest as well. As Piven and Cloward point out, urbanization had "formed a large laboring class" as well as a new middle class. Like the Northern ghetto, by mid-century the growing Southern ghettos were "concentrated, separated, and more independent of white domination than ever before, and with more cause for hope than ever before." This helped form the base from which "southern urban blacks bust forth in protest."[53] Another way to think of this is that this migration and ghetto formation was part of the process of class formation for both working and middle-class Blacks in the post-WWII era that, although restrictive in Jim Crow terms, also provided a growing power base for this mass movement.

While the civil rights movement (CRM) that emerged in the mid-1950s had long and deep antecedents, it was the convergence of these forces in the context of the high-profile contradiction between the era of prosperity and Black exclusion from it that made the movement primarily an urban phenomenon. Like the labor movement of the 1930s, the CRM would go through phases of development, produce new leaders and organizations, and draw in growing numbers of working-class people and eventually the poorest urban youth "untouchables," as Kelley put it.[54] New organizations such as the Montgomery Improvement Association that led the Montgomery Bus Boycott, the Southern Christian Leadership Conference (SCLC), and the Student Nonviolent Coordinating Committee (SNCC) are among the best known, but there were scores of local organizations such as Birmingham's Alabama Christian Movement for Human Rights (ACMHR), the Lowndes County Freedom Organization in Alabama (which gave us the original Black Panther logo), the Mississippi Freedom Democratic Party, Gloria Richardson's not always nonviolent Cambridge (Maryland) Nonviolent Action Committee, as well as some older organizations that saw growth and change such as the Congress of Racial Equality (CORE) and some local chapters of the NAACP.

The legislative culmination of the CRM was the Civil Rights Act of 1964 and the Voting Rights Act of 1965. The road to these legislative victories, however, was long, uphill, militant, and had very little to do with running for political office, which was all but impossible in the South and was largely sewed up in many Northern cities by the white-dominated party machine. It would also bypass the older legalistic strategy associated with the NAACP and the Urban League. In general, most accounts of the CRM place it between the Montgomery Bus Boycott of 1955–56 and the Selma to Montgomery March for voting rights in March 1965.[55] But this movement unfolded in phases as it achieved some victories and faced new barriers. Despite its nonviolent method of civil disobedience, it would be marked by violence, mostly from Southern authorities, but also increasingly from a growing contingent of Black unemployed proletarian youth who suffered some of the greatest deprivation under the Jim Crow regime.

Despite the central importance of legislation, voting was more a goal of the movement than an element in the victory. That is, while the rising Black vote in the North was important to both political parties at that time, these legislative achievements did not depend as much on the state of the political coalitions of the parties or even who was in office as on the force and growing militancy of the movement itself, as we will see below. Indeed, the congressional coalition of Southern Democrats (Dixiecrats) and conservative Republicans, along with the pragmatic and conservative attitudes of most white-dominated Democratic urban machines of that era, made the passage of any progressive legislation extremely difficult. While court decisions culminating in the famous 1954 *Brown v. Board of Education* undoubtedly contributed to a sense of hope, it was the movement that transformed the behavior of the politicians not the election of "liberals," per se, who were regarded with increasing suspicion and distrust by most movement activists and leaders. As one movement activist and civil rights lawyer put it in 1962 concerning liberal politicians, in a not too concealed critique of the Kennedy administration and other liberal politicians, "Negroes are dismayed as they observe that liberals, even when they are in apparent control, not only do not rally their organizations for an effective role in the fight against discrimination, but even tolerate a measure of racial discrimination in their own jurisdictions."[56] While there were many white liberals and socialists who actively supported and participated in the movement, white liberal politicians of both parties were less the allies of the movement than one of the political targets of its actions.

The first phase of the modern CRM began not at lunch counters, voter registration windows, or even in schools, but in the jostle of the Jim Crow transit systems of the urban South. Robin D. G. Kelley appropriately called the process of urbanization in the South that accelerated during and after World War II "congested terrain." Kelley quotes, of all people, "Bull" Connor, the police commissioner who would rain violence on protesters in Birmingham, Alabama, years later, who said of Birmingham "the war has brought unprecedented conditions. Stations, depots, carriers, busses, streetcars . . . are crowded to capacity."[57] Blacks and whites bumped into and jostled one another in these segregated sites on a daily basis. How to enforce segregation on crowded buses and streetcars? In fact, as Kelley shows there was constant resistance to moving to the "back of the bus" or giving up one's seat to a white person. There were countless acts of defiance by Black men and women on the buses of Southern cities, that Kelley labels "small war zones." Many of these acts were little different than Rosa Park's famous act of courage that set off the Montgomery Bus Boycott in December

1955.[58] The difference was a decade or more of changing Black consciousness, the formation of an urban working class across the South, the development of an urban Black culture distinct from that of the plantation or tenant farm, and an emerging confidence that comes with years of experience in the potential power of concentration and contestation.

The Montgomery Bus Boycott sparked by Rosa Park's actions and backed by E. D. Nixon of the Brotherhood of Sleeping Car Porters and local ministers, including the recently arrived Martin Luther King Jr., brought experienced organizer Bayard Rustin to town and launched the Montgomery Improvement Association. The boycott was a supreme example of Black self-organization, drawing in and based primarily on the Black working class of Montgomery who depended on the bus system. It lasted a year and won. Its inspiration set off similar transit boycotts in Birmingham, Mobile, Atlanta, and Tallahassee. As a result, transit systems in over twenty Southern cities voluntarily desegregated in order to avoid the disruption of a mass boycott. In response to the spreading movement, in December 1956 the Supreme Court ruled segregation in public transit illegal—the first in a series of national political victories. In the wake of this first wave, the SCLC that would lead many of the mass struggles that lay ahead was formed in early 1957. Sometimes, repression produced new Black self-organization. In Birmingham in 1956, for example, when the city actually outlawed the NAACP, a mass meeting called by Rev. Fred Shuttleworth formed the ACMHR that would lead many confrontations in years to come.[59]

Montgomery and the struggles that quickly followed had an almost immediate political impact, not on the liberals of the Democratic Party, but on the Eisenhower administration in Washington and the Republicans in Congress. In 1956, Eisenhower sent a civil rights bill to Congress in response to the *Brown* decision and the movement that had burst forth. As a result, the Republicans gained Northern Black votes at the expense of the Democrats in the 1956 election, largely because the Democrats played down the *Brown* decision and civil rights in general during the presidential campaign of Adlai Stevenson. Despite initial Democratic congressional resistance, the first civil rights bill enacted since 1875 passed in 1957. A second civil rights bill meant to firm up the legislation was passed in 1960 before the election of John F. Kennedy.[60] Though these bills would be rendered ineffective by massive Southern white resistance to desegregation, the movement had already set a pattern of political advance without intervening in electoral politics at all. Soon, the movement entered a new more militant phase of direct action on an increasingly massive scale.

The movement took a turn toward civil disobedience when in February 1960 Black students in Greensboro, North Carolina, sat-in at a segregated Woolworth's lunch counter. The movement grew and spread almost immediately across the South, drawing in adults in support actions. This was a new generation of activists. Many, however, had been inspired by the Montgomery movement. As John Lewis, later chair of SNCC, remembered, "Seeing Martin Luther King, Jr., and the black people of Montgomery organize themselves in such a way that fifty thousand people, for more than a year, walked rather than rode segregated buses had a tremendous impact on me."[61] There was continuity, but the new phase involved direct action and civil disobedience on an unprecedented scale. The militancy and intolerance for legalistic gradualism and political foot dragging of the new generation would be embodied in the slogan "Freedom Now!"[62]

The student sit-ins led to the formation of SNCC, which engaged in voter registration in rural areas as well as direct action and helped set the new militant tone of the movement for the next few years. But the major action, once again, came from the cities of the South. Almost from the start of his administration, President Kennedy sought to actively divert the new phase of the movement from mass direct action to voter registration. In June 1961, his attorney general told a meeting of representatives from SNCC, SCLC, CORE, and the National Student Association that voter registration would be "more constructive than freedom rides and demonstrations."[63] SNCC and other organizations did, indeed, engage in voter registration, but the movement continued to go far beyond that.

A 1961 SNCC campaign in Albany, Georgia, to desegregate local facilities became a mass movement with hundreds of arrests but failed to win or get the national attention accorded to the sit-ins or freedom rides, ironically because the police remained restrained. Bent on high-profile confrontation, a plan King labeled "Project C," he and other leaders decided to take the movement and its civil disobedience to Birmingham, Alabama, where confrontation was almost inevitable.[64] From Albany to Birmingham, the class base of the movement had expanded and deepened to mobilizations of virtually the entire Black community.[65]

In order to avoid a confrontation with the Southern Democrats in Congress, the Kennedy administration had not planned to submit further civil rights legislation. Instead the president proposed to use executive orders and court litigation to make marginal gains. This failed utterly. The Birmingham campaign called by King would change all of that. In April and May 1963, demonstrations grew as repression became more violent. Over four thousand demonstrators were arrested and the marches just kept coming. What made Birmingham different was the intervention of what some official movement leaders called the "onlookers" or "bystanders." As Robin D. G. Kelley shows, unlike the mostly middle-class and respectable working-class marchers, these were the "slum dwellers, teenagers and young adults alike" who showed up for the May demonstrations "on their own terms." This intervention became the era's first urban "riot."[66] The explosive events in Birmingham made national TV and sent a clear message to Washington that foot dragging would no longer work.

Furthermore, as noted in chapter 4, in May and June the events in Birmingham set off mass disruptive demonstrations in over 115 Southern cities and some in the North, including Washington, DC. There were between fourteen thousand and twenty thousand arrests that spring and early summer, according to various estimates. This avalanche of direct action reached a high point during the week of June 7. The immediate result was the collapse of formal segregation in public facilities in city after city as local authorities proved unable to contain the social explosion. The floodtide reached the White House, where JFK finally announced on June 11 that he was sending a civil rights bill to Congress. On June 19, the bill went to Congress. Later in June, according to Kennedy-admirer and historian Arthur Schlesinger, Kennedy himself told civil rights leaders that "the demonstrations in the streets had brought results, they had made the executive branch act faster and were now forcing Congress to entertain legislation which a few weeks before would have had no chance."[67]

It was also Birmingham and the May-June mass actions that set in motion the process that became the War on Poverty a year later. The August 28, 1963, March on Washington for Jobs and Freedom that brought 250,000 people to the nation's capital was a reminder of the deeper social convulsion gripping the country that could no longer be ignored. In fact, according to a Justice Department official, "Washington politicians were scared to death of the March," fearing yet another Birmingham-style riot in the nation's capital, while the Kennedy administration deployed troops across the Potomac just in case. And, at that, despite former Texas Dixiecrat and born-again liberal Lyndon Johnson's arm-twisting, it took Republican votes to pass the Civil Rights Act of 1964.[68]

The movement did not stop there. In 1963–64, the number of murdered leaders and activists grew, churches were bombed by whites, and mass demonstrations continued. The rejection of Black delegates from the Mississippi Freedom Democratic Party (MFDP) by Lyndon Johnson and a worthless compromise offered by Hubert Humphrey, Walter Reuther, and other liberals at the 1964 Democratic National Convention—the compromise Rustin called a victory but was soundly rejected by MFDP delegates—pushed the activists to greater contempt for the political establishment.[69] The climax came with the demonstrations and violent repression in Selma, Alabama, and the mass march of thirty thousand from Selma to Montgomery in the fall of 1964. As Louis Lomax argued, "The Selma police brutality caused the Congress to pass the comprehensive voting rights bill of 1965."[70] Nineteen sixty-four, of course, was also the year the urban riots that would characterize the rest of the decade erupted first in Cambridge, Maryland, Harlem, and Bedford-Stuyvesant in New York, Rochester, Jersey City, Paterson, Elizabeth, Philadelphia, and Chicago.[71] There can be little doubt that these, too, had an impact on legislation, including the Voting Rights Act and Johnson's War on Poverty.

In light of this experience it is remarkable that a number of socialists today look back to Bayard Rustin's February 1965 *Commentary* essay, "From Protest to Politics," and subsequent essays in which this once advocate and organizer of nonviolent confrontations with the powers that be proposed to leave direct action and civil disobedience behind in favor of a brand of electoral "coalition politics" that, in fact, included some of these powers that be. It was not, however, the idealized coalition of "Negros, trade unionists, liberals, and religious groups" in a "realigned" Democratic Party that Rustin called for,[72] but the real coalition of liberals, party hacks, machine politicians, and liberal Republicans that actually passed the Civil Rights Act of 1964, the Economic Opportunities Act of 1964 (War on Poverty), and the Voting Rights Act of 1965. It had been precisely mass confrontations that had forced the Kennedy and Johnson administrations and Congress to finally act.

The legislation, court rulings, executive orders, and policy changes the civil rights movement won in the 1960s changed much in American life and helped to encourage and inspire the social movements of Latinx people, students, women, LGBTQ people; the organization and growth of public employee unions; and many of the rank-and-file rebellions in industry and the unions that followed. At the same time, they failed to end racism or discrimination, or to head off mass incarceration and even the geographic segregation of today's ghettos that determine the life chances of millions of African Americans. All these things would require much deeper social and economic changes than were likely to come from Congress or the presidency then or now. It is hardly surprising that this phase of the long Black Freedom Movement should have been surpassed by the rise of still more militant leaders, activists, and organizations, as well as opportunists benefiting from some of the civil rights era gains, often under the banner of Black Power.

But, like the labor movement of the 1930s, the movements and actions of the civil rights era also showed that if meaningful, even though limited, reforms are to be wrenched from capitalism's representatives, it takes more than electing the "right" people, even when the "right" people do represent an improvement or a "lesser evil," much less making the right case for social justice or the salvation of the planet. Those who council that strikes, demonstration, occupations, riots, etc. are "not enough" have it backward. It is the deeply flawed "political process" of capitalist America that is not enough. Self-activity and self-organization of the oppressed and exploited from below are the first principle in any strategy for social change. To put it another way, it has generally been the case that in the US it takes revolutionary means to achieve meaningful reforms from an unwilling system.

Fortunately, we are not starting from nowhere. Who would have guessed that hundreds of thousands of primary and secondary school students around the world would strike twice in 2019 for emergency action on climate change? Climate change deniers beware! To cite Dylan once more, "Your sons and your daughters are beyond your command." Who would have guessed that over 370,000 education workers would strike with or without union "permission" or even collective bargaining rights in some cases in 2018? That thousands of mostly immigrant women hotel workers would also strike in 2018? Or that 36,000 retail workers at Stop & Shop stores and 49,000 General Motors workers would strike in 2019? Or that in the midst of the worst pandemic in a hundred years, workers of all sorts would take actions up to and including the strike without permission much less support from union leaders in most cases?

On the other hand, who could doubt anymore that Black people would go into the streets as more and more of their youths and family members were cut down by unaccountable cops? Or that in the face of the election of the Great

Groper that hundreds of thousands of women would march? And protest again when white male choice deniers in state after state tried to ban abortion? The demands may be different, but people are learning how to mobilize, strike, and disrupt, and as the examples of the original New Deal and the civil rights era show, it is more the mass direct action and disruption than conventional politics that brings results. The fact is, the best social legislation in the US, as limited as it has been, has followed the rhythm of mass social upheavals and movements far more closely than that of the ins and outs of the two major parties. Politics is about more than elections and officeholders, it is about power. While we cannot simply create a mass social upsurge, we can prepare and organize for an upswing in social and class conflict in order to maximize the political potential of such an upheaval.

CHAPTER 6

# Reversing the "Model": How Will the Millions Get Organized?

*The membership can only be a sounding board, even the delegates*
*... they can't make decisions. ... The idea of wisdom emanat-*
*ing from the bottom is full of shit, not because they are stupid*
*but because they have a job which is not running the union and*
*knowing all the intricate business about it. Consequently, their*
*inability to come up with initiatives is limited.[1]*
—Leon Davis, President, Hospital Workers' Union, 1199

It seems fairly obvious that mass actions leading to social upheaval will require the organizing of the unorganized at Amazon and Walmart, the high-tech outfits and platforms, the nonunion steel minimills and auto plants, warehouses and unorganized truckers, the rest of the nation's hospitals and sites of social reproduction, and other new and old industries that can provide the organized power and continuity to the sort of diverse upsurge already taking shape if the political impasse is to be broken. Breaking the impasse is inconceivable without a dynamic, powerful organized labor movement.

Yet, the pandemic has done massive damage to an already declining labor movement. In 2020 unions lost 428,000 private sector members. The largest hits were in hospitality and leisure, at 161,000 lost members, and manufacturing, down 110,000. The losses, of course, were mainly due to the sharp drop in employment in these two sectors. Ironically, this led to a slight increase in overall union density from 7.1 percent in 2019 to 7.2 percent. A surprising 77 percent of the decline was among white males, while Black, Latinx, and women workers made tiny gains.[2] Building the sort of powerful labor movement needed to break the impasse will obviously require a massive effort of a sort not seen since the 1930s. While many socialists would probably agree with that proposition, just how to go about that is a matter of controversy.

One of the most widely read and listened to experts on union organizing these days is Jane McAlevey, whose books, lectures, and online seminars have influenced many on the left.[3] An experienced organizer, McAlevey presents a well-worked-out model of successful organizing. One that, taken as a whole, is, however, itself controversial. Its advantage is that it seems practical and, indeed, many of her suggestions are well grounded. First is McAlevey's useful distinction between organizations that engage in advocacy and mobilization and those that engage in actual organizing. Advocacy is the sort of thing NGOs do that don't really involve their typically poor clients themselves except in walk-on parts. Mobilization is the practice of many unions in which the members are occasionally activated for a campaign or even a strike and then sent back in silence to the workplace. UAW organizer and dissident Jerry Tucker used to call this the "spigot approach"—turning the flow of worker action on and off by command. McAlevey pretty much dismisses these approaches to social change and insists that organizing is meant to produce permanent, sustainable worker organization and power. This, of course, is one reason why people pay attention when she speaks or writes.

Central to all three of her books and her approach to revitalizing the labor movement is her model of organizing. This model, and she insists it is a model, can be found in schematic form in *No Shortcuts*,[4] but is presented throughout these works in the context of gripping stories of her experiences as a union organizer, official, and consultant that bring the model to life. It has to be said, as well, that the organizing drives, contract negotiations, and campaigns she leads across these many pages, unlike many in recent decades, end up winning.

The model she advocates does not exist in a vacuum. It is explicitly counterposed to the more narrow approach she attributes to legendary community organizer Saul Alinsky and that is employed by many US unions, according to

McAlevey. This has particularly been the case in the years since John Sweeney became head of the AFL-CIO in the mid-1990s in an attempt to revive a slumping labor movement. Since it is painfully obvious that neither the top-down reforms implemented by Sweeney's "New Labor," as she calls it, nor the limited innovations in organizing tactics have succeeded in turning things around for the labor movement as a whole, McAlevey's counterposed organizing model has a lot of credibility.

The purpose of the model, McAlevey insists, is to activate workers so they can express and use the power they have in both the workplace and community. It is not simply to increase union numbers at any cost, as her former employer the Service Employees International Union (SEIU) often prioritizes, but to increase worker power. The initiative in her examples comes from the organizer whose job is to identify and develop the organic leaders in the workplace. This is not a simple task. Organic leaders are not necessarily the first person to step forward during an organizing drive, much less the "loudmouth" who sometimes stands up to the boss. Rather it is the person in the work group to whom others look for advice or help in various aspects of life as well as on the job. Such natural leaders may be anti-union, as some of her experiences reveal, but it is the job of the organizer to win them over if possible. Identifying such leaders is only the first step. She cites former syndicalist and Communist Party leader in the 1930s William Z. Foster to the effect that, "Organizers do not know how to organize by instinct, but must be carefully taught."[5] So, the next task is to train new leaders in organizing methods.

Part of the training of organic leaders and, more generally, the rank and file is the continuous charting or mapping of the workplace to locate the strengths and weaknesses of the organization and campaign. This becomes the basis for further actions. Along with this are what she calls "structure tests." These are essentially escalating collective actions that create confidence, demonstrate and test power, and build a solid majority of about 80 percent in order to win a representation election or eventually 90 percent to carry out a winning strike. Along with this goes "inoculation," preparing workers for the lies and barriers management or their hired union-busting guns will throw up to thwart the union drive. So far, all of this is pretty well known at least to the best union and workplace organizers. These ideas, without the official organizers' "lingo"—to use McAlevey's own term—can be found in *Secrets of a Successful Organizer*, published by the publication and worker education center *Labor Notes*, which draws on the experience of rank-and-file workplace organizers, activists, and leaders as well as union staff organizers.[6]

What is more original is McAlevey's approach to the post-representation phase of union organizing: the negotiation and campaign to win a first contract. As she points out, winning the first contract is a major stumbling block and almost half of new unions fail to gain a first agreement. Most unions separate the representation phase from that of negotiating the contract. Once the union has won recognition, the organizers are pulled and sent elsewhere and a new crew of professional negotiators along with lawyers are brought in. After all, negotiating a contract these days is complex. McAlevey argues convincingly that the two phases need to be continuous and connected in terms of personnel because, for one thing, the organizers have presumably developed the trust of the workers. For another, the employers and their unscrupulous hired guns don't stop fighting, lying, and throwing up barriers once negotiations start. Quite the opposite.

Not only does McAlevey insist that the organizers must still be in charge to lead the fight, but that negotiations should be open to any and all members. Many unions have rank-and-file "negotiating committees," but these famously sit in the hall or the next room, forced to thrive on pizzas while the officials and lawyers do the real negotiating. McAlevey brings the workers and their leaders into the negotiating session. Some are trained to present demands, many come and go at lunch or break time. The horrified faces of management that she describes and their ineffective protests at such unconventional interventions not only build the solidarity of the workers, but for the readers who haven't experienced anything quite like this make for terrific reading.

All of these organizing techniques, McAlevey argues, need to be in a strategic context. Simply responding to random "hot shops" where workers contact a union for help will not expand labor's power sufficiently to make a difference.[7] Union campaigns should be "industrial or geographic" in nature. In particular, she emphasizes service industries that can't be moved abroad, notably education and health care, which also have the advantage of close community connections. Her own experience in health care organizing is a clear example of an industrial orientation. In such strategic campaigns, for example, experienced organizers can draw "on workers in the same union but in a different unionized facility, who have experience winning hard-to-win NLRB elections and big strikes."[8] This strategic emphasis seems sensible, but certainly leaves an awful lot of unorganized workers who don't fit in the strategy de jour out of the picture.

Despite the vivid narrative and the positive ideas, as I read through these three books, I became more aware of McAlevey's emphasis on professional organizer (or officer or consultant) *initiative* in virtually every phase of union life. Although I had been on a panel with McAlevey and heard her speak a few years ago, I hadn't picked up this consistent, at times overarching, domination by staff organizers in representation elections, contract campaigns, and even strikes. Despite my own longtime emphasis on rank-and-file initiative and power, like most people concerned with the future of unions I recognize that organizers are an important part of the labor movement. I even did a stint as one back in the day. They are often thrust onto the front lines of combat with capital, make personal sacrifices, and do, indeed, help workers get organized to gain representation, win an initial contract, conduct a victorious strike, and sometimes build workplace organization. To be fair, in *No Short Cuts* McAlevey attacks the notion put forward by some organizing directors that "the workers often get in the way of union growth deals."[9] Nevertheless, throughout the three books it is *professional organizer initiative* that recurs again and again and plays the central and dominant role in all the campaigns she is directly involved in, and even in some cases where this emphasis is misplaced, such as her discussions of the teachers' unions in Chicago and Los Angeles.[10] The initiative of countless "untrained" workplace organizers and the part played by experience in their development is by and large absent.

Simple numbers and common sense dictate that unions cannot possibly be revitalized, democratized, and massively expanded through the initiative of professional organizers and other staffers alone. They simply cannot do everything and be everywhere, every day in a movement of millions trying to organize tens of millions. Failures aside, their successes at best produce incremental growth that cannot even keep up with membership attrition. Even the multiplication of such organizers several times over, though it would help matters, could not possibly produce the sort of exponential growth in both numbers and power needed to shift the balance of class forces that McAlevey and the rest of us desperately seek.

Without the grassroots initiative, day in and day out, of countless unidentified workplace organizers be they organic leaders, activists, or interested
members with titles no grander than shop steward or local union officer—if
that—unions cannot function let alone grow. McAlevey's idea of using unionized workers to approach the unorganized in the same industry is obviously a
good one. But if this is left only to the *initiative* of labor's too few, overworked
organizers it won't be nearly enough. Worse yet, if this sort of worker-to-worker
organizing occurs only with the *permission* of top leaders, which is typically the
case, it will never be enough or display the sort of initiative that can impress the
unorganized and give them a sense of ownership in the union. Clearly, it will
take much more of the sort of worker self-activity and initiative such as we saw
among industrial workers in the 1930s and public employees in the 1960s and
1970s, and have seen recently in the 2018–19 strikes of education workers, as
well as the first signs of action by workers at Amazon, Instacart, Uber, Google,
and other corners of the digitalizing economy in the midst of the COVID-19
pandemic. Later, I will look in greater detail at this question. To investigate this
problem further, however, we need to look at what McAlevey sees as the roots of
union decline over the last half century.

## "Who Killed the Unions?"

This is the title of a key chapter in McAlevey's most recent book, *A Collective
Bargain: Unions, Organizing, and the Fight for Democracy*, the most "big picture" of her three books. The bulk of her answer to this question is straightfor-
ward: Taft-Hartley and subsequent court decisions, professional union-busters, and globalization. Each of these has played an important role in throwing
up barriers to organizing—at least in those all too few cases where workers
or a union even attempt to seek representation. Taft-Hartley gives the boss a
legal advantage and the union-busters provide the muscle and intimidation,
while globalization allows employers to threaten to move abroad and close up
shop. As the record shows, these are, indeed, frequently effective in derailing
organizing drives and first-contract campaigns. This story is true as far as it
goes, although it downplays the far more persistent role of management in
fighting and demoralizing unions and workers day in and day out. It is also
the official union leadership's explanation for the decline, retreat, and crisis of

the organizations they lead. The problem with this story is that it lets the top leadership, the union hierarchy off the hook for their own role in the crisis of organized labor, certainly in the US.

This is not a question of good or bad people. All union leaders are not the same. Some are clearly much better than others, and that can make a difference. The problem lies in the whole practice of bureaucratic business unionism that emerged in the US most clearly during and after World War II. Taft-Hartley and McCarthyism played a role in this to be sure. But business unionism as a philosophy and practice had its roots way back in the era of Samuel Gompers and his "pure and simple" unionism. The post-WWII expansion and modernization of this old view, however, was based primarily in the simultaneous abandonment of the workplace and labor process in favor of wages and benefits—the US "private welfare state." This, in turn, led to an increased insulation of the leadership, administration, and the conduct of bargaining from the membership. Along with this came the union's turn from a broader social agenda, their political defeat, and Taft-Hartley. Labor historian Nelson Lichtenstein has controversially but correctly called this turn away from efforts to win broad social gains politically toward the private welfare state the "product of defeat, not victory."[11]

By the early 1950s, this defeat included productivity bargaining that linked wages and benefits to worker productivity increases and hence speedup and, more recently, lean production, extreme work standardization, digitally driven tasks, surveillance, etc. Even before this, the inclusion in most contracts of "management's rights" (to control the workplace) and "no-strike" (during the life of the contract) clauses became a feature of bargaining that surrendered the unions' ability to fight over working conditions and their members' ability to resist through direct action.

Instead, union members got the multilayered grievance procedure that postponed settlement and stripped workers of a major source of power. McAlevey is justifiably critical of such grievance procedures, but doesn't recognize their roots in this fundamental compromise with management. The surrender of shop-floor power to management also involved the sidestepping of labor's own racial problems in its organized work sites, which, among other things, led to the failure of "Operation Dixie," the CIO's attempt to organize the South in the late 1940s, further undermining labor's growth and bargaining power.

All of this led to a decade or so of worker rebellion in the 1960s and 1970s by Black and white workers often inspired by the civil rights movement and characterized by rank-and-file caucuses, Black caucuses, wildcat strikes, contract rejections, and the energizing of a new generation of industrial workers. With few exceptions, the union leadership did everything possible to crush the rebellion, helping to deplete rather than harness the energy of this social upsurge.[12] Such growth as labor experienced in that period came largely from the self-initiative of public sector workers, a process I participated in twice as a rank-and-file volunteer activist and leader and once as a staff organizer.

The decline of the unions in terms of numbers, organizing efforts and victories, and the use of the strike accelerated in the aftermath of this failed rebellion as union leaders turned to wage and benefit concessions, labor-management cooperation schemes, two-tier wage systems, and an increased reliance on rightward-moving Democratic politicians and pressure tactics that did not depend on worker self-activity. This disarmed the labor movement as a whole without in any way blunting capital's offensive against the unions and workers in general. In 1979, United Auto Workers' president Doug Fraser referred to capital's offensive as "one-sided class war."[13]

Among the shocks that introduced labor's retreat and the entire neoliberal era were the 1980–82 double-dip recession that destroyed millions of unionized manufacturing and other jobs, the Chrysler bailout and associated union concessions which ended pattern bargaining in auto, setting the precedent for other industries, and Reagan's firing of the striking air traffic controllers. But it was the subsequent behavior and practices of the union leadership of the major unions, with few exceptions, that further institutionalized long existing inclinations toward class collaboration. This, in turn, has made it even more difficult to organize the unorganized, a side of the story missing in McAlevey analysis of union decline.

Unions are contradictory organizations that are both institutions and social movements meant to combat the pressures of capital on wages and conditions.[14] Their tendency toward bureaucratization in unions is not an example of Robert Michels's "iron law of oligarchy," nor an inevitable "Weberian" cure for large organizations. The problem stems from the leadership's position as negotiators caught between the demands of capital not only for lower immediate costs, but for the long-term profitability and survival of the business in the vortex of real capitalist competition, on the one hand, and the needs of the membership, on the other. To deal with this contradictory situation the elected leadership tends to institutionally insulate itself and its institutional resources from membership pressure while nonetheless having occasionally to call on that membership to give it the power it needs in negotiations to resist management's pressure up to and including a strike. It is this dilemma that gives the "union"—that is, the top leadership in particular—the appearance of being a "third party" that McAlevey refers to in *No Shortcuts*.[15]

McAlevey, of course, is right that the union is not a "third party," as some management experts would have it, but a working-class institution. Nevertheless, it is one that necessarily attempts to mediate the contradictions inherent in the capital-labor relationship. This is one reason why almost all the "reforms" and "new" tactics of the 1990s and beyond implemented by the officialdom have emphasized forms of pressure that bypassed the self-activity of the membership: corporate and "leverage" campaigns; the fake counterposition of "organizing" and "service" models; union mergers that give the appearance of growth while increasing bureaucracy; the conglomerate nature and fragmented departmentalism of most unions resulting from mergers; the recruitment of former student radicals rather than members as organizers; "neutrality" or, as McAlevey calls them, "election procedure agreements" with management to facilitate organizing; the election of Democrats of any sort at all levels; and the insane split in the movement with the formation of the Change to Win federation in 2005.

In this context, it is also a fact that in most unions organizers are accountable to the union officialdom that hired them, not to the membership or those they are organizing. Some organizers manage a good deal of autonomy and initiative, as McAlevey did in her time with the SEIU in Las Vegas vividly described in *Raising Expectations*. Nevertheless, organizers are responsible to those who pay their wages, send them where *they* want them, and supply or deny them resources to carry out their assignment. There is, of course, no law that organizers cannot be chosen by the union membership just as the leaders are, but that would rub against the grain of business unionism even at its best.

There is an alternative or at least a strong countertendency to this long-standing trend toward bureaucratization of the unions and the routinization of collective bargaining away from the influence of the membership. It lies in union democracy stemming first of all from direct democracy and worker-initiative in the workplace, most commonly in the form of elected and *collective* workplace organization—not just isolated stewards buried in casework. The "representative democracy" characteristic of most unions is insufficient to create leadership and staff accountability because it involves only the occasional exercise of leadership selection in which the incumbent leaders have control of union resources and lines of communication. More often than not, the officialdom is capable of constructing a machine or loyal network strong enough to prevent the erosion of their power, even if the individuals at the top change from time to time. It is for this reason that simply running slates against incumbent leaders seldom changes things significantly.[16]

This is where the idea of rank-and-file movements based in strong workplace organization, caucuses, and networks that connect the various work sites comes into the picture. I will discuss this below in the context of McAlevey's discussion of the reform movements in the Chicago and Los Angeles teachers' unions as well as the 2018–19 upsurge in teacher strikes. But first, let's look at the final point in her explanation of "who killed the unions?" It's one of the top leadership's most effective alibies—globalization.

## Imports, Outsourcing, and the "Other"

One of the most common explanations for labor's decline and retreat in the United States coming from union organs, leaders, and sometimes friendly think tanks and academics is the loss of American jobs to overseas outsourcing and/or imports. To be sure, fingers are pointed at the employers who do this outsourcing and importing, but the focus is inevitably on the foreign "other." The foreign perpetrators have changed somewhat over time from the Japanese steel and automakers of the 1970s and 1980s, to the Mexican *maquiladoras* of the 1990s and 2000s, and most recently, of course, the Chinese who seem to make everything and be everywhere even though they account for just one-fifth of US imports. The story has just enough truth to be credible. Jobs in some industries such as textiles and garment have been all but wiped out by imports, while inputs to other goods production have gone overseas.

## The Case of Steel

One of the unions that routinely points to imports as the major source of lost jobs is the United Steelworkers of America (USWA). Steelworker employment has, indeed, plunged in the last four decades or more as has the steel membership of the USWA. Imports are one factor in this job loss, but by no means the only or even the most important cause. One is productivity. To put it simply, the workforce in US steel production fell by about 65 percent from the early 1980s to 2017, while the "man-hours" required to produce a ton of steel fell by 85 percent. The major reason for this was the rise of electric arc (AR) "minimills," which require far less labor per ton than traditional Basic Oxygen Furnace (BOF) mills.

Imports rose to about a quarter of US steel consumption by the 1980s and to an average 30 percent between 2012 and 2018, after which they fell back to 25 percent. Minimills, on the other hand, have risen from 31 percent of domestic production in the 1980s to around 60–65 percent in the last two decades. This is about 50 percent of total consumption, a far larger share than imports. Employment in BOF mills, where almost all union members work, of course fell over the years. What seems clear is that more of these lost union jobs fell to productivity, on the one hand, and the shift of domestic production to non-union minimills, on the other, than to imports. The USWA did little to resist job reorganization or to organize the minimills.[17]

One of the problems with citing imports, including outsourced intermediate inputs, as an explanation for the loss of union jobs, however, is that US manufacturing output as measured by the Federal Reserve grew by about 130 percent, or a fairly healthy 3.5 percent yearly average, over the neoliberal period from 1982 to 2019.[18] So, even if imports took a significant bite out of US production, growth on this scale should have created jobs. That is, imports could explain why domestic production grew somewhat more slowly than in the "golden" and more pre-global era of the 1950s and 1960s, but they cannot account for such a massive loss of manufacturing jobs within this level of growing domestic output. The reason for this scale of job loss lay primarily in the double whammy of recurrent recessions resulting from capitalist turbulence and productivity gains from management's application of lean production and work-pacing technology. That is, the contradictory course of capital accumulation, on the one hand, and management-led class struggle, on the other, drastically reduced employment in manufacturing despite significant growth in output. Table VIII shows the loss in manufacturing production jobs during the four major recessions of the neoliberal era.

*Table VIII: Manufacturing Production Jobs Lost During Recessions*

| Years* | Manufacturing |
| --- | --- |
| 1979–1982 | 2,751,000 |
| 1990–1991 | 663,000 |
| 2001–2003 | 2,198,000 |
| 2008–2010 | 1,797,000 |
| Total | 7,409,000 |

* From January of first year to December of last.

Source: BLS, "Production and Nonsupervisory Employees, Total Private, Manufacturing," *Data, Tables & Calculators by Subject*, 2018, https://www.bls.gov/webapps/legacy/cesbtab6.htm; National Bureau of Economic Research, "US Business Cycle Expansions and Contractions," 2012, https://data.nber.org/cycles/cyclesmain.html.

If repeated recessions eliminated jobs on a monumental scale, significant productivity growth between recessions prevented the recovery of the vast majority of these jobs once growth resumed. Between 1990 and 2000 productivity in manufacturing rose annually by 4.1 percent, while from 2000 to 2007, just before the Great Recession, it increased by an average of 4.7 percent a year.[19] This was sufficient to hold down job growth despite a significant increase in manufacturing output per year from recession trough to recovery highpoint in the 1980s (4.1 percent) and 1990s (6.4 percent). From 2001 to 2007 output grew by an annual average of only 2.8 percent, compared to 4.1 percent for productivity, costing some 2 million jobs even before the next recession. From 2009 to 2019 output grew by 2.4 percent a year and productivity increased by about 2.5 percent so that manufacturing employment grew only slowly by about 1 percent a year, mostly in lower-productivity jobs.[20]

In the case of the 2020 COVID-19 recession over 1 million production and nonsupervisory manufacturing jobs were lost between February and April as the virus and lockdown took hold, according to BLS figures. By the end of the third quarter in September the number of jobs was still over half a million below the February level despite a 12 percent increase in output. The culprit was a well above average productivity increase of 4.6 percent.[21] The embrace of labor-management cooperation by union leaders and the acceptance of lean production and work-intensifying technology that enabled these levels of productivity cost millions of jobs.

Pinning all this job loss on "globalization" lets the labor officialdom off the hook in two damaging ways. First it reinforces the sort of labor nationalism that sees the foreign "other" rather than the home-based boss as the culprit. At its worst, this has been expressed in the "Buy American" slogan of the 1970s and 1980s, a lingering sentiment that Trump has played effectively. Even at its most liberal where, for example, concerns for the negative impact of NAFTA on Mexican workers in the *maquiladora* plants are sometimes expressed, this approach still encourages nationalist sentiments and takes the fight for secure and decent employment out of the hands of workers and into those of the lobbyists and legislators who are supposed to stem this tide of foreign goods with "fair trade."

Second, while even the strongest of unions with the best of leaders could do little in the context of collective bargaining about capitalism's tendency toward recurrent crises, they could certainly have done a good deal about labor intensification resulting from lean production, and the work-pacing and surveillance technology that prevented the recovery of jobs between recessions. Instead, for nearly four decades most union top-level leaderships have engaged in joint "problem-solving" and cooperation with management, wage and benefit concessions, strike-avoidance tactics, one-sided political dependency, appeals to nationalism, and their own form of "social distancing" from the membership. Throughout these books, McAlevey's criticism of this type of union leader who has been the norm for decades is focused primarily on Andy Stern at the national level of SEIU and his associates. For all her contempt of some other top leaders and "clueless" unions, McAlevey lets the majority of the contemporary labor officialdom off the hook on all these counts.

## CIO "Model"?

McAlevey sees her model of organizing as rooted in the CIO's "high-participation model anchored in deep worker solidarities and cooperative engagement in class struggle."[22] Though high-participation and solidarity were certainly central to the birth of the new industrial unions of the 1930s that eventually formed the Congress of Industrial Organizations (CIO), to call the events that led to this a "model" is a stretch to say the least. This turbulent upsurge bore little resemblance to a well-organized and conducted NLRB or "election procedure agreement" (neutrality) representation election, collective bargaining campaign, or even the "model" strikes that McAlevey describes. Rather it arose from a mass grassroots-initiated strike movement that began in 1933 when the number of strikes more than doubled and that of strikers grew by over three and a half times, most without any official union leadership. This disorderly strike wave would continue through to its highpoint in 1937 when the victory of General Motors workers' unconventional and illegal sit-down strikes turned the tide in favor of the new unions.[23]

The course of events that led to that victory doesn't resemble that outlined in McAlevey's model or that of most representation campaigns in recent decades. As I wrote in the introduction for the republication of Sidney Fine's classic *Sit-Down:*

> The order of events in Flint in 1936–37 were the opposite: build the union
> in the workplace among those willing to join, take action according to plan
> even with a minority membership, demonstrate the power of the union, win
> recognition and bargaining, and recruit a majority.[24]

I am not suggesting this will necessarily work in today's circumstances, but that as circumstances change so might the way and order in which workers organize themselves. Like those of automobiles, organizing "models" can get out of date.

During the first three or so years of the upsurge of the early 1930s, the as yet unidentified or developed "organic leaders" and activists in hundreds of mines, mills, and factories led their fellow workers into action and organization without waiting for the professional organizers to arrive. This was the case even when in 1933 John L. Lewis sent his (often leftist) organizers into the coalfields in anticipation of the passage of Roosevelt's Section 7(a) of the National Industrial Relations Act (NIRA), which was supposed to grant the right to organize. As recent research by historians Michael Goldfield and Cody Melcher has shown, his organizers reported in 1933 that "the miners had been organizing on their own." As noted in chapter 5, labor historians have found that the coalminers had organized themselves, while steelworkers had joined the old Amalgamated Iron and Steelworkers by the thousands and struck before the passage of the NIRA in 1933.[25] This was even more the case in other industries like auto, rubber, and electrical goods where there was no pre-existing national union—at best federal locals of the AFL which rapidly proved ineffective and were abandoned by the workers.[26]

When the upsurge in auto began in 1933–35, the Communist organizers Bob Travis and Wyndham Mortimer, whom McAlevey cites, and the Socialist activists and organizers she doesn't, Kermit Johnson (in Chevy 4) and Roy Reuther (Travis's assistant in 1936–37), were rank-and-filers in various plants around the Midwest. While they were already leaders and organizers in their workplaces, Travis in Toledo, Mortimer in Cleveland, and Reuther in Detroit became staffers in Flint only after autoworkers across the Midwest had been in motion for almost three years. In other words, that era's "organic leaders" and activists stepped forward on their own as rank-and-file organizers, sometimes as part of worker-based political tendencies well before there were any full-time organizers. Along with the key role played by radical rank-and-file workplace leaders, the birth of the CIO was a classic example of collective worker self-activity.

More particularly, McAlevey credits her organizing techniques to Hospital Workers' Union Local 1199 prior to the merger of a majority of its local unions with the SEIU in 1998. Though her direct experience was with 1199 New England, which covers Connecticut and Rhode Island, she attributes the organizing model to the union's founding Local 1199 in New York under the leadership of Leon Davis. 1199 is, of course, famous for its militancy, atypical social unionism, "Bread and Roses" cultural program, embrace of the civil rights movement, and endorsement by Martin Luther King Jr., among other things. 1199's founding leaders, Leon Davis and Elliott Godoff, were Communists who originally formed a union of pharmacists in the 1930s. Their Communist-led union then organized hospital workers in New York City beginning in the late 1950s, before the air trails of McCarthyism and the House Un-American Activities Committee had been fully swept away by the winds of a new era of revolt—quite an achievement.

The subsequent history of 1199, however, does not reveal a democratic union adept at training grassroots leaders, at least above the workplace delegate (shop steward) level. When Davis retired in 1982, the union fell into a decade of leadership crisis as first Davis's handpicked successor, Doris Turner, and then her replacement Georgianna Johnson proved unprepared and incapable of leading or uniting the union. This was primarily because they had been given little leadership experience or responsibility, which remained in the hands of Davis and other top leaders. This story has been told in detail in *Upheaval in the Quiet Zone*, a history of 1199 by Leon Fink and Brian Greenberg that, oddly enough, McAlevey recommends.[27] What it revealed was that despite its elected delegate system of one delegate per twenty-five workers, 1199 was not a particularly democratic union, nor did it attempt to bargain over the nature of hospital work, or as Fink and Greenberg put it, "pressed no claims for work reorganization" and limited its bargaining to wages and benefits.[28] In both regards, it was, despite its militancy and social movement characteristics, fairly conventional in its organizational and bargaining practices. It was, in fact, a union with a highly centralized leadership in the person of Leon Davis, who said:

> The membership can only be a sounding board, even the delegates . . . they can't make decisions. . . . The idea of wisdom emanating from the bottom is full of shit, not because they are stupid but because they have a job which is not running the union and knowing all the intricate business about it. Consequently, their inability to come up with initiatives is limited.[29]

This, of course, is the more frequently unspoken assumption of business union leaders throughout the American labor movement. It is the central reason that genuine leadership development is *not* a part of most union cultures above routine stewards' training and why leadership transitions are mostly managed affairs even though there is an election. In the case of 1199 it led not only to a decade of internal chaos and racial conflict, but to this union's eventual subordination to the even more bureaucratic structure and bizarre leadership of the SEIU under Andy Stern. Ironically, this kind of all too typical top-down leadership also means that all those "organic leaders" back in the workplace never really have the opportunity to take initiative beyond grievance filing or to learn of the "complexities" that are the monopoly of the inner sanctum.

This doesn't mean that the organizing "model" proposed by McAlevey is wrong per se in today's limited context. What it does mean is that, by itself, it is insufficient to produce the kind of democratic, workplace-based, member-led unions, like those of the early CIO, needed to take on capital, expand, act as the backbone of the broader social upsurge, and lay the basis for bigger political changes. It should be obvious that most of today's unions in the US have failed to grow and win because they are bureaucratically incapable of deploying the collective power of the members beyond the framework of conventional bargaining and equally conventional strike strategies and tactics. There are exceptions in a number of the effective strikes of the last few years, or even a longer period, but they are exceptions. There is much more to winning a strike these days than just getting the 90 percent participation McAlevey proposes. The question then arises, one that McAlevey does not address despite her discussion of West Virginia, Chicago, and Los Angeles teachers' strikes: How we are to make our unions suitable for class struggle in an era in which the forces arrayed against workers are more massive than ever?

The question is: How or even if we are to transform most of today's bureaucratic unions into democratic organizations with genuinely accountable officials and staff? How are we to gain collective membership power beyond occasional "participation"? How are we to get unions in which workplace leaders are allowed to lead and there is a culture of debate and dissent rather than conformity in the name of "unity," as well as an atmosphere in which rank-and-file initiative in the fight with capital is encouraged? There are plenty of examples of efforts to democratize unions and improve their ability to fight the boss. These range from large-scale ones like the Teamsters' reform movement that nearly toppled the Hoffa bureaucracy in 2017 to scores of local rank-and-file caucuses and movements, the best-known example of which is, of course, the Coalition of Rank-and-File Educators (CORE) that toppled the old guard of the Chicago Teachers Union in 2010. What then does McAlevey say about this and other aspects of the democratic upsurge of teacher militancy and organization of the past several years?

## Reversing the "Model"

It would be unthinkable these days to write a book on US unions without mentioning the great teachers' rebellion of 2018–20. While McAlevey doesn't present this as the industry-wide upsurge it has become, she does include accounts of the strike of the West Virginia education workers and the reform movements in the Chicago Teachers Union (CTU) and the United Teachers of Los Angeles (UTLA). To my mind, these important struggles have more in common with the real CIO upsurge from 1933–37 and that of public sector workers and rank-and-file rebels in the 1960s and 1970s than most union struggles these days. These were struggles initiated, organized, and led in the first instance not by professional organizers, but by workers who had "a job which is not running the union," as Leon Davis so indelicately put it, yet were nonetheless organizers in the full sense of that word. Only after winning election to top positions and initiating the process of transforming the union did they hire full-time organizers to help firm up the union and prepare for the subsequent strikes.

Despite all the stressful hours teachers put in both in and out of school these days, these self-selected leaders and activists managed to organize grassroots caucuses, community alliances, stronger workplace organizations, and mass strikes that have rippled through the US education system. Grassroots leaders from West Virginia and half a dozen other "red" states, along with the successful caucus-based union takeovers in Chicago, Los Angeles, and partially in Massachusetts, and the formation of a national rank-and-file teachers' caucus, the United Caucuses of Rank-and-File Educators (UCORE), have changed the picture of teacher unionism dramatically in a few short years.

It is worth noting, therefore, that in the case of the Chicago and Los Angeles examples McAlevey discusses, the order of her "model" is reversed. First the "untrained" rank-and-file workers organize, lead a series of fights (structure tests?), and take over. Only then are the full-time organizers hired, most of whom themselves come from the ranks and have no formal training but a good deal of experience.[30] In these examples, and many others, it was in fact "wisdom emanating from the bottom" that made the elevation of struggle and the transformation and democratization of the union possible. McAlevey, of course, knows that workers can develop leadership skills in the course of struggle. But for her this seems to be something exceptional and "extraordinary." She writes of the workers at the Smithfield packing plant in North Carolina with a tone of surprise, "As the story of this fight will show, the intensity of the previous fight made some of the workers' leaders extraordinarily skilled, because of their experience in *struggle*."[31] That struggle involved two mass wildcat strikes in 2006 led by the immigrant Latinx workers in the plant before the organizer from the United Food and Commercial Workers arrived.

The "model" McAlevey proposes is less a replica of the early CIO's rise than an effort to stretch the essentially restraining and routinized Wagner Act/ Taft-Hartley framework of industrial relations to its limits. For decades, however, rank-and-file initiative in this context has been muted by a combination of the monopolization of real decision-making at the top, the routinization of bargaining and shop floor grievance handling, no-strike and management's rights clauses in most contracts, the ceremonial and boring nature of most union meetings and conventions, and has been further paralyzed by the fear generated by the economic insecurity of the neoliberal era. Substituting greater and more skilled organizer initiative cannot undo this routinized institutional framework by itself.

In this context, the attempt to find more effective ways to organize and fight can be traced to the debate over organizing that began in the 1990s, inspired by victories like the Los Angeles Justice for Janitors campaign in 1990 and the ascent of John Sweeney's "New Voice" team in 1995. It was carried further in the works of Kate Bronfenbrenner, Tom Juravich, Ruth Needleman, Bruce Nissen, Bill Fletcher Jr., and many others, as well as in the pages of *Labor Notes* and books it has published. At least two conclusions followed from that research and debate in terms of unionization drives: membership involvement in organizing produced more representation wins, and community support can make a difference.[32] That is, when these practices themselves do not just become more routinized rituals or temporary "mobilizations" in a top-down "strategy," as often happens.

The ideas McAlevey is proposing add to the best of these conclusions whatever their actual origins. They have been and will be used to extract victories from time to time. Nevertheless, even taken together all these innovations in organizing have not turned things around. On the contrary, they have at best contributed to the rearguard resistance to American labor's continued retreat in the face of relentless employers' aggression. So, we have to ask if they are sufficient for both the conditions and the possibilities that have emerged in recent years and are now taking shape? If not, what can we point to that might make a real difference?

Much has changed in the US labor movement and the context in which it struggles to survive over the past three or four decades. The working class and union membership are more racially diverse and women play a much larger role in both. Most unions have reversed the anti-immigrant positions many held prior to the acceleration of immigration after the mid-1980s. At the same time, the very nature of work and the labor process has morphed yet again from simple lean production to its digitally driven reign of super-standardization (eat your heart out Frederick Taylor), surveillance, and work intensification. This transformation of work now embraces virtually all types of labor. The increasing tendency of educated "millennials" to be pushed down into the working class brings a new source of energy but also uncertainty about one's social or class identity. The multiple connections of the production of goods and services have been tightened by the development of a global, information-driven logistics infrastructure that didn't exist even at the dawn of the twenty-first century.

All of this can seem overwhelming. Yet, some of these changes also present new opportunities for working-class organization and action. The tightening of work and the connections between workplaces, between goods producers and service producers, and their key points of convergence in major urban and metropolitan areas has rendered employers more vulnerable.[33] McAlevey makes note of this briefly, but it is an aspect of contemporary capitalism that needs analytical development as a strategic framework.[34] The downward mobility of so many "millennials" brings some new energy to the digitalized, sometimes irregular or platformed workforce from younger workers who are not that different from today's teacher insurgents. At the same time, increased racial diversity and the growing role of women often give today's struggles a more representative, universal, and solidaristic character than many of those in previous eras.

What may prove to be the most important development in creating a renewed labor movement, however, is the increase in worker self-activity found across the various divisions in the workforce. As David McNally has shown, this has increasingly taken the form of mass strikes across the world and by many different groups of workers and others, a major sign of changing times.[35] In the US, the teachers' movement is the most obvious example of this, but it is evident in the rise of nurse militancy and unionism as well. Direct actions by immigrant workers that go back to the 2006 "Day Without Immigrants" and Smithfield strikes McAlevey discusses, but arise almost continuously in unexpected corners of the economy such as small actions at Amazon as well as larger ones in the traditional "pastures of plenty" such as Washington State's apple orchards. Perhaps most unexpected, of course, are the many signs of worker self-activity that have arisen amidst the twin crises of renewed recession-cum-depression and the COVID-19 pandemic that accelerated it. Workers at Amazon, for example, have gone where traditional unions feared to tread. The worker-initiated Amazonians United has engaged in "deep organizing," as they call it, forming locals across the country, contacts around the world, and building on small actions (structure tests?) with an approach in which there are no professional organizers and that mixes up McAlevey's order of things.[36]

While it may seem remote from union activity, even the mass widespread protests at the police murder of George Floyd in Minneapolis represent a form of self-activity that is likely to influence events beyond even the protests' immediate focus on the depth of racism and police brutality in the US. Urban upheavals, protests, and riots were an integral part of the rebellion of the 1960s and 1970s. Black workers who rebelled in the streets of Detroit in 1967 were among those who struck and formed Black or integrated caucuses in the auto plants in the following years. My own experience in both public sector organizing in the 1960s and rank-and-file activity and a very long strike of telephone workers in the early 1970s convinced me of the impact Black militancy had on the thinking and actions of both Black and white workers in that period.

Furthermore, the protests and rioting in response to George Floyd's murder have been more visibly multiracial than those in the 1960s or even Ferguson. To a greater degree than in previous protests and riots over police murders of Black people, those over George Floyd's death have had more union support, although many top leaders including Rich Trumka of the AFL-CIO stopped short of criticizing the police "unions" for their complicity in defending killer cops.[37] Given the intensity of these mass demonstrations, there's no reason to doubt that today's protesters and rioters will return to their jobs cleaning the offices of the rich, assisting the sick in hospitals, stacking shelves in a supermarket, or picking and packing in a warehouse with anything but "attitude." Protest and militancy are contagious. Just as the upsurge that began in Ferguson created a new wave of activists and gave birth to Black Lives Matter, so this latest rebellion in the streets by working-class people may create unknown workplace leaders and activists who will be disinclined to take the boss's shit anymore.

This huge outpouring across the US and the world saw a multitude of handmade signs and few famous speakers in its first week or so—except for the ubiquitous Al Sharpton. It was truly an uprising of "untrained" organizers, "undeveloped" organic leaders, activists who skipped a structure test or two, and people who had never protested before. It can be argued that its very spontaneity will make it hard to sustain. Even if so, my guess is that, like the mass hunger marches and early strikes that preceded the CIO, this will prove to be one of the greatest organizer training sessions in a generation or two.

The rise of collective worker self-activity and, therefore, of natural workplace organizers will be the biggest "structure test" of US unions and labor leaders in generations. The advice McAlevey offers in her "model" is mostly good and useful. But it addresses institutional arrangements that have decayed without suggesting how to transcend them. At the same time, the "model" preserves or even enhances a dominant place for the professional organizer that can miss or even discourage the most fundamental ingredient of power—collective worker initiative from below. The time has come to reverse the "model."

## CHAPTER 7

# A Season of Inflammable Materials, Economic Dislocation, and Political Instability

*Perhaps the most useful assumption is that, under nineteenth- and early twentieth-century conditions, the normal process of industrial development tends to produce explosive situations, i.e., accumulation of inflammable material which only ignite periodically, as it were under compression.[1]*

—E. J. Hobsbawm, historian

*Working-class upsurges often happen in the context of deep social changes in society as a whole, such as abrupt and widespread economic dislocation, a profound loss of legitimacy by ruling elites, or abnormal political instability.[2]*

—Mark Meinster, United Electrical Workers (UE)

The impasse of American politics persists in a world of rising social turbulence. The Arab Spring can be considered the prelude to this new period of social uprisings, but in nation after nation in the past decade or so, angry masses have occupied the streets and squares of cities and workers have struck around the world. One estimate recorded "civil unrest" in forty-seven countries in 2019 alone.[3] The European Trade Union Institute counted sixty-four general strikes in Europe between 2010 and 2018.[4] The International Labour Organization reported 44,000 strikes in fifty-six countries between 2010 and 2019, but admitted "the number could be far higher than 44,000."[5] In China, the *China Labour Bulletin* counted some 6,694 strikes between 2015 and 2017 in a wide variety of industries. Yu Chunsen estimates 3,220 strikes by manufacturing workers from 2011 to May 2019 in spite of the government's ban on strikes.[6] The list of national democratic upsurges is simply too long to include here.

David McNally has analyzed "the return of the mass strike" in considerable detail. Looking at mass strikes since the 2008 recession, he wrote in 2020:

> Across the decade since the Great Recession, we have witnessed a series of enormous general strikes (Guadeloupe and Martinique, India, Brazil, South Africa, Colombia, Chile, Algeria, Sudan, South Korea, France, and many more) as well as strike waves that have helped to topple heads of state (Tunisia, Egypt, Puerto Rico, Sudan, Lebanon, Algeria, Iraq).[7]

In addition, there have been mass strikes of various sizes around the world often linked to issues of social reproduction, including, for example, the 2018–19 teachers' strikes in the US. As McNally emphasizes, the mass strike has also been adopted by the women's movement, notably in the International Women's Strikes that swept fifty nations in 2017 and 2018 in the name of the "feminism of the 99 percent." Some mass strikes, he reports, have occurred in the midst of broader mobilizations in streets and squares across the world such as those in Hong Kong, Chile, Thailand, Ukraine, Lebanon and Iraq.[8]

The most useful understanding of the potential of the current upsurge is best described by McNally, who writes, "the new strike movements are harbingers of a period of *recomposition* of militant working class cultures of resistance, the very soil out of which socialist politics can grow."[9] Whether this *recomposition* will help produce a general working-class upsurge is impossible to predict. But as United Electrical Workers (UE) rep Mark Meinster writes in *Labor Notes*, "Working-class upsurges often happen in the context of deep social changes in society as a whole, such as abrupt and widespread economic dislocation, a profound loss of legitimacy by ruling elites, or abnormal political instability."[10] That just about describes the situation labor faces across the world today.

While nothing like a "strike wave" or prolonged mass street occupation has emerged as of this writing in the United States and official strike statistics remain low, it has not been entirely immune to this epidemic of social conflict and rebellion even if the scale has been smaller so far. Nor have some of the protests in the US remained isolated to this country. The Black Lives Matter movement and the International Women's Strikes both spread internationally. The Puerto Rican uprising of 2019, which culminated in a mass march of eight hundred thousand people and the subsequent resignation of the Governor, carried rebellion to the US colonial periphery.[11] The roots of all these protests, strikes, and mass movements are ultimately found in the Great Recession of 2008; the massive level of inequality not seen in a hundred years; the climate crisis that has become tangible in the storms, floods, and wildfires that have swept the earth; and the COVID-19 pandemic which has stretched national health systems to the breaking point, killed thousands, and destroyed the livelihoods of millions. More generally, the multiple crises of the last decade or so have produced a crisis of social reproduction characterized by extreme inequality and increased insecurity.

The pandemic, of course, destroyed millions of jobs and it is not clear what will emerge if and when it is finally contained. But capitalism cannot function without sufficient labor to exploit. While manufacturing jobs continue to disappear, those involving key aspects of social reproduction as well as e-commerce and the movement of goods and capital have actually grown. As Ursula Huws points out, "The history of capitalism can be regarded synoptically as the history of the dynamic transformation of each of these types of labor into another, with (as Marx predicted) the overall effect of driving a higher and higher proportion of human labor into the 'productive' category where it is disciplined by, and produces value for, capitalists."[12]

On the other side of the class coin, the new billionaire class fraction in the US is evidence of this extreme inequality. Its members are actors in the further pressures on the labor process as they suck up profits for speculation. At the same time, a peculiar type of political instability not typical of US politics has arisen in the context of the impasse that has led to the recent turmoil in the presidential transition period, along with a growing sense that US political and economic elites are seriously out of touch with the majority, if not yet totally illegitimate in the eyes of everyone.

Crisis, of course, is the midwife of change—something the powers that be understand all too well. The economic crisis of the 1930s produced the great labor upheaval of that period as well as the New Deal, while that of the 1970s and early 1980s gave rise to the neoliberal era as capital and its political acolytes turned against virtually all the supporting elements of working-class life. The COVID-19 pandemic, the climate crisis, and depression have laid bare many of capitalism's fault lines, while making countless workers aware of their central place in the entire reproduction of life *and* the boss's profits. Simultaneously, it has exposed how little employers and politicians care about the daily plight of working-class people. This has driven some to direct action under very difficult circumstances. It is perhaps premature to say: It's our turn. But the increase in working-class self-activity is surely a sign of something new.

It is also a challenge for unions to adjust to a new reality. If there is a continued surge of collective self-organizing and actions, it may be something other than a simple series of "hot shops" or a neat industry- or sector-wide movement. The distinction between the two is likely to be blurred for one thing because interactions of "industries" and the supply chains and digital flows of finance that connect workplaces are complex and in flux as a result of the pandemic and depression. In this context, a static or linear view of strategy can become a barrier. Before assessing the potential for an upsurge that can break the political impasse in the US, we need to examine the changes in work itself that capital has wrought in the twenty-first century.

## Technology and the Control of Labor

Management, it should be remembered, exists because the cooperation of workers in their own exploitation cannot be taken for granted. From the origins of capitalism to its increasing dependence on digital technology, workers have displayed myriad forms of individual and collective resistance to the tyranny of capital on or off the job. These ranged from the observation of St. Monday, to selective machine breaking, the practice that Taylor called "soldiering," absenteeism, trade unions, strikes, slowdowns, work-to-rules, sick-ins, playing dumb, and just plain crankiness on the job. To counter the natural resistance of humans to the unnatural rhythms of capitalist exploitation, capital has developed management from simple coercion to modern management's multiple layers of theory from Taylor and the Gilbreths, to Mayo, to human resource management. The object of them all has been the intensification of labor: what Marx called the "real subsumption of labor" in the production of relative surplus value.[13]

What has changed most in the nature of work and its management in the last two decades is the degree, penetration, and application of digital technologies that monitor, quantify, standardize, modularize, track, and direct the work of individuals and groups.[14] Although capitalism is by nature a system requiring quantification, accelerated reliance on numerical metrics is frequently a function of capitalist crises. It was, after all, in the midst of the Great Depression of the 1930s that modern national income accounts and Keynesian demand management were developed. Similarly, it was in the mid-1980s in the wake of the 1980–82 recession, along with lean production, Six Sigma, and "Just-in-Time" delivery, that the use of the terms "metrics," "benchmarks," and "performance indicators" accelerated into common business usage, and management expert Tom Peters famously said, "What gets measured gets done."[15]

Today's digitalized statistical measurements build on but transcend the efforts of Taylorism and lean production to fragment, standardize, and thereby control individual and collective labor, regardless of what product or service it is meant to produce. The digitalization of much work-related technology means work can be measured and broken down into nanoseconds, as opposed to Taylor's minutes and seconds, and given a precision absent from lean production's simple elimination of "waste" via "management-by-stress." But it also means that every aspect of work becomes quantified. Simplification via quantification enables speed and speed demands quantification. Productivity can be measured where output is quantifiable or given a price, but not emotion, qualitative outcomes, the effects of professional training, or the tacit skills of all workers.

All of this applies to services already transformed in the twentieth century from domestic service and jobs performed by local tradesmen or small firms to corporate providers, then reorganized along lean lines, quantified, and now digitally driven everywhere, from call centers to hotels to building maintenance. Today's digitally driven measurements are also applied to professional work in fields such as health care and education. Data is harvested from the workers and then used against them here as in a factory or warehouse. So, teachers are measured by student grades (allegedly the teacher's product) in standardized tests based on "standardized knowledge" and forced to "teach to test," while hospital nurses can be tracked by GPS and directed by algorithmic Clinical Decision Support Systems that recommend standard treatments. Or, in both cases, workers can be replaced by less qualified and less costly workers performing standardized tasks. Because these are mostly women workers performing "emotional labor," the emotional content of the job is taken as an unacknowledged freebee for capital—the unpaid aspect of labor of social reproduction performed on the job rather than in the home.[16]

Amazon is the most cited exemplar of digitally driven workers for good reason. As a recent study of an Amazon fulfillment center in California described the context in which employees work, "In order to choreograph the brutal ballet that ensues once a consumer clicks 'place your order' for next-day delivery on Amazon Prime, the company leverages its algorithmic and technical prowess within its massive network of communication and digital technology, warehouse facilities, and machinery, as it numerically 'flexes' its workforce up and down in sync with fluctuating consumer demand." In identical facilities across the globe, the work itself is guided by scanners and hand-held or wrist-mounted computers that track, time, and guide workers to the correct product. Workers are allowed thirty minutes a shift of "off task" time; that is, time when they are not in motion for the company. In addition, they are pushed by Kiva robots who also pick products.[17] It is the prototype of work everywhere unless worker resistance curbs it.

There is another dimension to today's workplace technology that is seldom mentioned. Like the global workforce itself, that in the Amazon warehouse is multiracial and multinational. As the international Black Lives Matter upsurge of 2020 underlined, race and racism, while particularly deeply entrenched in the US, are worldwide and embedded since the days of slavery and colonialism. Racism under capitalism is not only a means of dividing working-class people, but of imposing working-class status on those racial or ethnic groups whose "life chances" are limited by racial or ethnic barriers to advancement. It is *itself* a force in class formation entirely integrated into capitalism's constant recreation of hierarchies of labor. Hence African Americans are disproportionately working-class and poor. While capitalism may have inherited racism from the era of slavery and colonial conquest, it has nevertheless allocated work and workers on an unequal racial, ethnic, gender, or national basis for generations.[18] Like management practices in general, the technology that sorts out workers by occupation, rank, skill, attitude, etc. bears the marks of that heritage.[19]

Artificial intelligence and algorithms are programmed by human beings raised in this historical context who more often than not possess many of its age-old, often unconscious assumptions, while at the same time using data necessarily based in the past. As one analyst noted, "The past is a very racist place. And we only have data from the past to train Artificial Intelligence."[20] As I discuss in the appendix, as one mathematician argues in terms of racial outcomes of AI programs used by police to "predict" high-crime areas, racially biased data "creates a pernicious feedback loop." So it is in every aspect of life affected by artificial intelligence that racial stereotypes are reinforced, including worker allocation and racial "life chances."[21]

One of the more outrageous examples is that of facial recognition technology, which is used by employers and police departments and which routinely fails to distinguish dark-complected individuals from one another.[22] It is scarcely an accident that most of the poorly paid, overworked workers in that California Amazon warehouse are Latinx or Black. Racism, after all, is one of capital's weapons of class struggle now embedded in its technology. The same applies to gender and sexism. For example, the Clinical Decision Support Systems imposed on nurses are based on clinical studies that "systematically excluded women and minorities."[23] This constant pressure to reduce human activity and labor to a mathematical minimum is of course the stuff of alienation. At the same time, it is its very dependence on precise measurement and execution that renders much of today's digitally driven work vulnerable to collective human intervention and resistance.

## Pandemic, Recession, and the Intensification of Labor

Technology is the enabler, but it is the action of capital that dials up the intensity of work to produce an increase in the rate of exploitation from which profits derive. Even where this involves investment in capital goods and equipment of the sort discussed above, labor intensification is almost always a consequence for the remaining workforce. As we saw in chapter 6, recessions destroy jobs, while the productivity gains derived mainly from work intensification that accompany recoveries prevent their return to pre-recession levels. So, the

COVID recession that began in the second quarter of 2020 destroyed a total of nearly 20 million jobs, yet by the end of the year over 11 million were still missing, even though the total value added produced by these workers had returned to 96 percent of its pre-recession level by the end of the third quarter (July–September), according to government figures. Employers simply increased production more than employment. The result was way above average increases in productivity of 10.6 percent in the second quarter and 4.6 percent in the third quarter. More output with fewer workers.[24] Bear in mind that official productivity figures cover all employees, including managers, executives, lawyers, etc. So, the impact on those actually producing goods and providing services, which includes nonmanagerial employees such as nurses and teachers, is significantly greater.

Most of this productivity was achieved in manufacturing. Looking at manufacturing beneath the official figures by comparing the numbers of production and nonsupervisory workers to the actual output and value added these workers create, the number of manufacturing production workers fell by 1.2 million between the third quarter (October–December) of 2019 and the second quarter (April–June) of 2020, but only 619,000 of them were recovered by the third quarter (July–September) with 533,000 still missing—down 6 percent overall. Real output *and* real value added, however, rose to 99 percent of their fourth quarter 2019 level, down just 1 percent. So, employers were getting more production with fewer workers.[25]

Given the rising demand for health care during the pandemic, you might think health care workers would be immune to layoffs. Not so. There are three major health care sectors for which there are figures on output and the number of production and nonsupervisory employees, which includes nonmanagerial professionals such as nurses. These workers in ambulatory care, hospitals, and nursing facilities lost 657,000 jobs over the ten-month period from the end of 2019 to September 2020, a drop of 5 percent. Yet, the output index for those sectors *rose* by 2.4 percent. Not a lot you might think, but that is still a spread of over 7 percent. Fewer workers, more work.

That much of this increased productivity came from intensifying or speeding up work rather than new investment is indicated by the fact that investment in equipment in this period slumped and then remained below pre-recession levels.[26] This is not the best situation for capital since additional investment in production technology would increase output more than additional human effort by itself could. But given the huge jumps in productivity in such a short space of time, significant advances in investment and technology would not have been possible. In any case, as Marx argued following J. S. Mill, mechanization increases work intensification. "On the basis of capitalist production the purpose of machinery is by no means *to lighten or shorten the day's toil* of the worker."[27] As Braverman put it, "Machinery offers to management the opportunity to do by wholly mechanical means that which it had previously attempted to do by organizational and disciplinary means."[28] As we saw above, today's digital capital is largely focused on surveillance, measurement, quantification, and standardization of tasks precisely to speed their application.

The contradictory contours of the COVID-induced recession of mid-2020, however, also offered the chance to intensify the labor of the workers in those industries that grew rapidly throughout the pandemic. With more and more people ordering things online during the pandemic, both the US Postal Service (USPS) and private parcel giant UPS saw huge increases in deliveries, but didn't see proportionate gains in their workforce. In 2020, the Postal Service saw package volumes rise by over 40 percent, but more than 50,000 of its 600,000 workers had to take pandemic-related leave.[29] At UPS, with its mixture of part-time and full-time workers, the company announced it would hire just 100,000 workers for the 2020 holiday season, the same it had in previous years, despite an average daily volume increase of 13.5 percent over that of 2019 and a predicted "nearly double" average of holiday package delivery. As a result, its third quarter net income rose by 12 percent above that for the same period in 2019 to $2 billion.[30] Amazon's contracted Flex drivers also face huge workloads, as many as four hundred deliveries per shift, as this e-commerce giant ups its competition with UPS and the Postal Service for the labor-intensive "last mile" of package delivery.[31]

That overwork was behind the productivity leaps is indicated by a number of surveys that revealed rising burnout, anxiety, and depression from the stress of overwork. Surveys done by Eagle Hill Consultants in April and August 2020 found that 58 percent of US workers had experienced burnout, while 47 percent "attributed burnout to their workload" and 28 percent to "performance expectations." A survey by FlexJobs and Mental Health America found that 40 percent of those experiencing burnout at work in 2020 did so "specifically during the pandemic."[32]

While mental health surveys taken throughout 2020 by the Centers for Disease Control and Census Bureau didn't relate their findings specifically to work, they nonetheless showed that symptoms of anxiety and depression rose during the pandemic and were most severe among young people, those without a college degree, and Blacks and Latinos—those most likely to work in manufacturing and many of the "frontline" occupations most affected during the pandemic.[33]

This type of pressure has been strong across the workforce throughout the pandemic and is likely to be repeated in 2021 as long as capital maintains the initiative. Along with the general crisis in social reproduction, this squeezing of the last possible ounce of work from the millions of workers who now see themselves as "essential," as they really always have been, is one more of those "inflammable materials" historian Eric Hobsbawm wrote about. In the sort of dialectical twist that capitalism is famous for, its best twenty-first-century efforts to speed profitability by accelerating the circuits of capital and production, however, offer the potential for the sort of workers' power needed to break the broader political impasse.

## Labor and the Control of the Corridors of Capital

The technology, employment patterns, and flows of goods, services, and capital that characterize both domestic production and shape the world of labor, rest, in turn, on a deepening international material infrastructure that enables the logistics that move products and value throughout the world. These material corridors of capital, both domestic and international, consist mainly of familiar roads, rails, shipping lanes, ports, pipelines, airports, and traditional warehouses, but also now include massive urban-based logistics clusters of facilities and labor, miles of fiber-optic cables employed widely only since the late 1990s, data centers that are even newer in application, and warehouses reconfigured for movement rather than storage and transformed by technology. This mostly embedded infrastructure itself is created by and dependent on the labor of millions of workers who build and maintain it. If technology imposes controls, the dependence of infrastructure on continuous labor inputs provides workers with their own potential control—the ability to slow down or stop capital's relentless movement of value and, hence, the process of accumulation.

Marx saw transportation and communications as part of value-production.[34] So, the tens of millions of workers across the world in these embedded repositories of fixed constant capital, and in the trucks, trains, ships, planes, cable stations, and data centers that move data, commodities, and finances across this infrastructure, are production workers as much as those in factories or sites of service delivery. They make the circuits of capital function and provide much of the speed at which they turn over. It is over and through these paths of transportation and communication that these circuits of capital move with Marx's familiar formula, M-C-M´, though in its extended form, sequentially and simultaneously repeated millions of times a day.[35] The speed at which this happens determines the potential profit.[36] And, of course, driven by global competition, speed and "just-in-time" delivery have become major features of contemporary production, logistics, and increasingly e-commerce.

This is as true of those working in the movement of data, information, and money as those driving on a road, steaming a container ship, maintaining a pipeline, or working in a factory: that is, all those workers who are merging living labor power with accumulated dead labor to produce value. None of this infrastructure or the capital equipment that runs over and through it comes to life without the hand and mind of labor. Even the most automated system requires constant maintenance and repair. For example, as of early 2020 Amazon's thirty-nine supposedly fully automated data centers in the US and Ireland employed ten thousand workers to keep them humming, and that doesn't include all those who provide energy, data conduits, replacement parts, etc.[37]

What is called the "cloud" or cyberspace is nothing more than an extended material complex of fiber-optic cables, data centers, transmitters, and computers. As a *New York Times* article argued, "People think that data is in the cloud, but it's not. It's in the ocean." Actually, it's also on and under the land as well as under the sea, following cable paths originally laid in the mid-nineteenth century for telegraph cables. Today's fiber-optic cables carry 95 percent of internet traffic. The whole connected material system and its parts are highly vulnerable and breaks or disruptions are frequent.[38]

It is laid and repaired by workers on cable ships, those in cable stations around the world, workers employed by national telecom companies, and in the proliferating number of huge data centers that, as James Bidle put it, "generate vast amounts of waste heat, and require corresponding quantities of cooling, from acres of air conditioning systems."[39] All of which, in turn, require human labor to run. At every point in this seemingly immaterial movement of data and money there are workers of various kinds and differing skills without which there would be no motion. There is no digitalization without human manipulation.

In a period of relatively low levels of capital investment, countless billions have been poured into the extension and deepening of this infrastructure. Looking at a somewhat broader measure of infrastructure, Price Waterhouse Coopers estimates that $1.7 trillion was invested by private sources in infrastructure from 2010 to 2017, in a sector in which government investment often plays the major role.[40] New cables are laid regularly, harbors and canals dug or dredged, new cross-continental rails embedded, more airports constructed and old ones expanded.[41] As large as these new investments are, they represent only the initial cost and labor input. As Akhil Gupta argues about the many new infrastructure projects around the world, "As soon as the project is completed, and officially declared to be open, it starts being repaired."[42] That is, the "dead" labor involved in infrastructure requires the constant input of living labor over its entire functioning "life."

A major force of this international infrastructure expansion has been Chinese President Xi Jinping's Belt and Road Initiative launched in 2013. This has funded, largely through loans, a network of super highways, rail lines (three from China to Europe), ports, and airports that "spreads into the Pacific, the Indian Ocean and deep into Africa" as well as the Middle East and Europe. By 2015 China had set aside $890 billion to spend on 900 projects.[43] By 2019, it was "focused on energy, infrastructure, and transportation with an overall potential investment estimated at about $1.4 trillion—a scale never before seen," according to analyst Daniel Yergin.[44] Such ventures mean the employment of huge numbers of workers across the vast spaces of Central and South Asia, the Middle East, and Africa who bring these projects to life and through collective action can shut them down as well.

In the United States, if the major highways and bridges remain under-repaired, freight-bearing railroad lines have been upgraded, new fiber-optic cable stretches across the nation beneath paths already set by the Interstate highways and major rail corridors, and corporate data centers proliferate particularly in northern Virginia among those belonging to the government's various intelligence agencies. And, of course, investment in infrastructure by the federal government is a perennial, if not always fulfilled, election promise. As elsewhere in the world, these transportation and communication links that keep capital, information, and goods flowing connect giant hubs of labor and capital sited in the country's major metropolitan areas.[45] It is in these metro areas that the bulk of the nation's economic life now takes place and some of these, as we saw in chapter 3, now include urbanized sections of rural America. And they are vulnerable to disruption from both the links that connect them and their own internal connections and interdependence.

The pandemic has forced more changes in the paths of trade and commerce as more and more people turned to the internet to buy everything from food to clothing to entertainment. Demands on e-commerce have jammed up the Pacific shipping routes, causing container shipping prices to triple over 2020. This, in turn has led to a fall in "on-time" arrivals affecting "just-in-time" supply chains. Furthermore, retailers have turned to fulfillment companies like UPS and XPO Logistics to warehouse their goods nearer to customers and deliver them. As brick-and-mortar retail jobs disappeared, those in e-commerce and warehousing grew almost certainly within large metropolitan markets.[46]

Indeed, not only are the largest "logistics clusters" centered in these metropolitan areas, but so are almost 80 percent of manufacturing jobs, according to a study by the Brookings Institution.[47] These metro regions are, of course, also the centers of transportation and communications, utilities, construction, and major services of social reproduction such as the US health care industry, public education, hotels, building maintenance, and food services. Even e-commerce finds itself rooted in these population and economic hubs. The workers who make these industries go and who live in the cites, suburbs, and "rural" counties of these metropolitan conurbations are disproportionately Black and Latinx.[48] They are the sites of today's revolts and centers of Hobsbawm's "inflammable materials" and "compression."

They are also, of course, the home of the Democratic Party's electoral base—a base whose needs and increasingly precarious lives this party can not sufficiently address. It is here that the impasse can be broken first. These metro areas overlap with and connect to the many rural counties in which manufacturing and other working-class jobs dominate. If the one-party nature of so many urban areas opens the door to challenge the hegemony of the Democratic Party in the urban United States, so the wildfire-like spread of class upsurge and conflict can upset the conservative and Republican one-party domination of much of rural United States as well.

## Class Struggle Changes Minds

Like a static understanding of organizing strategy, a static view of working-class attitudes is a hindrance in responding to a changing situation. In 2019 Gallup took two polls that indicate important changes in the way many Americans view society. The 2019 poll on whether or not Americans approve of labor unions found that 64 percent did, up from an all-time (since 1947) low of 48 percent in 2009.[49] As we saw in chapter 2, the Gallup poll on political attitudes that same year found that 43 percent of those who responded thought socialism would be a "good thing" for the country. In 2019, 58 percent of those between ages eighteen and thirty-four approved of socialism. It wasn't just those college-educated millennials who thought socialism was okay. Among all ages, those with a college degree liked it by 45 percent, while those without one thought it good for the country by 46 percent. "Non-whites" approved by 57 percent.[50]

Polls, of course, are static things. The formation of class consciousness is, on the other hand, a complex and contradictory process. Central to this process, however, is that minds are changed and consciousness altered in the course of prolonged struggle. The strikers that led to the CIO brought together people with a wide range of views on everything, turning some from apolitical people to activists, conservatives to radicals, and even followers of the right-wing demagogic Catholic priest Father Coughlin to good UAW members.[51] The people who walked the streets of Montgomery, Alabama, in 1955 in the boycott of that city's segregated bus service experienced a power they never knew they had, opening the eyes of millions and launching a mass movement that few at the time predicted. An upsurge of significant proportions could be part of activating those who seem passive or discouraged and even of winning some of those workers and union members who voted for Trump in 2016 and even 2020 to a militant labor movement and left politics.

So, more US residents as of 2019, including a lot of working-class people, not only like labor unions, but even think socialism is a good thing. Some, of course, were introduced to the idea of socialism via Bernie Sanders's two runs for president and were even willing to vote for a self-proclaimed democratic socialist in 2016 and 2020, but earlier polls showed a similar positive attitude toward socialism. Just what those who said they thought socialism was good for the country meant by "socialism" remains to be seen. But the fact is, in relation to the population, there were relatively few socialist organizers or agitators among the millions represented by those who answered in favor of socialism or voted for Bernie to convince them. Capitalism pushed them in this direction and many drew their own conclusions.

The Gallup organization didn't speculate on how these two sets of opinions might relate to one another and to the first green shoots of worker self-organization, but we should. We probably won't see red flags waving in the streets of the United States any time soon, but minds are opening just as more people are acting. As Gramsci wrote, "The first step in emancipating oneself from political and social slavery is that of freeing the mind."[52] The long festering problems and now almost 1930s-type underlying conditions are producing these changes, but it is the *convergence* of new thinking on organization and politics, on the one hand, and increased action, on the other, that are the major ingredients in, as McNally put it, a *"recomposition* of militant working class cultures of resistance" and a potential social explosion on a scale not seen for decades.

It is this explosion that can break the political impasse that has paralyzed US politics for too long. As I have argued throughout, the new Biden administration has no inclination toward major reforms and embodies huge barriers to reform in the party's increasingly wealthy voter base and super-wealthy funders. The tiny contingent of "progressive" officeholders elected in the last few years do not have the leverage to change this. The sort of power to break this gridlock will have to come from outside not only the Democrats, but the electoral arena itself as it has in the past.

Socialists and activists cannot create an upsurge, but they can be prepared for one and can certainly participate in events and actions that help move things along. Organizers and union strategists Rand Wilson and Peter Olney have pointed out that in 2021 some 450 union contracts covering a million and a half workers will expire. At least 160 of these cover 1,000 or more workers. These include such frontline essential workers as 200,000 in health care, 200,000 postal workers, 273,000 state and local public sector employees, 100,000 school workers, 48,500 grocery workers, and 37,000 airline employees.[53] There can be no doubt that most of these workers will face demands for concessions as employers, public or private, attempt to make up losses from the pandemic at the expense of their employees. Most of these contracts expire in June or later.

Activists who are members of these unions can propose grassroots contract campaigns and joint actions by different unions. Others can help organize mass solidarity, what Wilson and Olney call "swarming solidarity." While such actions need to have the support of the union members directly involved, they can help to put the plight *and* resistance of workers in the public light. A number of strikes occurred in early 2021, beginning in January. In New York, 1,400 Teamsters struck the Hunts Point Produce Market in the Bronx for a week and won. Hunts Point processes 60 percent of New York City's fresh fruit and vegetables. It is one of those "nodes" in the local economy's supply chains that becomes highly visible when its workers go on strike. That strike got wide support from other unionists and movement activists and, of course, AOC. It was an early example of what Wilson and Olney meant by "swarming solidarity." The 25,000-member Chicago Teachers Union voted to reject the school system's demand to return to unsafe classroom teaching and instead to continue teaching "safely and remotely." Other January strikes took place at a Marathon Petroleum refinery, an auto parts supplier to General Motors, and a steel mill, while a federal judge ruled that railroad workers on the Union Pacific who proposed to strike could not.[54]

Another event that can have a major impact on organized labor will be the Teamster elections in October 2021. With the old guard forces in disarray, it is almost certain the reformers backed by the Teamsters for a Democratic Union (TDU) will take control of this powerful union.[55] The sorts of critical rank-and-file victories we've seen in major teachers', transit, postal, and health care unions in the last several years could now come to a broad variety of industrial workers as this huge union sweeps away decades of conservative rule and prepares to take on the giants of transportation. Victories by this union could encourage others in logistics sectors such as warehousing, e-commerce, package delivery, etc. to organize.

A similar opportunity appears to be opening in the 400,000-member United Auto Workers (UAW). This union, whose forty-nine thousand members at General Motors struck for a month in 2019, saw its top leaders convicted of corruption. As a result of pressure from the rank-and-file group Unite All Workers for Democracy (UAWD), the Justice Department has agreed to allow the membership to vote on whether or not to have direct elections of top officers. This has been a demand of reform movements in the UAW for years, and now a vote to win direct elections will take place in September 2021. This represents an enormous challenge to the Administration Caucus which led the UAW into labor-management cooperation, two-tier wage systems, and workplace concessions for decades. If it passes, UAW members will directly elect new leaders in 2022, a challenge the Administration Caucus has never faced.[56]

Just as the rank-and-file victories by teachers in Chicago and Los Angeles and the mass strikes of 2018–19 inspired reform movements in other teachers' unions, so could similar victories in high-profile blue-collar unions like the Teamsters and UAW encourage more efforts to break with the business union practices that have been a major factor in union decline. Such a dynamic could also encourage new organization on a more democratic and militant basis among the millions of as yet unorganized workers across industries. It is from these fights and new efforts to organize at Amazon, Google, and other high-tech, e-commerce, and service outfits, along with Black Lives Matter, climate change actions, the new women's movement, and others, that the groundwork for breaking the impasse can be laid and larger, independent, class-based political possibilities created. It is critical that socialists are active in these events and movements.

## Toward the Formation of a Mass Working Class–Based Party

If there is to be a new working class–based political party of the left in the US, it will have to be much more than an electoral organization. As McNally put it, it will have to "move beyond electoralism," even as it runs candidates for office. It should differ not only from conventional major-party electoral campaigning in being an independent, permanent, democratic membership organization, but also from that of many third-party efforts, such as the Green Party, that have no real social base and rely on a limited issue constituency. From the start, it should seek to be a central piece in building the organized power of the working class in society independently of such positions as it seeks or holds in the capitalist state and its legislative bodies.

As such, like the mass working-class parties of the past, the efforts to build it must be rooted first and foremost in the daily lives of working-class people, in the workplaces and neighborhoods of this class in all its diversity as it confronts capitalism and its multiple crises. This party's own strength would flow from the participation of its members and activists in the day-to-day struggles around

housing, education, welfare, health care, childcare, police violence, unionization, wages, and working conditions; i.e., in class struggle. It is highly unlikely
and undesirable that such a party would be the result of the actions of the leaders
of most unions as they are today.

A sort of top-down model such as the Labour Representation Committee
that helped launch the British Labour Party over a hundred years ago is both im-
probable given the entanglements of the vast majority of the US union bureaucracy with the Democratic Party *and* undesirable from a democratic perspective.
Any union initiatives are far more likely to come from local unions, rank-and-file
caucuses, and new organizing movements as well as the other social movements.
A movement toward a workers' party will certainly involve a great deal of house-
cleaning and democratization of most of today's unions. It will also inevitably
involve winning those who have voted Democratic or even Republican in the
past, as well as those who haven't voted at all. It could hardly be otherwise. Call
it dirty or clean, what matters is the direction of the dynamic. To put it another
way, it is a reversal of the historical dynamic by which social and labor movement
activists and leaders have been drawn *into* the Democratic Party made possible
by today's underlying crisis conditions. The task now is to draw them *out* of this
party of capital and the prosperous, not lead them *in* again.

Furthermore, a workers' party's methods of gaining reforms such as the Green
New Deal, Medicare for All, free higher education, defunding the police, etc.,
should be informed more by mass actions and other grassroots activities outside
the Congress, state assembly, or city council than by parliamentary maneuvers inside. Of course, it will run candidates for political office and seek to establish itself
as a distinct political presence. But the effectiveness of a workers' or socialist party
and its ability to elect candidates flows from its real sources of power.

This perspective is based on the Marxist notion that the power of the working class derives from its position in the economy, the process of capital accumulation, and the social reproduction of life, as well as its organized numbers, not
from such political offices its representatives might hold in the capitalist state
as a result of electoral activity. Both the "hollowing out" and decline of most
traditional social democratic parties, and the new radical parties in Europe such
as Podemos all tell us that focusing mainly on elections even for member-based
parties leads to setbacks or defeat.[57] So does the focus on individual leaders and
candidates that often accompanies an electoral emphasis.

This is not, as some will say, a "build the movement first, run for office later" argument. The timing of any election is a matter of practical analysis of the forces available and the state of the opposition. Movements are already there. Many are still weak, although as recent events around Black Lives Matter and to a lesser extent the initial organizing efforts at Amazon and many other outfits during the coronavirus crisis show, there is already motion. Unions are weak nationally, but strong in many urban locations and some industries, and there are new organizing possibilities. The point is to be on the ground, in the class, in the workplace, in the tenants' organization, in the Black Lives Matter demonstrations, union reform movements, strikes, and organizing drives. That is, the party should be active in today's struggles and efforts to build durable democratic participatory organizations of these movements. For organization is always key, and a workers' party cannot become a force for change without significant support in these mostly working class–based movements. And that support is something that has to be fought for and earned through practice as well as ideas.

At the same time, hundreds of "one-party" Democratic urban electoral districts at various levels are there as a starting point for independent working-class political action. Given the likelihood of deepening crises in the first years of the Biden-Harris administration and the unwillingness of Democrats to lead a fight for programs adequate to the needs of working-class people, 2022 might be the year in which to launch some experimental, independent, working class–based congressional and/or state legislative election challenges in vulnerable "one-party" districts as the complacent Democrats chase the well-to-do suburban vote.

The urban areas, inner-ring suburbs, and edge cities containing these districts are home to the nation's concentrations of industrial, transportation, communications, and service workers in large workplaces such as hospitals, hotels, warehouses, etc. That is, home to some of the most powerful and diverse sections of today's working class. They are the key centers of the giant "logistics clusters" and infrastructure nodes on which production, circulation, and social reproduction depend.[58] So, incidentally, are some of DSA's larger chapters located in such areas. The potential mass base, concentrations of socialist activists, and the potential sites for an assault on the political status quo are there. The "spoiler" effect is largely absent. Duverger's Law is irrelevant in these districts.

As gains are made in these urban and metropolitan centers, it will become possible to organize within the equally one-party rural districts and communi-

ties currently dominated by the Republicans, particularly where union organizing has been successful. As we saw in chapter 3, there is a strong working-class,
even manufacturing presence in much of the rural United States that could help
to build a new working-class party even where it might not win elections for
some time. It should be borne in mind that many of these rural manufacturing
workers are connected to metropolitan-based industries by supply chains *and*
in many cases by Interstate highways such as I-75 and I-65 that compose "Auto
Ally," railroad corridors, and communications lines.[59]

Education toward independent political action and, where possible, some
experiments in electoral action should be part of what this new party does as it
forms. But it should flow from convincing activists in the movements, unions,
and issue campaigns that such electoral action can help build power and not just
be another strain on resources. This is not always simple because sometimes it *is*
a strain on resources, and the party should not attempt to demote direct action
or simply divert it into electoral campaigns. Again, working-class power does
not derive from holding office in the capitalist state even if that can enhance
its ability to win things under some circumstances. Rather working-class influence within the capitalist state derives from its fundamental social and economic
power. The point is to organize and activate that power at its sources.

This is not only an analytical proposition about the sources of class power,
but a necessary understanding of power because a new party, no matter what
its origins, will confront—as critics of this view never fail to point out—all the
barriers posed by the American electoral system. These include, of course, the
FPTP-SMD plurality problem at the state and national level, the various obstacles of ballot access in the early phases of development, a hostile media, the
mountains of money that will be deployed against it, and perhaps even some
measure of state repression. In addition, as the events of January 2021 revealed,
the possibility of violent opposition from the far right is now very real. Finally,
since it will be contesting the Democrats and Republicans in general elections
rather than primaries, it will have to mobilize a much larger electorate to become
credible even as a second party.

What its members and candidates *won't* face, however, is the prospect of
endless squabbles, patronizing efforts at co-optation, and institutional barriers
to success that exist *inside* the Democratic caucuses and the oligarchic hierarchies behind them that are present and active day in and day out in all legislative

bodies from Congress to city council. A new workers' party in the making will face this party of capital as the opponent it is from the vantage of independent class organization.

The potential mass base is there in all the statistics that Abbott and Guastella and others produce to show there is a base for socialist politics. The problem is how to activate what is now mostly just sentiment and separate though sometimes overlapping movements. The Sanders campaigns activated some of this base for a time, but in the end left it with no place to go beyond Biden and the conventional norms of American elections. Socialists want to take advantage of the inspiration, activation, and mobilization that Bernie set in motion, but it will have to do so independently of Bernie since he has tied himself, along with most of the other recently elected socialists, to pressuring the Democratic Party for the foreseeable future.

The chances of eventual success for a new working class–based party are increased by the convergence or clash of capitalism's multiple crises, the increasingly bitter political/ideological split within the ruling class, the altered realities of the US electoral system, and the movements in the streets and to a lesser extent so far in the workplaces. While this does not solve all the problems imposed by "Duverger's Law" in presidential or statewide elections where the "spoiler" effect remains, it opens the door to building a mass base potentially capable of overcoming even that situation.[60]

The ability to mount successful local independent political action is even greater in those cities with nonpartisan elections. Twenty-two of America's thirty largest cities have nonpartisan local elections.[61] That is, elections where there is no Democratic ballot line. The outstanding example of this is the Richmond (California) Progressive Alliance (RPA). The RPA has succeeded in electing city officials with union and working-class community support and combating corporate giant and local polluter Chevron.[62] In Chicago, where city council elections are nonpartisan, DSA succeeded in electing six of its members to the council following a wave of labor and community actions. All six had the active support of the Chicago Teachers Union and SEIU Healthcare Illinois-Indiana, along with several community groups. They formed their own Socialist Caucus distinct from the council's ineffective Democratic Party–linked Progressive Caucus.[63] In both cases, successful electoral action was possible because of active support from unions and working class–based community organizations that had long been in motion—and the temptation to run as Democrats was removed, although the pull of coalition with them remains a problem.

In the end, it is periods of deep crisis that tend to activate those that compose the potential mass base for social change in sufficient numbers to make a difference. Today, we see the convergence of economic, social, environmental, and even health crises in which the ruling class appears out of its depth. This is one reason why we get the stylistic extremes of a Trump and a Biden. 2020 was the year of the elite confrontation between centrism and the right in which those on the left working on the Democratic ballot line or in the party campaigns had little influence on policy or strategy. Despite all the "unity" task forces and even the relatively large voter turnout, the Democrats ran on a solidly centrist program as well as their suburban strategy. This is a cruel reminder of just how lasting have been the efforts of capital going back a hundred years to insulate electoral politics from the masses. But its aftermath, the inevitable failure of the centrists and liberals to deal effectively with these compounded crises, or indeed, their ability to exacerbate them, can be such an opening if the left is prepared.

Despite its size and continued growth, DSA cannot substitute itself for the mass grassroots organizations needed for effective working-class political action. It can, however, play a leading role in helping to build and educate the broader movements in socialist and class politics. To win the activists and constituencies described above to an independent political course will require both education and engagement. As it stands now, judging from the written materials, those who favor using the Democratic Party ballot line for whatever reasons appear to dominate the debate in and around DSA. Indeed, in their discussion of the "dirty break" strategy, Day and Uetricht argue that those who want to "build a true left-wing political alternative outside the Democratic Party," though "vocal," are "few and far between these days."[64] If so, this means that the dominant electoral *practice* on the left for the foreseeable future is likely to be within the Democratic Party's field of influence and control. This would be a step backward to DSA's social democratic past and the legacy that still haunts it, something its conventions appear to have rejected. It would also ignore what the new signs of upsurge from below promise. Furthermore, such long-term practice would tend to form habits and relationships of those engaged in it that would hinder an independent direction later. It is important then that the massive pressures to continue support for the Democrats in the hope of influencing policy or winning a bigger congressional majority in 2022 not lead to silence by those favoring genuine independent political action—even if we are "few and far between." The debate isn't over.

## Postscript

Of course, there is a deeper debate underlying that over electoral action. That is the question of socialist revolution or, as Vivek Chibber put it while dismissing it, "rupture" versus either the simple accumulation of reforms or a transition to socialism via normal political channels, perhaps backed up by after-the-fact mass action when capital reacts.[65] The concept of socialist revolution is not, as some would have it, "insurrectionism." What it does involve is a transition that is neither linear nor simply an *event*. The rupture is the radical democratic transition of class power from that of capital to that of the working class broadly defined (the vast majority), from an economy organized around profitability (and racism and environmental destruction) to one centered on human need and survival and commanded by the men and women who do the work whether it is currently paid or unpaid labor.

When Marx and/or Engels spoke of the working class taking political power in order to commence the transition from capitalism to socialism, they did not have in mind the president of the United States and Congress speaking and legislating from on high for a class of millions.[66] Rather, even while workers' parties used the electoral system, they assumed and argued for more direct and fluid forms of democracy at various levels in both politics and production. As Hal Draper, the Marxist most identified with the idea of "socialism from below," wrote, "Socialism as a political program may be most quickly defined, from the Marxist standpoint, as *the complete democratization of society*, not merely of political forms."[67] While the mechanics of the transition are themselves a matter of debate, such a *complete democratization* involves a rupture of historic proportions, including from the increasingly undemocratic character of the US electoral system. This requires mass, democratic organization at every level: unions, councils, parties, etc.

The rise of the far right as a mass, almost mainstream force as demonstrated in its attempt to negate the 2020 elections, its mass mobilization, self-confident racism, and violence demonstrated in January 2021 adds a new element to the whole question of a transition via the electoral process. The assumption of many of those who do see problems in the electoral road to socialism is usually that barriers to such a path would come mainly from the state acting on behalf of or in coordination with capital. It is becoming clear, however, that opposition to left electoral success will come from the organized mass far right well before the state sees the need for decisive intervention. This calls for a level of grassroots organizations and even self-defense that is not compatible with conventional, digitalized campaigning that is inevitably top-down despite the rhetoric of mobilization. Turning out the vote is not the same thing as permanent, democratic organization.

Central to this, however, is whether one assumes that such a transition or rupture is desirable or possible in the first place and, if so, whether it will require a radical discontinuity in political, economic, and social norms. That is, can such a rupture be made without the independent organizations of the working class in various forms including one or more class-based parties? Or can it somehow be extracted from capital through capital's own political institutions and parties via "permeation," as Draper called it, and incremental legislation? These counterposed long-term views, in turn, determine one's opinion on the necessity of political class independence as a guiding principle of electoral engagement based in concrete analysis, not faith in the here and now. As Draper put it in *The Two Souls of Socialism*, it is a matter of "Which Side Are You On?"[68]

# The Roots of Racial Policing in the US

The debate over the causes of mass incarceration and its class and racial roots has been one of the major sites of discussion on the role of race and racism in the United States and its demotion by some socialists. More recently, the multiple murders of Black men and women by police across the country has given new urgency to the role of the police in the larger question of racial oppression in the nation's communities of color. Rather than looking at incarceration itself, here I will examine the race and class origins and practices of policing in the US that inevitably underlie trends in incarceration, police violence, and criminal justice in general. My point of departure is a series of articles written by Cedric Johnson in *New Politics* and *Catalyst*, but could as well address the abovementioned works of several others writing on this subject in the last couple of years that contest the idea that race and racism is at the heart of mass incarceration.[1]

To put things in context, we need to examine the realities of the criminal justice system on which Cedric Johnson and others base their argument. Much of Johnson's argument demoting the role of race and racism in the rise of mass incarceration is drawn from James Forman Jr.'s important account of the role of Black communities and officials in supporting the escalation of "tough on crime" policies in the 1970s.[2] The racist framework of policing in the United States and many of the specific tactics that would characterize the War on Drugs, however, were already well established long before the escalation of incarceration, before Reagan declared the War on Drugs in the mid-1980s or even prior to Nixon's 1971 "war on drugs." Indeed, stop-and-frisk operations that have come to characterize American policing were upheld by the Supreme Court in the 1968 *Terry v. Ohio* ruling, which reversed the previous trend toward civil liberties represented by the *Miranda* ruling and helped set the tone for future police policies at all levels.

The escalation of incarceration was largely a political choice made under Reagan, increased under Clinton, and continued under Bush and Obama.[3] Since the second even more massive wave of Black Lives Matter demonstrations in 2020 and the election of Democrat Joe Biden as president and Kamala Harris as vice president, it has become impossible for the new administration to completely ignore the question of police violence and racism. While it is clear the new administration does not intend to "defund the police," as demonstrators have demanded, it is certain that if these reforms do not address the underlying nature of urban policing analyzed in this chapter, racism and violence against communities of color will continue to characterize American policing.

Local authorities, Black or white, that imposed draconian policies in the 1970s and later were following a well-trod path. In fact, the practice of what Forman perceptively calls "the paradox of the African American experience: the simultaneous over-*and*-under-policing of crime"—that is, a lack of emphasis on protecting Black residents, on the one hand, while over-policing and criminalizing low-income Black neighborhoods, on the other—goes further back to at least the post-WWII era as the Black working-class populations of Northern cities grew and new ghettos formed.[4] Walter Thabit, in *How East New York Became a Ghetto*, gives a clear example of this in the process of ghetto formation in Brooklyn in the 1960s. In addition to poor service from the sanitation and fire departments experienced by the residents of East New York, "the police were not as responsive to complaints as they should have been; yet they harshly ruled the streets, deciding which laws to enforce and when to enforce them."[5]

As a study of Milwaukee in the 1950s and early 1960s reveals, a policy known as "close surveillance," which focused on Black areas, "flooded the inner core with large numbers of police personnel, a concentration not found elsewhere in the city." As early as 1952 this led to "a staggering one arrest of a black resident for every three African Americans in the city." This same study notes a similar policy in Chicago about which the city's Black newspaper, the *Chicago Defender*, complained in 1958 that the Chicago Police "prey on racial districts."[6]

Historian Heather Ann Thompson quotes a Detroit resident about the police presence there: "The ugliest part of the problem in the '50s was police brutality against Black people." This led to rising complaints and efforts against police
brutality in the 1960s well before the 1967 rebellion.[7] In Birmingham, Alabama,
where deindustrialization in the 1950s and 1960s had increased poverty among
Blacks and brought about "the concentration of poverty in core city and North
Birmingham," police brutality and arrests of Blacks had become so extreme over
the years that in 1967 the local civil rights organizations put the fight against
police brutality at the head of their agenda for the first time.[8]

In the period of Northern Black ghetto formation following World War II,
the number of Black arrests grew significantly faster than those of whites. Reflecting this reality, the disproportionate percentage of Black citizens arrested
each year has been consistent over the decades even as the total number of arrests grew. African Americans accounted for 28 percent of all those arrested in
1950, 30 percent in 1960, and 27 percent in 1970, compared to 25 percent in
1980, 31 percent in 1999, and 28 percent in 2010 even after the number of annual arrests leveled off by the late 1990s.[9] Racism in policing, the entry point
into the criminal justice system and incarceration, has been a constant feature of
American law enforcement for generations.

Indeed, police brutality and "over-policing" in Oakland's Black ghetto in the
mid-1960s gave rise to the Black Panthers, who Johnson warns "can't save us now,"
well before Nixon declared war on crime in the nation's Black communities. The
Black and white politicians and police officials who made sentencing mandatory,
accelerated and lengthened sentencing in the 1970s and 1980s, and introduced
"broken windows" and "zero tolerance" policies later that accelerated incarceration were building on older practices and entrenched assumptions about policing.
More importantly, they were acting in the context of a class and racially biased
framework of law enforcement that had been established decades before and
which would make police targeting of Black and Latinx people virtually inevitable.

Given the weight that Johnson gives to Forman's arguments in diminishing
the importance of race, it is worth quoting Forman's own caveat to his readers:

> But in focusing on the actions of black officials, I do not minimize the role of
> whites or racism in the development of mass incarceration. To the contrary:
> racism shaped the political, economic, and legal context in which the black
> community and its elected representatives made their choices.[10]

## Street Crimes and the Racial Mapping

While the regulation and punishment of crime have a long history as a class- and race-based project, the criminal justice system as we know it had its origins in the rise of capitalism, wage labor, and increased urbanization. The first professional police forces were established in the early 1800s by Sir Robert Peel first in Ireland in 1822 with the Royal Irish Constabulary as a sort of colonial occupation force. This was followed in 1829 with the formation of the London Metropolitan Police to patrol the streets of London, its officers known as "Bobbies" and "Peelers" after their founder. The earliest penitentiaries and professional municipal police forces in the US were established between the 1820s and 1850s as capitalism began to take shape, concentrations of urban wage workers grew, the first efforts at trade unions and worker political action were attempted, and public "disorder" or riots committed by the "dangerous classes" became common.[11] Despite all the changes in society since that time, the police remain the dependable frontline, street-level defenders of capitalist "order" whether in protecting property, breaking up a union picket line, shooting down "rioters," or arresting and disbursing social protesters from suffragettes to civil rights and anti-war activists, Wall Street Occupiers, and Black Lives Matter demonstrators. At the same time, the police insulated the elite from both "street crime" and punishment for the crimes committed in elite circles.

The most basic evidence of the class and race bias of modern law enforcement from its origins to today is the historical focus of policing on "street crimes." In line with this focus, recent statistics on arrests show that the largest categories of crimes for which (suspected) offenders were "busted" in 2016 were drug-related activities (1,242,630), assaults (1,158,119), property crimes such as burglary and theft (1,074,136), drunkenness (299,248), and disorderly conduct (291,951), which together account for half of all arrests in this FBI count. And this does not include the many other "street crimes" pinned disproportionately on Black and Latinx people, including murder and robbery. These "street crimes" are typically confronted by police in public places and poorer neighborhoods, and are mostly traceable. Arrests for less visible white-collar, middle-class, or entrepreneurial crimes such as fraud (101,301), forgery and counterfeiting (44,831), embezzlement (12,592), or for that matter rape (18,606)—think Hollywood, #Me Too, etc.—count for little.[12]

Also important are the countless number of crimes for which no arrests are made because they are conducted under the cover of the opaque circuits of capital, the proprietary spaces of big business and finance, or the protected enclaves of the wealthy. "Respectable" middle-class neighborhoods forgo significant arrest rates because there is no dealer on the corner and drug use, assault, sexual violence, child abuse, cybercrime, and other offenses are kept indoors, private, or "in the family" aided by the absence of a snooping police presence. These are crimes that if they are pursued at all are generally beyond the daily sight or reach of the "cop on the beat," or more commonly these days, the patrol car.

Every once in a while some financier is arrested for crimes too big to conceal, like a Bernie Madoff, but the average offending banker or executive is more likely to get a bonus than a sentence. As Forman put it when in the 1980s law enforcement turned toward arresting drug users as well as dealers, "In D.C. and elsewhere, those with the financial means and networks quickly found alternative, and less risky, ways to buy drugs."[13]

This focus on "street crimes" and visible criminal activity was sharpened with the "mapping" of crime by urban police forces that began many decades ago. Crime "mapping" goes back to the mid-nineteenth-century European "cartographic" school of criminology which documented "the empirical regularity of crime." In the US it was further developed by the "Chicago School" in the 1930s, which found that visible crime correlated strongly with "disadvantaged" communities. In addition, in the work of this school the connection became explicitly racial. Its research claimed to produce a link between delinquency and "features of community structure like economic status, stability, and racial composition."[14]

This practice and its implications became common in police departments with the use of pins on a city map to locate "high-crime areas." Such areas became the focus of more police activity, more arrests, and hence higher recorded crime rates. As Blacks moved into Northern cities during and after the Second World War, Latinx people followed more recently, and many working-class whites departed to the suburbs, "disadvantaged" urban areas became increasing Black and Latinx. It was this population shift that underlay the inversion of the racial composition of convicts from 70 percent white at the end of World War II to 70 percent Black and Latinx now.[15] Thus, mapping that focused on these areas compounded the pre-existing racial bias of policing and the whole criminal justice system, creating a form of institutional or structural racism in the normal routines of daily policing that have become entrenched. By the 1970s, Black politicians that Johnson and Foreman focus on, like others, simply translated their constituents' desire for greater safety into policies that fit this already entrenched system.

The structural racial bias of the contemporary criminal justice system is clear. While African Americans composed only 13 percent of the population in 2016, they were 27 percent of those arrested.[16] This isn't just a matter of more crime in poor Black areas, but also of less detection in white areas. James Forman Jr. provides an example of how this works in terms of the Washington, DC, traffic stop and search program meant to find guns in the 1990s called "Operation Ceasefire." Cops could stop a "suspicious" car for a minor traffic violation and then search the car for guns, drugs, or other illegal items. The areas in which Operation Ceasefire were conducted specifically excluded Washington's mostly white middle-class and well-to-do Second District on the grounds there was little (though not no) gun crime committed there. Since whites use drugs at about the same rate as Blacks, this meant that well-off whites escaped being discovered, arrested, acquiring a criminal record, or being imprisoned for drug use.[17] This search of Black neighborhoods for guns is all the more suspicious since arrests for weapons are only about 10 percent of those for drugs and more whites than Blacks are arrested for possessing a weapon of any sort.[18]

Obviously, the same holds true for pedestrian stop-and-frisk operations in which the vast majority of those stopped are Black or Latinx. Partly as a result, the disproportion of Blacks is even worse in terms of those who go to jail. Blacks compose 34.4 percent of those in jail, two-and-a-half times their proportion of the population.[19] As Loïc Wacquant puts it, jails act as "frontline dams of social disorders in the city" and disrupt family life.[20]

## The Geography of Structural Racism and High-Tech Mapping

The intersection of poverty and race in the US is not geographically random. In this respect, white and Black poverty are very different. Black and Latinx people live in far greater geographic concentrations of poverty than whites. Major urban areas, including the "inner city" and inner ring of older suburbs, have become the main sites of "high-poverty areas," as they are designated, increasingly composed of Black and Latinx people. Ferguson, Missouri, a suburb within the St. Louis metro area made famous by the "rioting" that followed the failure to convict the police in the shooting of Michael Brown, is a good example of the spread *and* concentration of Black poverty. In 1990 Ferguson was three-quarters white. By 2014 it had become two-thirds Black. The poverty rate had risen from 7 to 22 percent and three of the town's ten neighborhoods are now officially "high-poverty areas."[21] The growth of white poverty is seldom concentrated in this manner.

Because poor whites do not face imposed residential segregation, they are far more geographically dispersed and far less frequently live in areas of concentrated poverty or in major "inner city" urban areas which are more intensely patrolled by police.[22] As a study of residential segregation by the Century Foundation points out, "Non-Hispanic white poor, despite more than doubling in number, are still less likely to live in high-poverty areas."[23] Racial segregation in almost all major American cities, on the other hand, has meant that "high-poverty areas," defined as areas with 40 percent or more living under the official poverty line, are primarily Black or Latinx. It is central urban areas, however, that have been the focus of police "mapping" and arrests for drugs and other "street crimes." And, as we saw above, drug busts are by far the largest source of arrests.[24]

The result of this difference is that while poor whites in concentrated "high-poverty areas" numbered 3.5 million by 2015, they composed only 20 percent of the nation's 17.3 million poor whites. The 5 million Blacks in "high-poverty areas," on the other hand, made up over half the 9.3 million African Americans living below the official poverty line, while the 4.3 million Latinxs in "high poverty" concentrations were 38 percent of the 11.2 million in poverty. Furthermore, the proportion of Blacks living in "high-poverty areas" has increased in three-fourths of the top 100 metropolitan areas since 2000.[25]

In other words, it is not simply that poor areas are more likely to have higher crime rates than more affluent neighborhoods, but as we will see, that the mapping and subsequent disproportionate deployment of police officers to these areas multiplies the number of arrests and, hence, the crime rates derived mainly from arrest records. The stigma grows and "overly aggressive law enforcement has continued to profile all ghetto residents as criminals," concluded a 2016 *New York Times* article.[26] As to racial profiling itself, in his *Washington Post* summary of studies of race and the criminal justice system, Radley Balko cites the well-known police joke: "It never happens . . . and it works."[27]

In the last two decades, however, the profiling of Black and Latinx neighborhoods has been supplemented and directed by predictive Geographic Information Systems (GIS) software in which geographic crime data are fed to an algorithm that not only locates "high-crime areas," but on the basis of that data "predicts" where the most offenses will take place. Probability-based programs such as CompStat and PredPol (Predictive Policing) are now used by police forces in 90 percent of cities with populations of 250,000 or more—precisely those where the largest concentrations of Black and Latinx poverty are located.[28] As the amount of arrest data grows, including large numbers of less serious crimes such as peddling or using small amounts of drugs, so does the deployment of police, and as a result more arrests and the predictions of crime location. As data scientist Cathy O'Neil describes the results:

> This creates a pernicious feedback loop. The policing itself spawns new data, which justifies more policing. And our prisons fill up with hundreds of thousands of people found guilty of victimless crimes. Most of them come from impoverished neighborhoods, and most are black or Hispanic. So even if our model is color blind, the result is anything but. In our highly segregated cities, geography is a highly effective proxy for race.[29]

Later she concludes, given our often-misplaced faith in technology, "the result is that we criminalize poverty, believing all the while that our tools are not only scientific but fair."[30]

These probability-based programs don't actually track criminals before or during the commission of a crime. Like earlier crime mapping, they simply point to high-risk areas on the basis of past data. As one analyst put it, "The past is a very racist place. And we only have data from the past to train Artificial Intelligence."[31] Unlike earlier mapping, however, these programs make predictions about the location of crime. As one mathematician said of PredPol, "It can't target individual people at all, only geography."[32] The geography, in turn, is targeted on the basis of "street crime" data "as opposed to corporate crime, cyber crime, or fraud" data in order to predict "high-crime areas" or "hotspots" of criminal activity.[33] Thus, the race bias is built in from the start.

The Los Angeles Police Department (LAPD), however, exploits PredPol's ability to locate "hot spots"—that is, areas already overpoliced—combined with other surveillance technology to gather the names and details of individuals in those "hot spots." Any contact with the police regardless of how trivial the "suspicion," including license plate and facial recognition scans, gets written up and put into the Los Angeles Strategic Extraction and Restoration (LASER) program's database. LASER is a points-based system in which officers get credit for the number of "points"—that is, people, they accumulate—so the incentive is to overpolice in overpoliced areas. Those, of course, were the ghettos and barrios of LA. LASER has been under attack for some time and was eventually discontinued in 2019. LAPD ended its contract with PredPol in April 2020, supposedly due to extra costs during the pandemic.[34]

Since most people living in those "high poverty" tracts predicted to be "high-crime areas" are not criminals, many are unfairly swept up in the digital dragnet simply because they are Black or Latinx. This, in turn, exaggerates the figures on arrests and "contact" with the police. The most outrageous examples of this, of course, are the stop-and-frisk operations that follow from these predictions. In 2011, 85 percent of those stopped by police during New York's infamous CompStat-directed stop-and-frisk program were Black or Latinx. Few violent crimes were found, but more busts for drug possession and other minor offenses were.[35] In Philadelphia the proportion of Blacks stopped was 72 percent, while in Boston it was 63 percent even though Blacks compose only 24 percent of Boston's population.[36]

Indeed, while all these policies of racial profiling and concentration have been launched in the name of curtailing violent crimes, actual arrests for violent crimes across the country remain 5 percent or less of all arrests.[37] The ghetto residents that Forman pointed to as demanding tougher sentencing for violent crimes back in the 1970s and 1980s couldn't have imagined the actual results. No wonder only 30 percent of African Americans of all classes had any confidence in the police by 2015–17, compared to 61 percent of whites, according to a Gallup poll.[38] No wonder also that the call to "defund the police" has entered mainstream debate.

This geographic approach to crime prediction and, hence, arrest has been underwritten by the Supreme Court in *Illinois v. Wardlow* in 2000, and subsequently in lower courts as well by creating a waver of a citizen's Fourth Amendment protection "against unreasonable searches and seizures." Specifically, these court rulings have given a legal basis to the focus on "high-crime areas" as at least one major criteria and justification for police targeting.[39] As legal scholar Andrew Ferguson noted in 2016, "In the years since *Wardlow* there have been more than one thousand federal and state cases that have used the term "high-crime area" in the context of Fourth Amendment reasonable suspicion."[40] The result is a compounded technological and legal basis for mass discrimination and the criminalization of Black and Latinx neighborhoods in law enforcement.

None of this is to say that crime is evenly distributed or that violent crime is not more prevalent in poor Black or Latinx neighborhoods than in most white residential areas, but rather that the historical "street crime" focus of local law enforcement, the geography of race that emerged in the twentieth century and intensified in the twenty-first, along with the juridical support of this view coming from courts and legislatures, and more recently the technological acceleration of this race bias have intensified the racial outcomes of law enforcement in the US. This is a structural reality of racism in the US that is missing in the downplaying of race in the growth of mass incarceration and even in Forman's well-documented account of the role of Black officials in tough-on-crime policy formation. It is a reality that is also absent in the calculations of those hoping to revive or create anew a race-blind social democratic politics. The underlying segregation cannot be eliminated simply by universal programs that address income inequality.

The United States' racial crisis exists in the context of capitalism's triple crises, on the one hand, and the political impasse that has characterized the country's right-center polarization for decades. While the 2020 elections seemed to hold out hope once Trump was forced from the White House, in fact they changed little in the balance of politics. At the same time, however, they demonstrated a silent realignment of capital and the voting public that has been driving US politics to the right and the holding the Democrats to dead center. If this impact is to be transcended, socialists would do well to look to the pre-1964 politics and practice of Rustin and Randolph with the emphasis on mass direct action.

The trends and resulting situations analyzed in the first four chapters have produced a political and class impasse that cannot be broken by electoral means alone or by simply "raising" issues and "universal" programs, which seem to be the primary methods of some on the left. It will have to be breeched in the way similar impasses in American history have been transcended: by mass action from below that not only disrupts "business as usual" but produces new levels and types of organizations among subordinate and oppressed people, from the anti-slavery movement of the 1850s and 1860s to populist upsurge and the labor upheavals of the late nineteenth and early twentieth centuries. In more recent times, something on a scale similar to or greater than the upheavals of industrial workers in the 1930s and of African Americans and others in the 1950s and 1960s is where the hope lies for the growth of socialism in the United States.

# Notes

## Chapter 1

1. Maurice Duverger, *Political Parties: Their Organisation and Activity in the Modern State* (1954; repr., London: Methuen, 1964), 205.
2. Mike Davis, "Trench Warfare: Notes on the 2020 Election," *New Left Review* 126 (November–December 2020): 30.
3. Roger H. Davidson et al., *Congress and Its Members*, 17th ed. (Washington, DC: CQ Press, 2020), 278.
4. Michael Roberts, *The Long Depression: How It Happened, Why It Happened, and What Happens Next* (Chicago: Haymarket Books, 2016), 65–94, 113–30; see also Anwar Shaikh, *Capitalism: Competition, Conflict, Crises* (New York: Oxford University Press, 2016), 56–74.
5. Dylan Riley, "Faultlines: Political Logics of the US Party System," *New Left Review* 126 (November-December 2020): 35.
6. Jared Abbott and Dustin Guastella, "A Socialist Party in Our Time?" *Catalyst* 3, no. 2 (Summer 2019): 7–63.
7. For example, two that I used while teaching US politics in the City University of New York system are the introductory Edward S. Greenberg and Benjamin I. Page, *America's Democratic Republic* (New York: Pearson Longman, 2005), 256–60; and the more advanced Roger H. Davidson and Walter J. Oleszek, *Congress and Its Members*, 10th ed. (Washington, DC: CQ Press, 2006), 188.
8. Duverger, *Political Parties*, 216–28, cited in Abbott and Guastella, "A Socialist Party," 18.
9. For a discussion of this, see Matthew M. Singer, "Was Duverger Correct? Single-Member District Election Outcomes in Fifty-Three Countries," *British Journal of Political Science* 43, no. 1 (2012): 201–20.
10. Duverger, *Political Parties*, 205. The original formulation of Duverger's "Law" appears on pages 216–28.
11. Duverger, *Political Parties*, 223.

12. Roger H. Davidson et al., *Congress and Its Members*, 17th ed. (Thousand Oaks, CA: Sage/CQ Press, 2019), 90–91.

13. Philip Bump, "The Decline and Fall of Split-Ticket Voting, Visualized," *Washington Post*, May 20, 2016, https://www.washingtonpost.com/news/the-fix/wp/2016/05/20/the-striking-evaporation-of-split-ticket-voting/.

14. Ed Kilgore, "2018 Midterms Offered More Proof That Split-Ticket Voting Is a Thing of the Past," *New York*, November 21, 2018, https://nymag.com/intelligencer/2018/11/2018-midterms-split-ticket-voting.html.

15. Gary C. Jacobson and Jamie L. Carson, *The Politics of Congressional Elections*, 10th ed. (Lanham, MD: Rowman & Littlefield, 2019), 283–92.

16. Chris Maisano, "A Left That Matters," *Socialist Forum*, Winter 2021, https://socialistforum.dsausa.org/issues/winteer-2021/a-left-that-matters/.

17. Kim Moody, *On New Terrain: How Capital Is Reshaping the Battleground of Class War* (Chicago: Haymarket Books, 2017), 95–99; Kevin B. Smith and Alan Greenblatt, *Governing States and Localities*, 5th ed. (Thousand Oaks, CA: CQ Press, 2016), 165–69.

18. Branko Marcetic, "The Good, Bad, and Extremely Ugly of the 2020 Election," *Jacobin*, November 11, 2020, https://www.jacobinmag.com/2020/11/election-2020-biden-trump-down-ballot-senate; Walker Bragman, "Hold Establishment Democrats Responsible for Down-Ballot Disasters," *Jacobin*, November 12, 2020, https://www.jacobinmag.com/2020/11/establishment-democrats-down-ballot-election-united-states.

19. For the relative decline and rise of the UK, see Charles P. Kindleberger, *World Economic Primacy, 1500–1990* (New York: Oxford University Press, 1996), 137–43, 172–74; Giovanni Arrighi, *The Long Twentieth Century: Money, Power, and the Origins of Our Times* (London: Verso, 1994), 58–61. Germany was the other major rising Western power but had a totally different political system.

20. Nelson Lichtenstein, *State of the Union: A Century of American Labor* (Princeton: Princeton University Press, 2002), 106.

21. Alfred D. Chandler Jr., *The Visible Hand: The Managerial Revolution in American Business* (Cambridge MA: Harvard University Press, 1977), 205.

22. Kim Moody, *Tramps & Trade Union Travelers: Internal Migration and Organized Labor in Gilded Age America* (Chicago: Haymarket Books, 2019), 10–14, 55–87, 153–82.

23. For some major works on this complex transition, see: Alan Trachtenberg, *The Incorporation of America: Culture and Society in the Gilded Age* (New York: Hill and Wang, 1982); C. Vann Woodward, *Origins of the New South, 1877–1913* (Baton Rouge: Louisiana State University Press, 1971); Michael Goldfield, *The Color of Politics: Race and the Mainsprings of American Politics* (New York: The New Press, 1997); Matthew Josephson, *The Politicos, 1865–1896* (New York:

Harcourt, Brace & World, 1938).

24. In the 1892 elections the Populists carried Kansas, North Dakota, Colorado, Idaho, and Nevada in the presidential election; became the second party in Nebraska, South Dakota, Oregon, Texas, Mississippi, and Alabama; and eventually elected three Senators, eleven House members, and the governors of Kansas, Colorado, and North Dakota. James L. Sundquist, *Dynamics of the Party System: Alignment and Realignment in Political Parties in the United States* (Washington, DC: The Brookings Institution, 1983), 123.

25. Walter Dean Burnham, "The System of 1896: An Analysis," in Paul Kleppner et al., *The Evolution of American Electoral Systems* (Westport, CT: Greenwood Press, 1981), 162.

26. Josephson, *The Politicos*, 319–40, 637–61; Trachtenberg, *Incorporation of America*, 164–65.

27. Frances Fox Piven and Richard A. Cloward, *Why Americans Don't Vote* (New York: Pantheon Books, 1989), 67, 71, 64–95; Walter Dean Burnham, *Critical Elections and the Mainsprings of American Politics* (New York: W.W. Norton, 1970), 71–90; R. Hal Williams, *Realigning America: McKinley, Bryan, and the Remarkable Election of 1896* (Lawrence: University Press of Kansas, 2010). There were no primary elections in the 1890s. The Populists were absorbed into the Democratic Party via its conventions and fusion tickets over the issue of silver coinage. By that time, the Democrats were dominated by capital. Lawrence Goodwyn, *Democratic Promise: The Populist moment in America* (New York: Oxford University Press, 1976), 470–92, 534–37.

28. Julie Greene, "Negotiating the State: Frank Walsh and the Transformation of Labor's Political Culture in Progressive America," in *Organized Labor and American Politics, 1894–1994*, ed. Kevin Boyle (Albany: State University of New York Press, 1998), 71–102.

29. Burnham, "System of 1896," 163–65.

30. Piven and Cloward, *Americans Don't Vote*, 78–95, 100–101. The Northern Progressives were not necessarily involved in the rise of Jim Crow per se. Rather their targets were most immigrants and industrial workers who may or may not have been represented by urban "machines." But Southern progressives did implement Black disenfranchisement at least in Virginia, and it was the "progressive" Democrat Woodrow Wilson who, as president, segregated jobs in several federal agencies including the Post Office. Goldfield, *Color of Politics*, 168; Burham, *Critical Elections*, 78.

31. Martin Shefter, *Political Parties and the State: The American Historical Experience* (Princeton: Princeton University Press, 1994), 77.

32. Samuel P. Hays, *The Response to Industrialism, 1885–1914* (Chicago: University of Chicago Press, 1957), 152–58.

33. C. Vann Woodward, *Origins of the New South, 1877–1913* (Baton Rouge: Louisiana State University Press, 1971), 369–95.

34. Michael Goldfield, *The Color of Politics: Race and the Mainsprings of American Politics* (New York: The New Press, 1997), 168.

35. Burnham, *Critical Elections*, 76–81.

36. Piven and Cloward, *Americans Don't Vote*, 54–56, 64–95; Burnham, "System of 1896" 169.

37. Jacobson and Carson, *Politics of Congressional Elections*, 158.

38. Piven and Cloward, *Americans Don't Vote*, 72.

39. Arthur Lipow, *Political Parties and Democracy: Explorations in History and Theory* (London: Pluto Press, 1996), 20.

40. Duverger, *Political Parties*, 61.

41. Lipow, *Political Parties*, 15–17. Lipow focuses on the Socialist Party as a democratic membership party, but these other parties also had members and grassroots participation.

42. Moisei Ostrogorski, *Democracy and the Organization of Political Parties*, vol. 2 (New York: The Macmillan Company, 1902), 292. The pre-1896 Democratic and Republican Parties, of course, had their own elites who used sectional loyalties and demagogic appeals—in the case of the Democrats, overt racism North and South—to help beat each other in a closely matched alignment.

43. The Greenback-Labor Party, for example, drew over 12 percent of the presidential vote and elected thirteen members of Congress in 1878 as well as many state and local officials.

44. Micah L. Sifry, "Obama's Lost Army," *New Republic,* February 9, 2017, https://newrepublic.com/article/140245/obamas-lost-army-inside-fall-grassroots-machine.

45. In 2020 more than 13 million donors gave to Democrats through internet "single-click" fundraiser ActBlue. ActBlue, "Meet ActBlue Express Lane," accessed November 20, 2020, https://secure.actblue.com/.

46. New Deal Strategists, Justice Democrats, Sunrise Movement, Data for Progress, "What Went Wrong for Congressional Democrats in 2020," November 10, 2020, https://www.politico.com/f/?id=00000175-b4b4-dc7f-a3fd-bdf660490000. This memo holds up the example of Ilhan Omar's 2020 campaign, which, "while the Biden-Harris campaign resisted in-person canvassing, Omar's campaign kept doing it, *hiring* dozens of people to knock on doors and pull out votes" (emphasis added—KM).

47. Burnham, *Critical Elections*, 72–74.

48. Presidential primaries were introduced separately and did not become common until the 1970s.

49. Joseph A. Pika and John Anthony Maltese, *The Politics of the Presidency*, 6th ed.

(Washington, DC: CQ Press, 2005), 33–36; Thomas E. Cronin and Michael A. Genovese, *The Paradoxes of the American Presidency* (New York: Oxford University Press, 2004), 42–45.

50. Cronin and Genovese, *The Paradoxes*, 44.
51. Quotes from Lipow, *Political Parties*, 15–17.
52. John C. Fortier and Joshua Ferrer, "Primary Election Results Show Improved Voter Turnout, but Not Enough," *Bipartisan Policy Center*, September 21, 2018, https://bipartisanpolicy.org/blog/2018-primary-election-results/.
53. Davidson et al., *Congress and Its Members*, 66.
54. Matt Karp, "Bernie Sanders's Five-Year War," *Jacobin*, no. 38 (Summer 2020): 67, 68.
55. Steven P. Erie, *Rainbow's End: Irish-Americans and the Dilemmas of Urban Machine Politics, 1840–1985* (Berkeley: University of California Press, 1988), 52; Moody, *Tramps*, 153–75.
56. Shefter, *Political Parties*, 175.
57. Dennis R. Judd and Todd Swanstrom, *City Politics: Private Power and Public Policy* (New York: Pearson Longman, 2004), 57; Sundquist, *Dynamics*, 148; Moody, *Tramps*, 157–62.
58. Ostrogorski, *Democracy*, 207–13.
59. Elaine B. Sharp, "Political Participation in Cities," in *Cities, Politics, and Policy: A Comparative Analysis*, ed. John P. Pelissero (Washington, DC: CQ Press, 2003), 72; Erie, *Rainbow's End*, 218–19.
60. Erie, *Rainbow's End*, 3–17, 140–44, 200; Piven and Cloward, *Americans Don't Vote*, 74.
61. Oliver Hall, "Death by a Thousand Signatures: The Rise of Restrictive Ballot Access Laws and the Decline of Electoral Competition in the United States," *Seattle University Law Review* 29, no. 407 (2006): 418. Piven and Cloward, *Americans Don't Vote*, 72, 64–95; Burnham, *Critical Elections*, 76.
62. I'm not including here those third parties that exist today by virtue of "fusion" via the Democrats' ballot line, such as the Working Families Party and the Vermont Progressive Party. A partial exception was the Minnesota Farmer-Labor Party, which dominated that state's politics from the early 1920s to 1948 when it merged with the Democratic Party. An account of this is in Eric Blanc, "The Ballot and the Break," *Jacobin*, December 14, 2017, https://www.jacoginmag.com/2017/12/democratic-party-minnesota-farmer-labor-floyd-olsen. This is the historical precedent for Blanc's argument for the "dirty break" strategy. It should be noted that the Minnesota labor movement in 1920 intervened in major party primaries in only one election cycle when it didn't win any offices before launching the Farmer-Labor Party in 1922. Thus, the problem of functioning in a major capitalist party over time did not face the Minnesota move-

ment's socialist leaders. The other major exception was the Progressive Party of Wisconsin from 1934 to 1942. Burnham, *Critical Elections*, 22–23.

63. Kim Moody, "The Rank-and-File Strategy," in Kim Moody, *In Solidarity: Essays on Working-Class Organization in the United States* (Chicago: Haymarket Books, 2014), 75–161; Kim Moody, "Reversing the 'Model': Thoughts on Jane McAlevey's Plan for Union Power," *Spectre* 1, no. 2 (Fall 2020).

64. For the restructuring of the US working class, see Moody, *On New Terrain*, 23–41; Kim Moody, "The New Terrain of Class Conflict in the United States," *Catalyst* 1, no. 2 (Summer 2017): 41–74.

65. Holly Otterbein, "Tlaib Getting Help from Working Families Party," *Politico*, July 23, 2020, https://www.politico.com/news/2020/07/23/rashida -tlaib-working-families-379228; David Duhalde, "Socialist and Super PACs," *Jacobin*, June 27, 2020, https://www.jacobinmag.com/2020/06/socialists -super-pacs-campaign-fiance-justice-democrats.

66. Scott Bland and Maggie Severns, "Document Reveals Massive 'Dark-Money' Group Boosted Democrats in 2018," *Politico*, November 19, 2019, https:// www.politico.com/news/dark-money-democrats-midterms-071725; Scott Bland, "Liberal Dark-Money Behemoth Raised Nearly $140M Last Year," *Politico*, November 20, 2020, https://www.politco.com/news/2020/11/20/ liberal-dark-money-ffundraising-438667; Anna Massoglia and Karl Evers-Hill-strom, "New 'Dark Money' Group Devotes Multi-Million Dollar Budget to Ads Helping Democrats," OpenSecrets, August 22, 2019, https://www.opensecrets .org/news/2019/06/drakmoney-grp-devotes-multi-million-dollars -democrats/?utm_source=CRP+Mail+List&utm_campaign=57dca-fa3d9-EMAIL_CAMPAIGN_2019_17_11_12_COPY-02&urtm.

67. Elena Schneider, David Siders, and Zach Montellaro, "State Democrats Mount Big Comeback in 2020," *Politico*, July 30, 2020, https://www.politco.com/ news/2020/07/30/dems-pour-record-cash-into-state-parties-389082; Bland and Severns, "Document Reveals."

68. Roger H. Davidson et al., *Congress and Its Members*, 17th ed. (Thousand Oaks, CA: Sage/CQ Press, 2020), 62, 93–94; Jacobson and Carson, *Congressional Elections*, 37–41; Andrew Perez, "Senate Democrats' Machine Spent $15 Million to Destroy Progressive Candidates in Primaries," *Jacobin*, July 7, 2020, https://www.jacobin.com/2020/07/senate-democrats-majority-pac-dscc ; Malcom E. Jewell and Sarah M. Morehouse, *Political Parties and Elections in American States*, 4th ed. (Washington, DC: CQ Press, 2001), 202–3; Kyle Kondik, "House 2020: Incumbents Hardly Ever Lose Primaries," *Rasmussen Reports*, May 30, 2019, https://www.rasmussenreports.com/public_content/political _commentary/commentary_by_kyle_kondik/house_2020_incumbents_hardly _ever_lose_primaries; Russell Berman, "The 2020 Congressional-Retirement

Tracker," *The Atlantic*, December 19, 2019, updated February 27, 2020, https://www.theatlantic.com/politics/archive/2019/12/retirement-congress-2020-hurd-alexander/596965/.

69. Maisano, "A Left." Maisano specifically argues that "the most promising route" to a new party is "to keep squeezing establishment Democrats out of one-party districts through primary elections." The rate of incumbency in primaries makes that route highly problematic.

70. Stephen Ansolabehere, John Mark Hansen, Shigeo Hirano, and James M. Snyder, "The Decline of Competition in U.S. Primary Elections, 1908–2004," in *The Marketplace of Democracy: Electoral Competition and American Politics*, ed. Michael P. McDonald and John Samples (Washington, DC: Brookings Institute Press, 2006), 81–83.

71. Jacobson and Carson, *Congressional Elections*, 38–39; Davidson et al., *Congress*, 65, 93–95; Ballotpedia, "United State Congress Elections, 2016," accessed August 20, 2020, https://ballotpedia.org/United_States_Congress_elections,_2016#House_primary_competitiveness.

72. Sarah Bryner, "A Center for Responsive Politics Report," Center for Responsive Politics, June 30, 2020, https://www.opensecrets.org/news/reports/gender-and-race-2020; Nicholas Fandos, "Cori Bush Defeats William Lacy Clay in a Show of Progressive Might," *New York Times*, August 5, 2020, https://www.nytimes.com/2020/08/05/us/cori-bush-missouri-william-lacy-clay.html: Ella Nilsen, "Progressive Democrats Running in Competitive House Districts Had a Bad Night on Tuesday," *Vox*, November 7, 2018, https://www.vox.com/2018/11/7/18071700/proressive-democrats-house-midterm-elections-2018. Although Rashida Tlaib beat Brenda Jones in the 2018 Democratic primary, the seat had been John Conyers's, not Jones's, who won a special election when Conyers resigned in disgrace. Jones served for only two months and was not considered an incumbent. Even if you consider her so, it doesn't change the percentage much.

73. Robert G. Boatwright, *Getting Primaried: The Changing Politics of Congressional Primary Challenges* (Ann Arbor: University of Michigan Press, 2014), 8.

74. Ballotpedia, *Annual Congressional Competitiveness Report, 2020*, November 9, 2020, https://ballotpedia.org/Annual_Congressional_Competitiveness_Report,_2020; Ballotpedia, *Annual Congressional Competitiveness Report, 2018*, October 11, 2018, https://ballotpedia.org/Annual_Congeressional_Competitiveness_Report,_2018#Incumbents_who_did_not_seek_re-election_in_2018; Ballotpedia, *United States House of Representatives Elections, 2016*, https://ballotpedia.org/United_States_House_of_Representatives_elections,_2016#Retired_incumbents.

75. Jacobson and Carson, *Congressional Elections*, 145.

76. Jacobson and Carson, *Congressional Elections*, 61, 145–46.

77. Hans J. G. Hassell, *The Party's Primary: Control of Congressional Nominations* (Cambridge: Cambridge University Press, 2018), 39–63.

78. Boatwright, *Getting Primaried*, 7.

79. Boatwright, *Getting Primaried*, 108–9; OpenSecrets, "Incumbent Advantage," By Type of Candidates, House Races, 2019–2020, https://opensecrets.org/ elections-overview/incumbent-advantage. The ratio of incumbent to challenger funds in Senate primary races is slightly higher at seven to one.

80. Hassell, *Party's Primary*, 27–38, 58; Adam Bonica, "Professional Networks, Early Fundraising, and Electoral Success," *Election Law Journal: Rules, Politics, and Policy* 16, no. 1 (2017): 153–71.

81. Bonica, "Professional Networks," 153–71.

82. These interconnected national party committees include the Democratic National Committee (DNC), which links state parties to the national structure through grants, election assistance, and representation on the DNC; the Democratic Congressional Campaign Committee (DCCC), which raises funds for House candidates, the Democratic Senatorial Campaign Committee (DSCC), which does the same for senatorial candidates; and the Democratic Legislative Campaign Committee (DLCC), which raises funds for state legislative candidates.

83. Hassell, *Party's Primary*, 13–16, 25–38, 71–73; OpenSecrets, "Democratic Congressional Campaign Committee," Expenditures, 2020 Cycle, accessed September 13, 2021, https://www.opensecrets.org/parties/expend.php?cmte=DCCC &cycle=2020; OpenSecrets, "Democratic Congressional Campaign Committee," Independent Expenditures and Coordinated Expenses, 2020 Cycle, https://www .opensecrets.org/parties/indexp.php?cycle=2020&cmte=DCCC.

84. Ryan Grim and Rachel M. Cohen, "The Democratic Party's Consultant Factory," *The Intercept*, April 6, 2021, https://theintercept.com/2021/04/06/ democratic-party-dccc-political-consultant-factory/. The DCCC has additional problems. Despite some efforts to improve representation of Blacks and Latinxs among its consultants, less than 10 percent of its spending went to consulting firms led by people of color in 2020.

85. Bonica, "Professional Networks," 153–71; Hassell, *Party's Primary*, 31–33, 72; Boatwright, *Getting Primaried*, 136–38.

86. Hassell, *Party's Primary*, 121–28.

87. Hassell, *Party's Primary*, 31, 176; also see Hans J. G. Hassell, "Principled Moderation: Understanding Parties' Support of Moderate Candidates," *Legislative Studies Quarterly* 43, no. 2 (May 2018): 343–69.

88. OpenSecrets, "Democratic Congressional Campaign Committee," Expenditures, 2020 Cycle, accessed September 13, 2021, https://www.opensecrets.org/parties/ expend.php?cmte=DCCC&cycle=2020; OpenSecrets, "Democratic Congres-

sional Campaign Committee," Independent Expenditures and Coordinated Expenses, 2020 Cycle, https://www.opensecrets.org/parties/indexp .php?cycle=2020&cmte=DCCC; Ballotpedia, "New Democrat Coalition," Members – 117th Congress, https://ballotpedia.org/New_Democrat_Coalition; Ballotpedia, "Congressional Progressive Caucus," Membership – 117th Congress, https://ballotpedia.org/Congressional_Progressive_Caucus; Ballotpedia, "Blue Dog Coalition," https://ballotpedia.org/Blue_Dog_Coalition.

89.  Doug Mataconis, "38% of Congressmen Represent 'Safe' Districts," *Outside the Beltway*, October 7, 2013, https://www.outsidethebeltway.com/38-of -congressmen-represent-safe-districts/; Matt Taibbi, "Far Too Many House Seats Have Been Uncontested for Too Long," *Rolling Stone*, November 6, 2018, https://www.rollingstone.com/politics/politics-features/uncontested -house-seats-history-752658/; Michael Collins, "Fewer and Fewer U.S. House Seats Have Any Competition," *USA Today*, November 6, 2016, https://usa-today.com/story/news/politics/elections/2016/11/04/fewer-and-fewer-us-house-seats-have-any-competition/93295358.

90.  Proximity One, "113th/114th Congressional District Urban-Rural Characteristics," August 12, 2020, http://proximityone.com/cd113_2010_ur.htm; Scott Keeter and Ruth Igielnik, *Democrats Made Gains from Multiple Sources in 2018 Midterm Victories*, Pew Research Center, September 8, 2020, pp. 9, 10, https:// www.pewresearch.org/methods/2020/09/08/democrats-made-gains -from-multiple-sources-in-2018-midterm-victories/. This poll was based on over thirteen thousand validated voters, not simply "likely" or "registered" voters as with many polls, and is therefore more accurate in terms of who actually voted.

91.  Matt Karp, "Sanders's Five-Year War," 62.

92.  Moody, *On New Terrain*, 158.

93.  "City Council," *New York Times*, November 5, 2013, www.nytimes.com /projects/elections/2013/general/city-council/results.html.

94.  Hall, "A Thousand Signatures," 412.

95.  Andrew DePietro, "After the Midterms, One Party Controls All the Wealthiest Congressional Districts," *Yahoo Finance*, November 8, 2018, https://finance .yahoo.com/news/midterms-one-party-controls-wealthiest-184200649.html.

96.  Keeter and Igielnik, *Democrats*, 9, 14, 15, 16. According to this poll, Democratic voters in 2018 were 65 percent white, 16 percent Black, 11 percent Latinx, and 8 percent mixed race, Asian, Native, or "other," while half had a college degree or more. Edison Research, "National Exit Polls: How Different Groups Voted," *New York Times*, November 3, 2020, https://www.nytimes.com/interactive /2020/11/03/us/elections/exit-polls-president.html.

97.  Anwar Shaikh, *Capitalism: Competition, Conflict, Crises* (New York: Oxford University Press, 2016), 56–74; Michael Roberts, *The Long Depression: How It*

*Happened, Why It Happened, and What Happens Next* (Chicago: Haymarket Books, 2016), 45–94.

98. David Harvey, *A Brief History of Neoliberalism* (New York: Oxford University Press, 2005), 39–86.

99. For an interesting liberal Republican account of this through the Tea Party invasion, see Geoffrey Kabaservice, *Rule and Ruin: The Downfall of Moderation and the Destruction of the Republican Party from Eisenhower to the Tea Party* (New York: Oxford University Press, 2012).

100. Davidson et al., *Congress*, 278.

101. Thomas Ferguson and Joel Rogers, *Right Turn: The Decline of the Democrats and the Future of American Politics* (New York: Hill and Wang, 1986), 78–113; Moody, *On New Terrain*, 107–46; Kim Moody, *An Injury to All: The Decline of American Unionism* (London: Verso, 1988), 127–48.

102. Dennis R. Judd and Todd Swanstrom, *City Politics: The Political Economy of Urban America*, 9th ed. (New York: Routledge, 2015), 213–22, 358–61.

103. Moody, *On New Terrain*, 103.

104. Ballotpedia, "Congressional Progressive Caucus," accessed August 20, 2020, https://ballotpedia.org/Congressional_Progressive_Caucus; Ballotpedia, "New Democrat Coalition," accessed August 20, 2020, https://ballotpedia.org/New_Democrat_Coalition; Blue Dog Democrats PAC, "Members of the Blue Dog Caucus," accessed August 20, 2020, https://bluedogdems.com/.

105. Ryan Grim, "Congressional Progressives Are Revamping Their Caucus with an Eye toward 2021," *The Intercept*, October 26, 2020, https://theintercept.com/2020/10/26/congressional-progressives-are-revampinh-tyheir-caucus-with-an-eye-toward-2021.

106. Luke Savage, "This Week, Democratic Leaders Rejected Medicare for All Again," *Jacobin*, July 29, 2020, https://www.jacobinmag.com/2020/07/covid-19-democrats-medicare-for-all; Michelle Cottle, "Just How Far Will Joe Biden Go?" *New York Times*, July 24, 2020, https://www.nytimes.com/2020/07/24/opinion/sunday/joe-biden-2020.html; Holly Otterbein, "Where Progressives Won—and Lost—in the Democratic Platform," *Politico*, July 22, 2020, https://www.politico.com/news/2020/07/22/progress-settle-medicare-biden-378348; Laura Barron-Lopez and Holly Otterbein, "A Democratic Turf War Is Raging—Even as Progressives Try to Elect Biden," *Politico*, August 29, 2020, https://www.politico.com/news/2020/08/29/democrats-turf-war-joe-biden-404549.

107. Johnathan Martin and Astead W. Herndon, "In Kamala Harris, a Choice at Once Safe and Energizing," *New York Times*, August 11, 2020, https://www.nytimes.com/2020/08/11/us/politics/kamala-harris-joe-biden-running-mate.html?action=click&module=Spotlight&pgtype=Homepage. For more on her real politics and connections to big tech, big health care, big pharma, etc., see

Branko Marcetic, "Joe Biden Has Found His Neoliberal Match in Kamala Harris," *Jacobin*, August 12, 2020, https://www.jacobinmag.com/2020/08/joe-biden-kamala-harris-vice-president-neoliberalism.

108. Branko Marcetic, "Biden Wants to Bring the Dems Responsible for the 1994 Crime Bill Back to the White House," *Jacobin*, December 16, 2020, https://www.jacobinmag.com/2020/12/bill-clinton-biden-crime-bill-1994-rahm; Meagan Day, "Joe Biden's BlackRock Cabinet Picks Show the President-Elect Is Ready and Eager to Serve the Rich," *Jacobin*, December 3, 2020, https://www.jacobinmag.com/2020/12/weal-street-joe-biden-transition-cabinwt-black-rock; Claire Kelloway, "Tom Vilsack for Agriculture Secretary Is Everything That's Wrong with the Democratic Party," *The Intercept*, December 11, 2020, https://theintercept.com/2020/12/11/democrat-tom-vilsack-farms/; Nick Turse and Alex Emmons, "Biden Defense Secretary Nominee Llyod Austin Comes Under Fire for Industry Connections," *The Intercept*, December 9, 2020, https://theintercept.com/2020/12/08/biden-defense-secretary-lloyd-austin-raytheon/.

109. Jacobson and Carson, *Congressional Elections*, 284.

110. The DSOC (Democratic Socialist Organizing Committee) was the precursor of DSA.

# Chapter 2

1.    Heather Gautney, *Crashing the Party: From Bernie Sanders Campaign to a Progressive Movement* (London: Verso, 2018), 133.

2.    Jared Abbott and Dustin Guastella, "A Socialist Party in Our Time?" *Catalyst* 3, no. 2 (Summer 2019): 33.

3.    DSOC/DSA members John Conyers (D-MI), Ron Dellums (D-CA), and Major Owens (D-NY) held House seats throughout the 1980s and 1990s and into the 2000s. Conyers held his seat from 1965 until 2017, when he resigned in disgrace over sexual scandals. All three were African American. Danny K. Davis, also a Black DSA member, has been a representative from Chicago's 7th District since 1996 but is seldom mentioned by DSAers or considered part of "the squad."

4.    Influence Watch, "Medicare-for-All," accessed September 1, 2020, https://www.influencewatch.org/movement/medicare-for-all/.

5.    For evidence of AOC's adaptation to Democratic rules and protocol, see Catie Edmondson, "How Alexandria Ocasio-Cortez Learned to Play by Washington's Rules," *New York Times*, September 18, 2019, updated April 17, 2020, https://www.nytimes.com/2019/09/18/us/politics/alexandria-ocasio-cortez-washington.html; Alex Thompson and Holly Otterbein, "AOC Breaks with Bernie on How to Lead the Left," *Politico*, March 30, 2020, https://www

.politico.com/news/2020/03/30/new-aoc-divides-the-left-150767; Aida Chávez, "AOC: Nancy Pelosi Needs to Go, but There's Nobody to Replace Her Yet," *The Intercept*, December 16, 2020, https://theintercept.com/2020/12/16 /aoc-nancy-pelosi-needs-to-go-but-theres-nobody-to-replace-her-yet/.

6. Walter J. Oleszek, Mark J. Oleszek, Elizabeth Rybicki, and Bill Heniff Jr., *Congressional Procedures and the Policy Process*, 11th ed. (Thousand Oaks, CA: CQ Press, 2020), 113.

7. 116th Congress (2019–20), All Actions H.Res.109—116th Congress (2019–20) (accessed 5/01/2020 and 8/11/2020), https://www.congress.gov /bill/116th-congress/house-resolution/109/all-actions; Nancy Pelosi, Speaker of the House, "Pelosi Names Members of the Select Committee on the Climate Crisis," *Newsroom*, February 7, 2019, https://www.speaker.gov/newsroom /2719/; H.R. 9, 116th Congress, "To direct the President to develop a plan for the United States to meet its nationally determined contribution under the Paris Agreement, and for other purposes," House Of Representatives, March 27, 2019, https://www.congress.gov/116/bills/hr9/BILLS-116hr9ih.pdf; H.R. 9, 116th Congress, "To direct the President to develop a plan for the United States to meet its nationally determined contribution under the Paris Agreement, and for other purposes," Senate of the United States, May 6, 2019, https://www .congress.gov/bill/116th-congress/house-9/text; Clerk House, Final Vote Results for Roll Call 184, H.R. 9, Recorded Vote 2-May-2019, www.clerk .house.gov/evs/2019/roll184.xml.

8. Sarah Ferris and Heather Caygle, "Kathleen Rice Beats Out AOC for Spot on Coveted House Committee," *Politico*, December 17, 2020, https://politico.com /news/2020/12/17/kathleen-rice-aoc-house-committee-448001.

9. Rachael Bade and David Weigel, "Pelosi Endorses Rep. Tlaib in Primary Fight, Moves to Help Members of the 'Squad,'" *Washington Post*, July 29, 2020, https:// www,washingtonpost.com/powerpost/pelosi-endorses-rep-tlaib-in-primary -fight-to-help-members-of-the-squad/2020/07/29/028b5692-d16-11ea -af089b63ac21_story.html.

10. Alan Fram, "On House Floor, Dem Women Call Out Abusive Treatment by Men," Associated Press, July 23, 2020, https://apnews.com /e593ba2f117a3ac201b8571ffd2481f1.

11. Center for Responsive Politics, "Democratic Party," *Top Industries, 2020 Cycle*, accessed August 27, 2020, https://www.opensecrets.org/parties/indus.php ?cycle=2020&cmte=DPC; Center for Responsive Politics, "Election Overview," accessed August 27, 2020, https://www.opensecrets.org/elections-overview/; Center for Responsive Politics, "Outside Spending," accessed August 27, 2020, https://www.opensecrets.org/outsidespending/fes_summ.php.

12. Davidson et al., *Congress*, 211–15, 143–50.

13. Oleszek et al., *Congressional Procedures*, 36.

14. Nelson Lichtenstein, *Labor's War at Home: The CIO in World War II* (Cambridge: Cambridge University Press, 1982), 173.

15. Keven Boyle, "Little More than Ashes: The UAW and American Reform in the 1960s," in *Organized Labor and American Politics, 1894–1994*, ed. Kevin Boyle (Albany: State University of New York, 1998), 221.

16. David Sirota and Andrew Perez, "Beltway Liberals Aren't Fighting Biden's Pro-Corporate Admin Picks Hard Enough," *Jacobin*, December 4, 2020, https://www.jacobinmag.com/2020/12/joe-biden-cabinet-nominations-kerry-tanden.

17. Jennifer Ludden, "John Kerry Tapped For Newly Created Role as Presidential Climate Envoy," National Public Radio, November 23, 2020, https://www.npr.org/sections/biden-transition- updates/2020/11/23/938150511/john-kerry-tapped-for-newly-created-role-as-presidential-climate-envoy; Branko Marcetic, "It's Joe Biden's Swamp," *Jacobin*, December 3, 2020, https://www.jacobinmag.com/2020/12/joe-biden-cabinet-picks-donald-trump.

18. Sirota and Perez, "Beltway Liberals."

19. Matt T. Huber, "Still No Short Cuts for Climate Change," *Catalyst* 4, no. 4 (Winter 2021): 137–38.

20. OpenSecrets, "Democratic National Committee," accessed January 24, 2021, https://www.opensecrets.org/parties/indus.php?cmte=DNC&cycle=2020; https://www.opensecrets.org/parties/indus.php?cmte=DNC&cycle=2000.

21. OpenSecrets, "Democratic Congressional Campaign Committee," accessed 24, 2021, https://www.opensecrets.org/parties/indus.php?cmte=DCCC&cycle=2020; https://www.opensecrets.org/parties/indus.php?cmte=DCCC&cycle=2000.

22. OpenSecrets, "Democratic Senatorial Campaign Committee," accessed January 24, 2021, https://www.opensecrets.org/parties/indus.php?cycle=2020&cmte=DSCC; https://www.opensecrets.org/parties/indus.php?cmte=DSCC&cycle=2000.

23. For some examples, see Jonathan H. Martin, ed., *Empowering Progressive Third Parties in the United States: Defeating Duopoly, Advancing Democracy* (New York: Routledge, 2016), 117, 223–24, 231, 247.

24. Abbott and Guastella, "Socialist Party," 61–62. The Labour Representation Committee (LRC), which became the Labour Party in 1906, might be considered a party-surrogate, but it was a delegated body of leaders from unions and socialist groups, not a mass membership organization. The whole Lib-Lab period has been viewed by most socialists as a roadblock to independent labor politics. The LRC was meant to end that, although it did so via a backroom deal with the Liberals.

25. The brief "capture" of the Democratic nomination by George McGovern in 1972 was really the last gasp of 1960s liberalism rather than a prelude to change. The movement of the party toward the center really began in 1974 just as the first major recession of the era rocked confidence in the Keynesian underpinnings of New Deal and Great Society liberalism.

26. For a version of this argument, see Frances Fox Piven and Richard A. Cloward, *Poor People's Movements: Why They Succeed, How They Fail* (New York: Vintage Books, 1979). For another as yet unpublished view of this, see Kim Moody, "The Politics of Winning by Mass Action," available from the author.

27. Abbott and Guastella, "Socialist Party," 33.

28. Jesse McKinley, "Jamaal Bowman, Progressive Insurgent, Defeats Eliot Engel in House Primary," *New York Times*, July 17, 2020, https://www.nytimes.com /2020/07/17/jamall-bowman-eliot-engel.html?action=click&module=Top %20Stories&pgtype=Homepage; Roma Venkateswaran and Amber Herrle, "How Have Progressives Fared in the 2020 Congressional Primaries?" Brookings, April 7, 2020, https://www.brookings.edu/blog/fixgov/2020 /04/07/how-have-progressives-fared-in-the-2020-congressional-primaries; Davidson et al., *Congress*, 65.

29. Jewell and Morehouse, *Political Parties*, 281.

30. The degree to which gentrifiers played a role in AOC's 2018 primary election victory is a matter of controversy. See Zaid Jilani and Ryan Grim, "Data Suggests That Gentrifying Neighborhoods Powered Alexandria Ocasio-Cortez's Victory," *The Intercept*, July 2, 2018, https://theintercept.com/2018/07/01 /ocasio-cortez-data-suggests-that-grentrifying-neighborhoods-powered -ocasio-cortez-victory-over-the-democratic-establishment; Kevin Morris, "Data for Politics #19: Young Voters, Not Gentrification, Drove Ocasio-Cortez's Victory," Data For Progress, September 6, 2018, https://dataforprogress .org/blog/2018/9/5/data-for-politics-19-young-voters-not-grantrification -drove-aoc-victory.

31. Ballotpedia, "New York's 14th Congressional District Election, 2018," https://ballotpedia.org/New_York%27s_14th_Congressional_District _election,_2018; New York State Board of Elections, "Enrollment by Congressional District," April 2018, https://www.elections.ny.gov/EnrollmentCD.html.

32. Clare Foran, "Alexandria Ocasio-Cortez Wins Democratic Primary against Michelle Caruso-Cabrera, CNN Projects," *CNN Politics*, updated June 24, 2020, https://edition.cnn.com/2020/06/23/politics/aoc-ny-primary-14th-district /index.html; New York State Board of Elections, "Enrollment by Congressional District," February 2020, https://www.elections.ny.gov/EnrollmentCD.html.

33. In the late nineteenth century some states allowed resident immigrants to vote in local elections. The "reformers" put an end to that.

34. Jeffery C. Mays, "If A.O.C. Is So Heavily Favored, Why Has Her Race Drawn $30 Million?" *New York Times*, October 24, 2020, https://www.nytimes.com /2020/10/24/nyregion/aoc-money-campaign-spending.html?action=click &module=Well&pgtype=Homepage&section=New%20York; Center for Responsive Politics, *New York District 14 2020 Race, Top Contributors*, "Alexandria Ocasio-Cortez," accessed October 24, 2020, https://www.opensecrets.org /races/contributors?cycle=2020&id=NY14&spec=N.

35. As one text put it, "In short, the legislative process favors opponents of legislation and hinders proponents." Davidson et al., *Congress*, 220–22.

36. Davidson et al., *Congress*, 165–66, 178–79.

37. Chávez, "AOC: Nancy Pelosi Needs to Go."

38. Kevin B. Smith and Alan Greenblatt, *Governing States and Localities*, 5th ed. (Los Angeles: Sage CQ Press, 2016), 210–16.

39. Blanc, "The Ballot."

40. Eric Blanc, "Bernie Supporters, Don't Give Up," *Jacobin*, April 8, 2020, https:// www.jacobinmag.com/2020/04/bernie-sanders-campaign-supporters -2020-election; Nick French and Jeremy Gong, "Why Workers Need A Political Party," *The Call*, June 15, 2020, https://socialistcall.com/2020/15/bernie -2020-workers-party/

41. Eric Blanc, "The Birth of the Labour Party Has Many Lessons for Socialists Today," *Jacobin*, February 15, 2021, https://www.jacobinmag.com/2021/02 /labour-party-uk-lessons-socialists.

42. Blanc, "The Ballot"; Blanc, "The Labour Party." For what it is worth, throughout their involvement with the British labor movement, Marx and Engels bitterly opposed the union leaders' and workers' practice of being what Engels called in 1881 in *The Labour Standard*, "the Tail of the 'Great Liberal Party.'" He stated, "A labour organ must be neither Whig nor Tory, neither Conservative nor Liberal, or even Radical." As Marx wrote in 1871, "Considering that against this collective power of the propertied classes, the working class cannot act, as a class, except by constituting itself into a political party, distinct from, and opposed to all old parties formed by the propertied classes." More evidence for this view could easily be produced, but the record on this is clear.

43. Paul Foot, *The Vote: How It Was Won and How It Was Undermined* (London: Penguin Books, 2006), 242; J.H. Stewart Reid, *The Origins of the British Labour Party* (Minneapolis: University of Minnesota Press, 1955), 177-204.

44. George Dangerfield, *The Strange Death of Liberal England, 1910–1914* (New York: Capricorn Books, 1961).

45. Foot, *The Vote*, 250–52.

46. Blanc, "The Ballot"; French and Gong, "Why Workers"; Meagan Day and Micah Uetricht, *Bigger Than Bernie: How We Go from the Sanders Campaign to Demo-*

*cratic Socialism* (London: Verso, 2020), 99–139.

47. For example, French and Gong, "Why Workers."
48. Natalia Tylim, "We're Not Just Along for the Ride," *New Politics* 18, no. 1, whole number 69 (Summer 2020): 51–54.
49. Gallup News Service, "April Wave 2," April 17–30, 2019, https://news.gallup.com/poll/257639/four-americans-embrace-from-socialism.aspx; Frank Newport, "Socialism Viewed Positively by 36% of Americans," Gallup News Service, February 4, 2010, https://news.gallup.com/poll/125645/Socialism-Viewed-Positively-Americans.aspxt; Frank Newport, "Democrats More Positive about Socialism Than Capitalism," Gallup News Service, August 13, 2018, https://news.gallup.com/poll/240725/democrats-positive-socialism-capitalism.aspx.
50. Gautney, *Crashing the Party*, 18, 35–37.
51. RealClearPolitics, "2020 Democratic Popular Vote," accessed August 1, 2020, https://www.realclearpolitics.com/epolls/2020/president/democratic_vote_count.html; RealClearPolitics, "2016 Democratic Popular Vote," accessed August 1, 2020, https://www.realclearpolitics.com/epolls/2016/president/democratic_vote_count.html; NBC News, "2020 Primary Results National Results & Map," accessed August 1, 2020, https://www.nbcnews.com/politics/2020-primary-elections/results-map; Gautney, *Crashing*, 99.
52. Spencer Bokat-Lindell, "What Does the Democratic Party Stand For?" *New York Times*, August 18, 2020, https://www.nytimes.com/2020/08/18/opinion/democratic-party-trump-aoc.html?action=click&module=Opinion&pgtype=Homepage; Branko Marcetic, "The Democrats' DNC Plans Show They Aren't Even Pretending Anymore," *Jacobin*, August 17, 2020, https://www.jacobinmag.com/2020/08/dnc-biden-clinton-cuomo-democrats. Following the convention rules, AOC nominated Bernie, who still had delegates. She later apologized for any confusion and tweeted, "I extend my deepest congratulations to Joe Biden—let's go win in November."
53. Niall Stanage, "Five Takeaways from the Democratic National Convention," *The Hill*, August 21, 2020, https://thehill.com/homenews/campaign/513053-five-takeaways-from-the-democratic-national-convention.
54. Luke Savage, "Joe Biden's Promises Were Meant to Be Broken," *Jacobin*, September 12, 2020, https://www.jacobinmag.com/2020/09/joe-biden-trump-2020-election.
55. Charlie Cook, "Centrism or Bust in the 117th Congress," *Cook Political Report*, December 22, 2020, https://cookpolitical.com/analysis/national/narional-politics/cenrtrism-or-bust-117th-congress.
56. David Duhalde, "Our Revolution Failed to Live Up to Its Potential. But the Bernie Movement Needs a Mass Organization Now," *Jacobin*, April 28, 2020, https://www.jacobinmag.com/2020/04/our-revolution -bernie-sanders; Shane

Goldmacher, "Former Aides to Bernie Sanders Form a Super PAC to Support Joe Biden," *New York Times*, April 28, 2020, https://www.nytimes.com/2020/04/28 /us/politics/bernie-sanders-biden-progressive-super-pac.html.

57. Gautney, *Crashing*, 133.

58. On the impact of *this* demographic trend on the 2020 presidential primaries, see Karp, "Sanders's Five-Year War," 67–69.

## Chapter 3

1. Quoted in Mike Davis, "Trench Warfare: Notes on the 2020 Election," *New Left Review* 126 (November–December 2020): 9.

2. Davis, "Trench Warfare," 5.

3. Janet Hook, "Biden's Cabinet: Expertise, Diversity, and an Obama Class Re-union," *Los Angeles Times*, December 19, 2020, https://www.latimes.com /politics/story/2020-12-19/bidens-cabinet-expertise-diversity-and-an-obama -class-reunion; Meagan Day, "Joe Biden's BlackRock Cabinet Picks Show the President-Elect Is Ready and Eager to Serve the Rich," *Jacobin*, December 3, 2020, https://www.jacobinmag.com/2020/12/wall-street-joe-biden-transition -cabinet-blackrock; Claire Kelloway, "Tom Vilsack for Agriculture Secretary Is Everything That's Wrong with the Democratic Party," *The Intercept*, December 11, 2020, https://theintercept.com/2020/12/11/democrat-tom-valsack-esda -secretary-farms/; Michael Crowley and David E. Sanger, "Biden to Tap More Former Obama Officials for Top National Security Jobs," *New York Times*, Janu-ary 5, 2021, https://www.nytimes.com/2021/01/05/us/politics/biden-national -security-state-officials.html?action=click&module=Latest&pgtype=Homep-age; Julia Rock and Andrew Perez, "Joe Biden Has Preserved Key Loopholes for New Appointees," *Jacobin*, January 22, 2021, https://www.jacobinmag.com /2021/01/biden-administration-ethics-loopholes-lobbying.

4. Samuel Farber, "Trumpism Will Endure," *Jacobin*, January 3, 2021, https:// www.jacobinmag.com/2021/01/donald-trump-white-working-class-trumpism.

5. *Fortune* 500, Most Profitable, 2020, https://fortune.com/fortune500/2020 /search/?f500_profits=desc; *Fortune* 500 Archive, https://archive.fortune.com /magazine/fortune.fortune500_archive/full/2000

6. Kim Moody, *On New Terrain: How Capital Is Reshaping the Battleground of Class War* (Chicago: Haymarket Books, 2017), 45–58; Doug Henwood, *Wall Street: How It Works and for Whom* (London: Verso, 1997), 265–77; Kim Moody, *From Welfare State to Real Estate: Regime Change in New York City, 1974 to the Present* (New York: The New Press, 2007), 198–206.

7. Doug Henwood, "Trump and the New Billionaire Class," *Socialist Register 2019* (London: The Merlin Press, 2018), 119.

8. Davis, "Trench Warfare," 18–19.

9. Carter Coudriet, "The States with the Most Billionaires," *Forbes*, November 4, 2020, https://www.forbes.com/sites/cartercoudriet/2020/04/09/the-states -with-the-most-billionaires-2020/?sh=3578cf4e392a#72ca628e392a; "Number of Billionaires in the United States, 1987–2012," Statista Research Department, May 7, 2012, https://www.statista.com/statistics/220093/number-of -billionaires-in-the-united-startes/.

10. "Billionaires List 2018—US Only," Billionaire Mailing List, January 2019, https://www.billionairemailinglist.com/billionaires-list.html.

11. Karl Evers-Hillstrom and Brendan Quinn, "OpenSecrets Looks Back at 2020, a $14 Billion Year," OpenSecrets, December 22, 2020, https://www.opensecrets. org/news/2020/12/2020-opensecrets-year-in-review/; "2020 Election to Cost $14 Billion, Blowing Away Spending Records," OpenSecrets, October 28, 2020, https://www.opensecrets.org/news/2020/10/cost-of-election-14billion-update; "Total by Type of Spender, 2020," through January 4, 2021, OpenSecrets, https:// www.opensecrets.org/outsidespending/fes_summ.php.

12. "2020 Election to Cost $14 Billion"; "Elections Overview," Cycles 1991-92- 2019-20, OpenSecrets, accessed December 3, 2020, https://www.opensecrets .org/elections-overview.

13. Ian Vanderwalker, "The 2018 Small Donor Boom Was Drowned Out by Big Do- nors Thanks to Citizens United," Brennan Center for Justice, January 10, 2020, https://www.brennencenter.org/our-work/analysis-opinion/2018-small -donor-boom-was-drowned-out-by-big-donors-thanks-to-citizens-united.

14. Ian Vanderwalker and Lawrence Norden, "Small Donors Still Aren't as Import- ant as Wealthy Ones," *The Atlantic*, October 18, 2016, https://www.theatlantic .com/politics/archive/2016/10/campaign-finance-fundraising-citizens-united/ 504425.

15. "Who Are the Biggest Donors?" 2020 Cycle, Top 100 Donors, 2019–2020, OpenSecrets, https://www.opensecrets.org/election-overview/biggest-donors. The largest Republican donation was just over $180 million from the right-wing Las Vegas billionaire Adelson family.

16. "Biggest Donors"; "Billionaires List 2018"; Adam Bonica, Nolan McCarty, Keith T. Poole, and Howard Rosenthal, "Why Hasn't Democracy Slowed Rising Inequality?" *Journal of Economic Perspectives* 27, no. 3 (Summer 2013): 107.

17. Jonathan A. Rodden, *Why Cites Lose: The Deep Roots of the Urban-Rural Political Divide* (New York: Basic Books, 2019), 79–84.

18. "Large Versus Small Individual Donations," OpenSecrets, https://www .opensecrets.org/elections-overview/large-vs-small-donations.

19. Meagan Day, "Joe Biden's BlackRock Cabinet Picks Show the President-Elect Is Ready and Eager to Serve the Rich," *Jacobin*, December 3, 2020, https://www

.jacobinmag.com/2020/12/wall-street-joe-biden-transition-cabinet-blackrock.

20. Kalyeena Makortoff, "Yellen Files £5 Million Speech Fees in Ethics Check for US Treasury," *The Guardian*, January 2, 2021, p. 9.

21. See, for example, Walter Dean Burnham, *Critical Elections and the Mainsprings of American Politics* (New York: W.W. Norton, 1970), 1–10.

22. "Understanding the 2020 Electorate: AP Vote Cast Survey," National Public Radio, November 3, 2020; Edison Research, "National Exit Polls: How Different Groups Voted," *New York Times*, November 3, 2020, https://www.nytimes.com/interactive/2020/11/03/us/elections/exit-polls-president.html.

23. Dave Leip's Atlas of U.S. Elections, "2020 Presidential Election Results," https://uselectionatlas.org/RESULTS.

24. M. T. Wroblewski, "The Average Income of Small Business Owners," *CHRON*, November 13, 2020, https://smallbusiness.chron.com/average-income-small-business-owners-5189.html; Mike Juang, "A Secret Many Small-Business Owners Share with Mark Zuckerberg," CNBC, July 19, 2017, https://www.cnbc.com/2017/07/19/survey-shows-majority-of-business-owners-lck-college-degree.html.

25. Dante Chinni, "The 2020 Results: Where Biden and Trump Gained and Lost Voters," American Community Project, November 9, 2020, https://www.americancommunities.org/the-2020-results-where-biden-and-trump-gained-and-lost-voters/.

26. Team AOC, "We Need a Federal Jobs Guarantee," October 28, 2020, email, Ocasio-Cortez.com, news@jacobinmag.com.

27. All of the election figures in this and subsequent paragraphs are drawn from the same sources list with Table II and III; for the union household vote back to 1948, see Stephen Amberg, "The CIO Political Strategy in Historical Perspective," in *Organized Labor and American Politics, 1894–1994*, ed. Kevin Boyle (Albany: State University of New York, 1998), 175.

28. Quoted in Jon Schwarz, "Chuck Schumer: The Worst Possible Democratic Leader at The Worst Possible Time," *The Intercept*, November 14, 2016, https://theintercept.com/2016/11/14/chuck-schumer-the-worst-possible-democratic-leader-at-the-worst-possible-time/.

29. Darel E. Paul, "The New Party of the Rich," *First Things*, November 8, 2019, https://www.firstthings.com/web-exclusives/2019/11/the-new-party-of-the-rich.

30. Matt Karp, "Bernie Sanders's Five-Year War," *Jacobin*, no. 38 (Summer 2020): 68.

31. Jonathan A. Rodden, *Why Cities Lose: The Deep Roots of the Urban-Rural Political Divide* (New York: Basic Books, 2019), 69, 106–13.

32. "36 Facts about the 2020 Elections," *Cook Political Report*, December 22, 2020, https://cookpolitical.com/analysis/national/national-politics/36-facts-abour-2020-elections.

33. New York City Department of Planning, *NYC 2000: Results from the Census*, 2000, https://www1.nyc.gov/assets/planning/download/pdf/planning-level /nyc-population/census2000/sociopp.pdf; Census Reporter, "New York County, NY," 2019, https://censusreporter.org/profiles/05000US36061-new-york -county-ny/; Board of Elections in the City of New York, "General Elections," New York County, 2020, https://vote.nyc/page/election-results-summary.

34. Rodden, *Cities Lose*, 109.

35. Ryan Williamson and Jamie Carson, "Why Did the Democrats Lose Seats in the 2020 Elections? More Incumbents Ran in More Competitive Districts," *USAPP* (blog), London School of Economics Phelan US Centre, November 12, 2020, https://blogs.lse.ac.uk/usappblog/2020/11/12/why-did-democrats-lose-seats -in-the-2020-elections-more-incumbents-ran-in-more-competitive-districts/.

36. Emily Badger and Quoctrung Bui, "How the Suburbs Moved Away from Trump," *New York Times*, November 9, 2020, https://www.nytimes. com/2020/11/06/upshot/suburbs-shifted-left-president.html?action=click &module=RelatedLinks&pgtype=Article.

37. New Democrat Coalition, "Members, 117th Congress," accessed January 12, 2021, https://newdemocratcoalition.house.gov/members; Blue Dog Coalition, "Members," accessed January 12, 2021, https://bluedogcaucus-costa.house. gov/members; Congressional Progressive Caucus, "Caucus Members," accessed January 12, 2021, https://progressives.house.gov/caucus-members/; WikiMili. com, "Congressional Progressive Caucus," updated January 9, 2021, https:// wikimili.com/en/Congressional_Progressive_Caucus; Problem Solvers Caucus, "Featured Members," 116th Congress, accessed January 12, 2021, https:// problemsolverscaucus-gottheimer.house.gov/members; Problem Solvers Caucus, "About," accessed January 12, 2021, https://problemsolverscaucus -gottheimer.house.gov/about.

38. Alexander Burns, "Democrats Beat Trump in 2020. Now They're Asking: What Went Wrong?" *New York Times*, February 20, 2021, https://www.nytimes.com /2021/02/20/us/politics/democrats-beat-trump-in-2020-now-theyre-asking- what-went-wrong.html?action=click&module=Top%20Stories&pgtype =Homepage; Ballotpedia, "270 Strategies," accessed February 20,2021, https://ballotpedia.org/270_Strategies.

39. Alexander Bolton, "Centrist Democrats Pose Major Problems for Progressives," *The Hill*, February 9, 2021, https://thehill.com/homenews/senate/537925 -centrist-democrats-pose-major-problem-for-progreessives; Niv Elis, "Senate Democrats Likely to Face Key Test of Unity on 2022 Budget," *The Hill*, February 9, 2021, https://thehill.com/policy/finance/537921-senate-democrats- likely-to-face-key-test-of-unity-on-2022-budget; Walter Shapiro, "Moderate Democrats Rule Washington Now," *New Republic*, January 6, 2021, https://

newrepublic.com/article/160806/moderate-democrats-rule-washington-now; Daniel Strauss, "Joe Manchin: The Conservative Democrat with Leverage in a Split Senate," *The Guardian*, January 17, 2021, https://www.theguardian.com /us-news/2021/jan/17/joe-manchin-democrat-split-senate-leverage.

40. Russell Berman, "The Failure That Could Haunt Democrats for a Decade," *The Atlantic*, November 10, 2020, https://www.theatlantic.com/politics/archive /2020/11/democrats-2020-elections-state-legislatures/617047/; Ballotpedia, "State Legislative Elections, 2020," December 4, 2020, https://ballotpedia.org /State_legislative_elections_2020; "36 Facts."

41. Stephen Semler, "Congressional Democrats Are Raking in Huge Donations from War Profiteers," *Jacobin*, December 17, 2020, https://www.jacobinmag .com/2020/12/congressional-democrats-war-profiteers-donations-ndaa.

42. Bonica et al., "Why Hasn't Democracy Slowed?" 118.

43. Bonica et al., "Why Hasn't Democracy Slowed?" 106.

44. Jared Abbott and Dustin Guastella, "A Socialist Party in Our Time?" *Catalyst* 3, no. 2 (Summer 2019): 33.

45. Dennis R. Judd and Todd Swanstrom, *City Politics: The Political Economy of Urban America* (New York: Routledge, 2016), 219–20.

46. Judd and Swanstrom, *City Politics*, 219–22.

47. Amanda Albright, "Biden Relief Plan Tosses $350 Billion Lifeline to States, Cities," *Bloomberg*, January 15, 2021, https://www.bloomberg.com/news/articles /20201-01-15/biden-plan-rescues-states-cities-from-pandemic-s-financial-toll.

48. Branko Marcetic, "So Far, the Biden Administration Is Shaping Up to Be Obama's Third Term," *Jacobin*, February 10, 2021, https://www.jacobinmag. com/2021/02/joe-biden-administration-trump-obama-status-quo.

49. Luke Savage, "Joe Biden's Climate Policies Are a Step Back from 'Death Wish.' But We Need More Than That: An Interview with Kate Aronoff," *Jacobin*, February 16, 2021, https://www.jacobinmag.com/2021/02/joe-biden-climate -change-fossil-fuels.

50. Adam Cancryn, Susannah Luthi, and Rachel Roubein, "Biden Picks Brooks- LaSure to Run Medicare, Medicaid Agency," *Politico*, February 17, 2021, https://www.politico.com/news/2021/02/17/chiquita-brooks lasure-cms-nominee-469562.

51. United States Department of Agriculture (USDA), *Rural America at a Glance, 2016 Edition*, Economic Information Bulletin 162, November 2016, p. 1.

52. Michael Ratcliffe, Charlynn Burd, Kelly Holder, and Alison Fields, *Defining Rural at the U.S. Census Bureau* (Washington, DC: US Census Bureau, 2016), 6. Unless specified all statistics on rural countries are from this source and *Rural America at a Glance*.

53. Karl Marx and Frederick Engels, *The Communist Manifesto*, in Karl Marx and

Frederick Engels, *Selected Works in One Volume* (London: Lawrence and Wishart, 1991), 39.

54. United States Department of Agriculture, *Farm Computer Usage and Ownership* (Washington, DC: US Department of Agriculture, 2019), 6–7.

55. USDA, *Rural America*, 3; Ratcliffe et al., *Defining Rural*; Bureau of Labor Statistics, "Employment by Major Industry Sector," September 1, 2020, https://www.bls.gov/emp/tables/employment-by-major-industry-sector.htm; Cindy Estrada and Chris Schwartz, "Organizing Rural Manufacturing Workers Matters," *The Forge*, October 19, 2020, from *Portside*, moderator@portside.org.

56. USDA, Rural America.

57. Rodden, *Why Cities Lose*, 46–69.

58. Rodden, *Why Cities Lose*, 87–88.

59. Larry Buchanan, Quoctrung Bui, and Jugal K. Patel, "Black Lives Matter May Be the Largest Movement in U.S. History," *New York Times*, July 3, 2020, https://www.nytimes.com/interactive/2020/07/03/us/george-floyd-protests-crowd-size.html.

60. Davis, "Trench Warfare," 26–27.

61. Chinni, "The 2020 Results."

62. Rodden, *Why Cities Lose*, 190–96.

63. George Ingram and Annababette Wils, "Misrepresentation in the House of Representatives," Brookings Institution, February 22, 2017, https://www.brookings.edu/blog/fixgov/2017/02/22/misrepresentation-in-the-house/ ; Office of the Clerk, US House of Representatives, "Congressional Election," February 28, 2019, https://clerk.house.gov; "U.S. House Election Results," *New York Times*, January 1, 2020, https://www.nytimes.com/interactive/2020/11/03/us/elections/results-house.html?action=click&pgtype=Article&state=default&module=styln-elections-2020&region=TOP_BANNER&context=election_recirc.

64. Nicole Chavez, "There's No Such Thing as the 'Latino Vote.' 2020 Results Reveal a Complex Electorate," CNN, November 9, 2020, https://edition.cnn.com/2020/11/09/politics/latino-voters-florida-texas-arizona/index.html.

65. US Small Business Administration, *2018 Small Business Profile*, n.d., https://www.sba.gov/sites/default/files/advocacy/2018-Small-Business-Profiles-US.pdf.

66. Sabrina Tavernise and Robert Gebeloff, "They Did Not Vote in 2016. Why They Plan to Skip the Election Again," *New York Times*, October 26, 2020, https://www.nytimes.com/2020/10/26/us/election-nonvoters.html; Pew Research Center, *The Party of Nonvoters*, October 31, 2014, https://www.pewresearch.org/politics/2014/10/31/the-party-of-nonvoters-2/; Colin Woodard, "Half of Americans Don't Vote. What Are They Thinking?" *Politico*, February 19, 2020, https://www.politico.com/news/magazine/2020/02/19/knight-nonvoter-study-decoding-2020-election-wild-card-115796.

67. Knight Foundation, *The Untold Story of American Non-Voters*, February 2020, https://knightfoundation.org/wp-content/uploads/2020/02/The-100-Million -Project_KF_Report_2020.pdf; Pew Research Center, *Nonvoters*. More non-voters do lean Democratic, but as they are packed in cities and blue states, party strategists don't worry about them.

68. Davis, "Trench Warfare," 9.

69. William J. Barber II and Liz Theoharis, "What Biden and Harris Owe the Poor," *New York Times*, December 25, 2020, https://www.nytimes.com/2020/12/25 /opinion/biden-harris-agenda-poverty.html?action=click&module=Opin-ion&pgtype=Homepage.

70. For two slightly different accounts of the role of Democratic administrations in the growth of US imperialism, see Sidney Lens, *The Forging of the American Empire* (New York: Thomas Y. Crowell Company, 1971, a more recent edition is available from Haymarket Books), 292–436; Leo Panitch and Sam Gindin, *The Making of Global Capitalism: The Political Economy of American Empire* (London: Verso, 2012), 89–192.

## Chapter 4

1. Quoted in Herbert Garfinkel, *When Negroes March: The March on Washington Movement in the Organizational Politics for FEPC* (New York: Atheneum, 1969), 128.

2. Philip S. Foner, *Organized Labor and the Black Worker, 1619–1973* (New York: International Publishers, 1976), 339.

3. Bayard Rustin, "From Protest to Politics: The Future of the Civil Rights Movement," *Commentary*, February 1965, https://www.commentarymagazine.com /articles/from-protest-to-politics-the-future-of-the-civil-rights-movement/; A. Philip Randolph Institute, *A "Freedom Budget" for All Americans: Budgeting Our Resources, 1966–1975, to Achieve "Freedom from Want"* (New York: A. Philip Randolph Institute, 1966), https://archive.org/details/freedomBudgetForAl-lAmericansBudgetingOurResources1966-1975To/page/n13/mode/2up.

4. Cedric Johnson, "The Panthers Can't Save Us Now," *Catalyst* 1, no. 1 (2017): 57–85: Cedric Johnson, "Who's Afraid of Left Populism?" *New Politics* 17, no. 2, whole number 66 (2019): 21–37; Touré Reed, "Black Exceptionalism and the Militant Capitulation to Economic Inequality," *New Politics* 17, no. 2, whole number 66 (2019): 43–51; Mark Jay, "Cages and Crises: A Marxist Analysis of Mass Incarceration," *Historical Materialism* 27, no. 1 (2019): 182–223; John Clegg and Adaner Usmani, "The Economic Origins of Mass Incarceration," *Catalyst* 3, no. 3 (Fall 2019): 41; Leo Casey, "The Teacher Strike: Conditions for Success," *Dissent*, December 2, 2020, https://www.dissentmagazine.org

/online_articles/the-teacher-strike-conditions-for-success; Preston H. Smith II, "Which Black Lives Matter," *Catalyst* 4, no. 3 (Fall 2020): 132.

5. Herbert Aptheker, *American Negro Slave Revolts* (New York: International Publishers, 1963); W. E. B. Du Bois, *Black Reconstruction in America, 1860–1880* (New York: The Free Press, 1992), 55–83; Jack Bloom, *Class, Race and the Civil Rights Movement* (Bloomington: Indiana University Press, 1987), 148–54.

6. For a Marxist explanation of how the dynamics of capitalism create these recurring forms of inequality, see Howard Botwinick, *Persistent Inequality: Wage Disparity under Capitalist Competition* (Chicago: Haymarket Books, 2018); for a history of the role of race in allocating Blacks and other people of color to the lowest rungs of the working class, see David R. Roediger and Elizabeth D. Esch, *The Production of Difference: Race and the Management of Labor in U.S. History* (New York: Oxford University Press, 2012). Mark Jay's dismissal of race as central relies in part on a quantitative "adjustment" for the impact of race in the incarceration of young males "once one controls for class" measured by household income, education, assets, and home ownership. Not a Marxist view of class. Jay, "Cages and Crises," 184.

7. Johnson, "The Panthers," 67.

8. While slightly more whites are killed by police than Blacks, Latinos, and other non-whites, the figures reverse when the victims are unarmed. In those police shootings "minorities" account for almost twice the number of whites killed. German Lopez, "There Are Huge Racial Disparities in How US Police Use Force," *Vox*, November 14, 2018, https://www.vox.com/identities /2016/8/13/17938186/police-shootings-killings-racism-racial-disparaties.

9. Johnson, "The Panthers," 66.

10. Michael Goldfield, *The Color of Politics: Race and the Mainsprings of American Politics* (New York: The New Press, 1997), 240–49.

11. Philip Foner, *Organized Labor and the Black Worker, 1619–1973* (New York: International Publishers, 1976), 215, 262–67.

12. Theodore G. Vincent, *Black Power and the Garvey Movement* (Palo Alto, CA: Ramparts Press, 1971), 44–45.

13. Foner, *Organized Labor*, 177–87, 213–14.

14. Garfinkel, *Negroes March*, 37–61.

15. Garfinkel, *Negroes March*, 128.

16. Garfinkel, *Negroes March*, 83–96; Manning Marable, *Black American Politics: From the Washington Marches to Jesse Jackson* (London: Verso, 1985), 84–87.

17. Foner, *Organized Labor*, 314.

18. Herbert Hill, "The Racial Practices of the Contemporary Labor Movement," in *The Negro and the American Labor Movement*, ed. Julius Jacobson (New York: Anchor Books, 1968), 286–357.

19. Nelson Lichtenstein, *The Most Dangerous Man in Detroit: Walter Reuther and the Fate of American Labor* (New York: Basic Books, 1995), 374–79.

20. Lichtenstein, *Most Dangerous Man*, 374–79; Foner, *Organized Labor*, 333–39; J. David Greenstone, *Labor in American Politics* (New York: Vintage Books, 1969), 256–59.

21. Foner, *Organized Labor*, 334; Jervis Anderson, *A. Philip Randolph: A Biographical Portrait* (New York: Harcourt Brace Jovanovich, 1973), 302.

22. Anderson, *A. Philip Randolph*, 302–8; Foner, *Organized Labor*, 334, 345–46, 349; Hill, "Racial Practices," 288.

23. Anderson, *A. Philip Randolph*, 343–44.

24. Foner, *Organized Labor*, 339.

25. Stephen Steinberg, "Bayard Rustin and the Rise and Decline of the Black Protest Movement," *New Politics* 6, no. 3 (Summer 1997), http://nova.wpunj.edu /newpolitics/issue23/steinb23.htm; Randall Kennedy, "From Protest to Patronage," *The Nation*, September 11, 2003, https://www.thenation.com/article /protest-patronage/; Bloom, *Class, Race*, 127, 154.

26. SNCC Digital Gateway, "Bayard Rustin," 2019, https://snccdigital.org /bayard-rustin/.

27. Jervis Anderson, *Bayard Rustin: Troubles I've Seen* (Berkeley: University of California Press, 1998), 277.

28. Maurice Isserman, *If I Had a Hammer . . . : The Death of the Old Left and the Birth of the New Left* (New York: Basic Books, 1987), 73–75.

29. Isserman, *If I Had a Hammer*, 192.

30. Peter Drucker, *Max Shachtman and His Left: A Socialist's Odyssey Through the "American Century"* (New Jersey: Humanities Press, 1994), 259–72; Anderson, *Bayard Rustin*, 286; Steinberg, "Bayard Rustin."

31. Howard Brick and Christopher Phelps, *Radicals in America: The U.S. Left since the Second World War* (New York: Cambridge University Press, 2015), 186; Drucker, *Shachtman*, 304–8.

32. For background, see Walter Dean Burnham, *Critical Elections and the Mainsprings of American Politics* (New York: W.W. Norton, 1970), 1–10.

33. Anderson, *Bayard Rustin*, 286.

34. Brick and Phelps, *Radicals*, 116–17; Anderson, *Bayard Rustin*, 286–87.

35. Anderson, *Bayard Rustin*, 279–80; Anderson, *A. Philip Randolph*, 343.

36. Kennedy, "From Protest."

37. Anderson, *Bayard Rustin*, 277–80; Bloom, *Class, Race*, 182–83; for a blow-by -blow description see Todd Gitlin, *The Sixties: Years of Hope, Days of Rage* (New York: Bantam Books, 1989), 151–62.

38. Julius Jacobson, "Union Conservatism: A Barrier to Racial Equality," in Jacobson, ed., *The Negro*, 24.

39. Louis Lomax, "When 'Nonviolence' Meets "Black Power," in *Martin Luther King, Jr.: A Profile*, ed. C. Eric Lincoln (New York: Hill and Wang, 1984), 165.
40. Steinberg, "Bayard Rustin."
41. Anderson, *Bayard Rustin*, 337.
42. Quoted in Kennedy, "From Protest."
43. Thanks to Kate Doyle Griffiths for pointing this out. Kate Doyle Griffiths, "The Rank and File Strategy on New Terrain, Part 3," *Spectre*, September 4, 2020, https://spectrejournal.com/the-rank-and-file-strategy-on-new-terrain-3/.
44. Johnson, "The Panthers," 66–67.
45. Marable, *Black American Politics*, 89–90.
46. Frances Fox Piven and Richard A. Cloward, *Poor People's Movements: Why They Succeed, How They Fail* (New York: Vintage Books, 1979), 244.
47. Steinberg, "Bayard Rustin."
48. Anderson, *Bayard Rustin*, 285.
49. Bloom, *Class, Race*, 211. Strictly speaking, the term "Black Power" had been used by James Boggs in his unfortunately short-lived Organization for Black Power in 1965. Stephen M. Ward, "An Ending and a Beginning: James Boggs, C. L. R. James and *The American Revolution*," in *New Insurgency: The Port Huron Statement and Its Times*, ed. Howard Brick and Gregory Parker (Ann Arbor: Michigan Publishing, 2015), 275–76.
50. Rustin, "From Protest."
51. Piven and Cloward, *Poor People's*, 246.
52. Rustin, "'Black Power."
53. Mike Davis, *Prisoners of the American Dream: Politics and Economy in the History of the US Working Class* (London: Verso, 1986), 121–24.
54. Aaron Brenner, Robert Brenner, and Cal Winslow, *Rebel Rank and File: Labor Militancy and Revolt from Below During the Long 1970s* (London: Verso, 2010).
55. Robert Brenner, *The Boom and the Bubble: The US in the World Economy* (London: Verso, 2002), 7–41; Anwar Shaikh, *Capitalism: Competition, Conflict, Crises* (New York: Oxford University Press, 2016), 56–74.
56. Moody, *On New Terrain*, 107–46; Thomas Ferguson and Joel Rogers, *Right Turn: The Decline of the Democrats and the Future of American Politics* (New York: Hill & Wang, 1986).
57. Paul Jargowsky, *The Architecture of Segregation* (Washington, DC: The Century Foundation, 2015); Reshaad Shirazi, "It's High Time to Dump the High-Crime Area Factor," *Berkeley Journal of Criminal Law* 21, no. 2 (2016): 77–79.
58. US Equal Employment Opportunity Commission, "Charge Statistics (Charges Filed with EEOC), FY 1997 through FY 2017," 2018, https://www1.eeoc.gov//eeoc/statistics/enforcement/charges.cfm?renderforprint=1.
59. Mia White, "In Defense of Black Sentiment: A Comment on Cedric Johnson's

Essay: Re: Black Power Nostalgia," *New Politics* 17, no. 2, whole number 66 (2019): 50.

## Chapter 5

1. H. Res. 109, 116th Congress, "Recognizing the Duty of the Federal Government to Create a Green New Deal," House of Representatives, February 7, 2019, pp. 5–6, https://www.congress.gov/116/bills/hres109/BILLS-116hres109ih.pdf.
2. Li Zhou and Ella Nilsen, "Senate Democrats Broadly Shut Down Republican Trolling on the Green New Deal," *Vox*, March 26, 2019, https://www.vox.com /2019/3/26/18281323/green-new-deal-democrats-vote 1/5; Susan Davis, "Senate Blocks Green New Deal, but Climate Change Emerges as a Key 2020 Issue," NPR, March 26, 2019, https://www.npr.org/2019/03/26/705897344 /green-new-deal-vote-sets-up-climate-change-as-key-2020-issue.
3. H. Res. 109, "Recognizing the Duty," 1.
4. Nancy Pelosi, Speaker of the House, "Pelosi Names Members of the Select Committee on the Climate Crisis," Newsroom, February 7, 2019, https://www .speaker.gov/newsroom/2719/.
5. H.R. 9, 116th Congress, "To direct the President to develop a plan for the United States to meet its nationally determined contribution under the Paris Agreement, and for other purposes," House of Representatives, March 27, 2019, https://www .congress.gov/116/bills/hr9/BILLS-116hr9ih.pdf; H.R. 9, 116th Congress, "To direct the President to develop a plan for the United States to meet its nationally determined contribution under the Paris Agreement, and for other purposes," Senate of the United States, May 6, 2019, https://www.congress.gov/bill/116th-congress /house-9/text; Clerk House, Final Vote Results for Roll Call 184, H.R. 9, Recorded Vote 2-May-2019, www.clerk.house.gov/evs/2019/roll184.xml.
6. H. Res. 332, 117th Congress, "Recognizing the Duty of the Federal Government to Create a Green New Deal," House of Representatives, April 20, 2021, https://www.govtrack.us/congress/bills/117hres332/text.
7. About 3 percent of proposed bills ever pass Congress. See Roger H. Davidson et al., *Congress and Its Members*, 17th ed. (Thousand Oaks, CA: SAGE/CQ Press, 2020), 228; "Historical Statistics about Legislation in the U.S. Congress," GovTrack, 2019, https://www.govtrack.us/congress/bills/statistics.
8. This is from memory of the Sanders session which I chaired, but it has always stuck in my mind. Whether Bernie would say that today is another matter. See Program Book, *7th Labor Notes Conference*, April 23–25, 1993, Dearborn, Michigan, "A Bill of Rights for American Workers: Beyond the Clinton Agenda," US Representative Bernie Sanders (Independent, Vermont), Chair: Kim Moody, 6.
9. Davidson et al., *Congress and Its Members*, 220–22.

10. Colby Itkowitz, Dino Grandoni, and Jeff Stein, "AFL-CIO Criticizes Green New Deal, Calling it 'Not Achievable or Realistic,'" *Washington Post*, March 12, 2019, https://www.washingtonpost.com/politics/afl-cio-criticizes-green-new -deal-calling-it-not-achievable-or-realistic/2019/03/12/842784fe-44dd-11e9 -aaf8-4512a6fe3439_story.html?utm_term=.ede62f5a447b.

11. See, for example, Joe Maniscalco, "New Calls for a General Strike in the Face of Coming Climate Catastrophe," *Labor Press*, May 13, 2019, https://www .laborpress.org/new-calls-for-a-general-strike-in-the-face-of-coming-climate -catastrophe/.

12. "Lobbying," Top Spenders, Industry, Sector, 1998–2019, OpenSecrets, 2018, https://www.opensecrets.org/lobby/top.php?showYear=a&indexType=s; "Political Parties," Democratic Party, OpenSecrets, 2018, https://www .opensecrets.org/parties/indus.php?cycle=2018&cmte=DPC; Kim Moody, "From Realignment to Reinforcement," *Jacobin*, January 26, 2017, https:// www.jacobinmag.com/2017/01/democratic-party-campaign-fundraising -wasserman-schultz; Kim Moody *On New Terrain: How Capital Is Reshaping the Battleground of Class War* (Chicago: Haymarket Books, 2017), 119–46.

13. For the Second New Deal, see: William E. Leuchtenburg, *Franklin D. Roosevelt and the New Deal: 1932–1940* (New York: Harper & Row, 1963), 143–66; James MacGregor Burns, *Roosevelt: The Lion and the Fox* (New York: Harcourt, Brace & World, 1956), 223–26; Eric Foner, *Give Me Liberty!: An American History* (New York: W.W. Norton, 2005), 810–13.

14. Burns, *Roosevelt*, 166.

15. John Newsinger, *Fighting Back: The American Working Class in the 1930s* (London: Bookmarks, 2012), 70–71.

16. Burns, *Roosevelt*, 170; Leuchtenburg, *Franklin D. Roosevelt*, 60.

17. Irving Bernstein, *The Lean Years: A History of the American Worker, 1920–1933* (Baltimore: Penguin Books, 1966), 469–70.

18. Burns, *Roosevelt*, 196; Leuchtenburg, *Franklin D. Roosevelt*, 120.

19. Burns, *Roosevelt*, 196, 220; Leuchtenburg, *Franklin D. Roosevelt*, 121–24.

20. Burns, *Roosevelt*, 144; US Census, *Historical Statistics of the United States: Colonial Times to 1970*, part 2 (Washington, DC: Bureau of the Census, 1975), 1071.

21. Bernstein, *Lean Years*, 475.

22. Francis Fox Piven and Richard A. Cloward, *Poor People's Movements: Why They Succeed, How They Fail* (New York: Vintage Books, 1979), 48–76; Jeremy Brecher, *Strike!* rev. ed. (Boston: South End Press, 1997), 159–63; Bernstein, *Lean Years*, 416–35.

23. Bernstein, *Lean Years*, 432–41.

24. Sidney Lens, *Left, Right & Center: Conflicting Forces in American Labor* (Hinsdale, IL: Henry Regnery Company, 1949), 268.

25. Art Preis, *Labor's Giant Step: Twenty Years of the CIO* 2nd ed. (New York: Pathfinder Press, 1972), 14–15; Piven and Cloward, *Poor People's Movements*, 119; Irving Bernstein, *Turbulent Years: A History of the American Worker, 1933–1941* (Boston: Houghton Mifflin, 1969), 322; Burns, *Roosevelt*, 192–94.

26. Burns, *Roosevelt*, 209.

27. Leuchtenburg, *Franklin D. Roosevelt*, 185.

28. Michael Goldfield, *The Color of Politics: Race and the Mainsprings of American Politics* (New York: The New Press, 1997), 202–5.

29. Burns, *Roosevelt*, 193, 231.

30. Bernstein, *Turbulent Years*, 30.

31. Burns, *Roosevelt*, 216.

32. Piven and Cloward, *Poor People's Movements*, 129.

33. Sidney Fine, *Sit-Down: The General Motors Strike of 1936–1937* (Ann Arbor: University of Michigan Press, 1969), 31.

34. Preis, *Giant Step*, 15–16.

35. Preis, *Giant Step*, 12; Robert M. Schwartz, ed., *The Labor Law Source Book* (Cambridge, MA: Work Rights Press, 1999), 2.

36. Lens, *Left*, 272.

37. Sidney Fine, *The Automobile Under the Blue Eagle* (Ann Arbor: University of Michigan Press, 1963), 27.

38. Nelson Lichtenstein, *The Most Dangerous Man in Detroit: Walter Reuther and the Fate of American Labor* (New York: Basic Books, 1995), 33.

39. Bernstein, *Lean Years*, 343.

40. Preis, *Giant Step*, 12.

41. Burns, *Roosevelt*, 216.

42. Michael Goldfield and Cody R. Melcher, "The Myth of Section 7(a): Worker Militancy, Progressive Labor Legislation, and the Coal Miners," *Labor: Studies in Working-Class History* 16, no. 4 (December 2019): 49–65.

43. David Brody, "The Origins of Modern Steel Unionism: The SWOC Era," in *Forging a Union of Steel: Philip Murray, SWOC, & the United Steelworkers*, ed. Paul F. Clark, Peter Gottlieb, and Donald Kennedy (Ithaca, NY: ILR Press, 1987), 15–16.

44. Bernstein, *Turbulent Years*, 41, 173.

45. Preis, *Giant Step*, 19–33; Brecher, *Strike!*, 166–84; Newsinger, *Fighting Back*, 85–100.

46. Bernstein, *Turbulent Years*, 198–317; Newsinger, *Fighting Back*, 100–104.

47. Newsinger, *Fighting Back*, 138.

48. Burns, *Roosevelt*.

49. For various Marxist accounts of the period of growth and prosperity and its end, see Robert Brenner, *The Economics of Global Turbulence: The Advanced Capital-*

*ist Economies from Long Boom to Long Downturn, 1945–2005* (London: Verso, 2006), 1–9; David McNally, *Global Slump: The Economics and Politics of Crisis and Resistance* (Oakland, CA: PM Press, 2011), 25–30; Anwar Shaikh, *Capitalism: Competition, Conflict, Crises* (New York: Oxford University Press, 2016), 56–74.

50. Jack M. Bloom, *Class, Race, and the Civil Rights Movement* (Bloomington, IN: Indiana University Press, 1987), 60; Goldfield, *Color of Politics*, 277–79.

51. Bloom, *Class, Race*, 12–13, 128–29.

52. Robin D. G. Kelley, *Race Rebels: Culture, Politics, and the Black Working Class* (New York: The Free Press, 1994), 75.

53. Piven and Cloward, *Poor People's Movements*, 208.

54. Kelley, *Race Rebels*, 77–100.

55. Louis Lomax, "When 'Nonviolence' Meets 'Black Power,'" in *Martin Luther King, Jr.: A Profile*, rev ed., ed. C. Eric Lincoln (New York: Hill and Wang, 1984), 167; Piven and Cloward, *Poor People's Movements*, 208–55; Bloom, *Class, Race*, 120–85; Manning Marable, *Black American Politics: From the Washington Marches to Jesse Jackson* (London: Verso, 1985), 87–97.

56. Joanne Grant, ed., *Black Protest: History, Documents, and Analysis 1619 to the Present* (Greenwich, CT: Fawcett Publications, 1968), 434.

57. Kelley, *Race Rebels*, 57.

58. Kelley, *Race Rebels*, 56–70.

59. Bloom, *Class, Race*, 146–50, 172; Piven and Cloward, *Poor People's Movements*, 208–11; Grant, *Black Protest*, 284–89.

60. Piven and Cloward, *Poor People's Movements*, 214–17; Bloom, *Class, Race*, 220–21.

61. Bloom, *Class, Race*, 157.

62. Jervis Anderson, *Bayard Rustin: Troubles I've Seen* (Berkeley: University of California Press, 1998), 256.

63. Piven and Cloward, *Poor People's Movements*, 232–33.

64. Bloom, *Class, Race*.

65. Goldfield, *Color of Politics*, 290.

66. Kelley, *Race Rebels*, 88.

67. Piven and Cloward, *Poor People's Movements*, 244–46, 270; Marable, *Black American Politics*, 90; Anderson, *Bayard Rustin*, 254.

68. Piven and Cloward, *Poor People's Movements*, 244–46, 270; Anderson, *Bayard Rustin*, 254.

69. Bloom, *Class, Race*, 182–83; for a blow-by-blow description, see Todd Gitlin, *The Sixties: Years of Hope, Days of Rage* (New York: Bantam Books, 1989), 149–62.

70. Lomax, "When 'Nonviolence,'" 167.

71. Piven and Cloward, *Poor People's Movements*, 248.

72. Bayard Rustin, "From Protest to Politics: The Future of the Civil Rights Movement," *Commentary*, February 1965, https://www.commentarymagazine.com/articles/from-protest-to-politics-the-future-of-the-civil-rights-movement/.

## Chapter 6

1. Leon Fink and Brian Greenberg, *Upheaval in the Quiet Zone: A History of Hospital Workers' Union Local 1199* (Urbana: University of Illinois Press, 1989), 203–4.

2. Bureau of Labor Statistics, "Union Members – 2020," Economic News Release, January 22, 2021, https://www.bls.gov/news.release/union2.nr0.htm#.

3. Jane McAlevey with Bob Ostertag, *Raising Expectations (and Raising Hell): My Decade Fighting for the Labor Movement* (London: Verso, 2014); Jane McAlevey, *No Shortcuts: Organizing for Power in the New Gilded Age* (New York: Oxford University Press, 2016); Jane McAlevey, *A Collective Bargain: Unions, Organizing, and the Fight for Democracy* (New York: Ecco, 2020).

4. McAlevey, *Shortcuts*, 54–55.

5. McAlevey, *Shortcuts*, 33.

6. Alexandra Bradbury, Mark Brenner, and Jane Slaughter, *Secrets of a Successful Organizer* (Brooklyn: A Labor Notes Book, 2016).

7. *No Shortcuts*, 202–3.

8. McAlevey, *Collective Bargain*, 158–59.

9. McAlevey, *Shortcuts*, 51.

10. McAlevey, *Shortcuts*, 101–42; McAlevey, *Collective Bargain*, 199–231.

11. Nelson Lichtenstein, *State of the Union: A Century of American Labor* (Princeton: Princeton University Press, 2002), 99–100.

12. For multiple examples of this, see Aaron Brenner, Robert Brenner, and Cal Winslow, *Rebel Rank and File: Labor Militancy and Revolt from Below during the Long 1970s* (London: Verso, 2010); Heather Ann Thompson, *Whose Detroit? Politics, Labor, and Race in a Modern American City* (Ithaca, NY: Cornell University Press, 2001).

13. Kim Moody, *US Labor in Trouble and Transition: The Failure of Reform from Above, the Promise of Renewal from Below* (London: Verso, 2007), 104.

14. See, for example, Sheila Cohen, *Ramparts of Resistance: Why Workers Lost Their Power and How to Get It Back* (London: Pluto Press, 2006), 149–73.

15. McAlevey, *Shortcuts*.

16. For the best detailed discussion of building union democracy, see Mike Parker and Martha Gruelle, *Democracy Is Power: Rebuilding Unions from the Bottom Up* (Detroit: A Labor Notes Book, 1999).

17. International Trade Administration, "Steel Imports Report: United States," May

2020, *Global Steel Trade Monitor,* https://Legacy.trade.gov/steel/countries /pdfs/imports-us.pdf; Bruce A. Blonigen, Benjamin H. Liebman, and Welsey W. Wilson, "Trade Policy and Market Power: The Case of the US Steel Industry," *NBER Working Paper Series,* Working Paper 13671, December 2007, https:// www.researchgate.net/publication/5188626_Trade_Policy_and_Market _Power_The_Case_of_the_US_Steel_Industry/figures?lo=1; Frank Giarratani, Ravi Madhavan, and Gene Gruver, "Steel Industry Restructuring and Location," Center for Industry Studies, University of Pittsburgh, May 7, 2012; Nicholas Tolomeo, Michael Fitzgerald, and Joe Eckelman, "US Steel Sector Thrives As Mills Move Up Quality Ladder," *Insight* (blog), S&P Global Platts, May 9, 2019, https://blogs.platts.com/2019/05/09/us-steel-mills-quality/; Associated Press, "As Trump Weighs Tariffs, US Steelmakers Enjoy Rising Profits," March 13, 2018, https://apnews.com/cae426730cd74e64932e4be7fa5cdebc /As-Trump-weighs-tariffs,-US-steelmakers-enjoy-rising-profits#/pq=FGkzCO.

18. Federal Reserve Statistical Release, *Industrial Production and Capacity Utilization,* G.17 (419), December 17, 2019, https://www.federalreserve.gov/releases /g17/20191217/g17.pdf.

19. Bureau of Labor Statistics, "Labor Productivity and Costs," https://data.bls. gov/cgi-bin/print.pl/1pc/prodybar.htm; Conference Board, *International Comparisons of Manufacturing Productivity and Unit Labor Costs Trends, 2012* (New York: Conference Board, 2013), 7.

20. Bureau of Labor Statistics, "Production and Nonsupervisory Employees," 2019; "How's Manufacturing? Depends on the Sector," *The FRED\* Blog,* February 1, 2018; https://fredblog.stlouisfed.org/2018/02/hows-manufacturing/; for a more detailed analyses of why imports are not the major culprit and productivity matters, see Kim Moody, *On New Terrain: Howe Capital Is Reshaping the Battleground of Class War* (Chicago: Haymarket Books, 2017), 8–13, 191–95; Kim Moody, "Productivity, Crises and Imports in the Loss of Manufacturing Jobs," *Capital & Class* 44, no. 1 (2020): 47–61.

21. Bureau of Labor Statistics, "Manufacturing: NAICS 31–33," *Industries at a Glance,* January 8, 2021, https://www.bls.gov/iag/tgs/iag31-33.htm.

22. McAlevey, *Shortcuts,* 30.

23. See, for example, Irving Bernstein, *Turbulent Years: A History of the American Worker, 1933–1941* (Boston: Houghton Mifflin, 1969); and Sidney Fine, *Sit-Down: The General Motors Strike of 1936–1937* (Ann Arbor: University of Michigan Press, 2020).

24. Kim Moody, introduction to Sidney Fine, *Sit-Down: The General Motors Strike of 1936-1937* (Ann Arbor: The University of Michigan Press, 2020).

25. David Brody, "The Origins of Modern Steel Unionism: The SWOC Era," in *Forging a Union of Steel: Philip Murray, SWOC, & the United Steelworkers,* ed.

Paul F. Clark, Peter Gottlieb, and Donald Kennedy (Ithaca, NY: ILR Press, 1987), 15–16.

26. Bernstein, *Turbulent Years*, 440–43, 604–7.

27. Fink and Greenberg, *Upheaval*, 181–243.

28. Fink and Greenberg, *Upheaval*, 202

29. Fink and Greenberg, *Upheaval*, 203–4.

30. McAlevey, *Shortcuts*, 120–21; McAlevey, *Collective Bargain*, 199.

31. McAlevey, *Shortcuts*, 154–55.

32. For some of the works in this research and debate, see: Kate Bronfenbenner et al., eds. *Organizing to Win: New Research on Union Strategies* (Ithaca, NY: Cornell University Press, 1998); Lowell Turner, Harry Katz, and Richard W. Hurd, eds., *Rekindling the Movement: Labor's Quest for Relevance in the 21st Century* (Ithaca: Cornell University Press, 2001.); and Ruth Milkman and Kim Voss, eds., *Rebuilding Labor: Organizing and Organizers in the New Union Movement* (Ithaca: Cornell University Press, 2004).

33. Kim Moody, "Labour and the Contradictory Logic of Logistics," *Work Organization, Labour & Globalisation* 13, no. 1 (Spring 2019): 79–95.

34. For some more works on this, see Deborah Cowen, *The Deadly Life of Logistics: Mapping Violence in Global Trade* (Minneapolis: University of Minnesota Press, 2014); Jake Alimahomed-Wilson and Immanuel Ness, eds., *Choke Points: Logistics Workers Disrupting the Global Supply Chain* (London: Pluto Press, 2018); and Moody, *On New Terrain*, 59–69.

35. David McNally, "The Return of the Mass Strike: Teachers, Students, Feminists, and the New Wave of Popular Upheavals," *Spectre* 1, no. 1 (Spring 2020): 13–37.

36. For this and a summary of such actions up to June 2020, see Jane Slaughter "In a Pandemic, Finding Ways to Fight New and Old Foes," *Labor Notes* 495 (June 2020): 1, 3–4.

37. Saurav Sarkar, "Twin Cities Labor Mobilizes against George Floyd Murder," *Labor Notes*, May 29, 2020, https://www.labornotes.org/blogs/2020/05/twin-cities-labor-mobilizes-against-george-floyd-murder; Alexia Fernández Campbell, "As Protests Grow, Big Labor Sides with Police Unions," Center for Public Integrity, June 5, 2020, https://publicintegrity.org/inequality-poverty-opportunity/as-protests-grow-big-labor-sides-with-police-unions.

# Chapter 7

1.  E. J. Hobsbawm, *Labouring Men: Studies in the History of Labour* (London: Weidenfeld and Nicolson, 1964), 139.

2.  Mark Meinster, "Let's Not Miss Any More Chances," *Labor Notes* 500 (November 2020): 3.

3.  Miha Hribernik and Sam Haynes, "47 Countries Witness Surge in Civil Unrest – Trend to Continue in 2020," Maplecroft, January 16, 2020, https://www .maplecroft.com/insights/anaysis/47-countries-witness-surge-in-civil-unrest/; Saeed Kamali Dehghan, "One in Four Countries Beset by Civil Strife as Global Unrest Soars," *The Guardian*, January 16, 2020, https://www.theguardian.com /global-development/2020/jan/16/one-in-four-countries-beset-by-civil-strife -as-global-unrest-soars.

4.  European Trade Union Institute, *Strikes in Europe*, April 7, 2020, https://www .etui.org/sites/default/files/2020-06/Strikesmap_20200407_1.pdf.

5.  Rosina Gammarano, "At Least 44,000 Work Stoppages since 2010," International Labour Organization, November 4, 2019, https://ilostat.ilo.org/at-least -44000-work-stoppages-since-2010.

6.  Yu Chunsen, "All Workers Are Precarious: The 'Dangerous Class' in China's Labour Regime," in *Socialist Register 2020*, ed. Leo Panitch and Greg Albo (London: The Merlin Press, 2019), 156.

7.  David McNally, "The Return of the Mass Strike: Teachers, Students, Feminists, and the New Wave of Popular Upheavals," *Spectre* 1, no. 1 (Spring 2020): 20.

8.  McNally, "Mass Strike," 15–27.

9.  McNally, "Mass Strike," 16.

10. Mark Meinster, "Let's Not Miss Any More Chances," *Labor Notes* 500 (November 2020): 3.

11. Rafael Bernabe, "The Puerto Rican Summer," *New Politics* 17, no. 4, whole number 68 (Winter 2020): 3–10.

12. Ursula Huws, "Social Reproduction in Twenty-First Century Capitalism," in Panitch and Albo, *Socialist Register 2020*, 169.

13. For a useful history of management theory, see Gerard Hanlon, *The Dark Side of Management: A Secret History of Management Theory* (New York: Routledge, 2016); Tony Smith, *Technology and Capital in the Age of Lean Production* (Albany: State University of New York Press, 2000), 55–73.

14. Ursula Huws, *Labor in the Global Digital Economy* (New York: Monthly Review Press, 2014), 94–96.

15. Fritz Bos, "The History of National Accounts," National Accounts Research Division, NA—48 (The Hague: Netherlands Central Bureau of Statistics, 1992), 8–14, https://papers.ssnr.com/sol3/papers.cfm?abstract_id=1032598; Jerry Z. Muller,

*The Tyranny of Metrics* (Princeton: Princeton University Press, 2018), 6, 17.

16. Institute for Health and Socio-Economic Policy, *Health Information Basics* (Oakland, CA: Institute for Health and Socio-Economic Policy, 2009), 4–7; Lois Weiner, "Walkouts Teach U.S. Labor a New Grammar for Struggle," *New Politics* 17, no. 1, whole number 65 (2019): 3–13; Will Johnson, "Lean Production," in *Class Action: An Activist Teacher's Handbook*, ed. Shawn Gude and Bhaskar Sunkara (Bronx, NY: Jacobin Foundation, 2014), 11–31; Huws, *Digital Economy*, 34–41.

17. Jason Struna and Ellen Reese, "Automation and the Surveillance-Driven Warehouse in Inland Southern California," in *The Cost of Free Shipping: Amazon in the Global Economy*, ed. Jake Alimahomed-Wilson and Ellen Reese (London: Pluto Press, 2020), 90–92; James Bridle, *New Dark Age: Technology and the End of the Future* (London: Verso, 2018), 114–16.

18. For example, see David R. Roediger and Elizabeth D. Esch, *The Production of Difference: Race and the Management of Labor in U.S. History* (New York: Oxford University Press, 2012).

19. Contrary to some interpretations of Marx, Braverman, and others, the breaking down of skills into tasks or the creation of new ones, their quantification, and even standardization do not create the *homogenization* of labor. "Abstract" labor can be measured by time or equivalence in exchange but does not imply uniformity of tasks. Rather, the multiplication of standardized tasks produces a proliferation and differentiation of tasks suited to specific aspects of production or service delivery that can be compensated differently. That, along with the matter of speed, is a goal of both deskilling and the process now underway in high-tech industries of breaking down such new skills as this work produces. Karl Marx, *Capital, Volume I* (London: Penguin Books, 1976), 142, 150.

20. Bridle, *Dark Age*, 144–45.

21. Cathy O'Neil, *Weapons of Math Destruction: How Big Data Increases Inequality and Threatens Democracy* (London: Penguin Books, 2016), 87.

22. Bridle, *Dark Age*, 139–44.

23. Institute for Health, *Health Information Basics*, 4–7.

24. Bureau of Labor Statistics, "Productivity and Costs," Third Quarter Revised, USDL 20-2215, Table 2; US Bureau of Economic Analysis, "Gross Domestic Product (Third Estimate), Corporate Profits (Revised), and GDP by Industry, Third Quarter 2020," news release, BEA 20-67, December 22, 2020, Table 11; Bureau of Labor Statistics, "Nonfarm Business," *Employment, Hours, and Earnings from the Current Employment Statistics Survey (National)*, January 10, 2021.

25. Bureau of Labor Statistics, "Manufacturing," *Employment, Hours, and Earnings from the Current Employment Statistics Survey (National)*, January 10, 2021; US Bureau of Economic Analysis, "Gross Domestic Product (Third Estimate),

Corporate Profits (Revised), and GDP by Industry, Third Quarter 2020," BEA 20-67, December 22, 2020, Table 17; US Bureau of Economic Analysis, "Real Value Added by Industry," December 22, 2020, https://apps.bea.gov/iTable /iTable.cfm?reqid=150&step=2&isuri=1&categories=gdpxind.

26. US Bureau of Economic Analysis, Table 5.2.6U, "Real Gross and Net Domestic Investment by Major Type," 2020Q1 to 2020Q3.

27. Quoted from Marx's 1861–1863 *Manuscripts* on "Machinery" in Tony Smith, "The Chapters on Machinery in the 1861–1863 Manuscripts," https://www .academia.edu/12000286/The_Chapters_on_Machinery_in_the_1861_63 _Manuscripts?email_work_card=view-paper.

28. Harry Braverman, *Labor and Monopoly Capital: The Degradation of Work in the Twentieth Century* (New York: Monthly Review Press, 1998), 134.

29. Alexandra Bradbury, "It's Been a Long Nightmare before Christmas for UPS and Postal Workers," *Labor Notes*, December 18, 2020, https://labornotes.org /2020/12/its-been-long-nightmare-christmas-ups-and-postal-workers.

30. Dawn Geske, "UPS Isn't Hiring More Than Usual for the Holidays, Despite Pandemic Revenue Boost," *International Business Times*, October 28, 2020, https://www.ibtimes.com/ups-isnt-hiring-more-usual-holidays-despite -pandemic-revenue-boost-30711692.

31. Jake Alimahomed-Wilson, "Building Its Own Delivery Network, Amazon Puts the Squeeze On Drivers," *Labor Notes*, December 17, 2020, https://labornotes.org /2020/12/building-its-own-delivery-network-amazon-puts-squeeze-drivers.

32. Brie Weller Reynolds, "FlexJobs, Mental Health America Survey: Mental Health in the Workplace," *FlexJobs*, August 21, 2020, https://www.flexjobs.com /blog/post/flexjobs-mha-mental-health-wokrplace-pandemic; Eagle Hill Consulting LLC, "Employee Burnout from COVID-19 on the Rise, with 58% of US Workers Reporting Burnout," Eagle Hill Consulting LLC, Arlington, VA, September 2, 2020, https://www.eaglehillconsulting.com/news/employee- burnout-from-covid-19-on-the-rise-with-58-of-u-s-workers-reporting-burnout.

33. Centers for Disease Control and National Center for Health Statistics, "Anxi- ety and Depression," *Household Pulse Survey*, April and November-December, 2020, https://www.cdc.gov/nchs/covid19/pulse/mental-health.htm

34. Karl Marx, *Grundrisse: Introduction to the Critique of Political Economy* (Har- mondsworth, UK: Penguin Books, 1973), 533–34; Karl Marx, *Capital, Volume II* (Harmondsworth, UK: Penguin Books, 1978), 226–27.

35. Karl Marx, *Capital, Volume II* (Harmondsworth, UK: Penguin Books, 1978), 180–93.

36. Marx, *Grundrisse*, 517–18.

37. "Amazon AWS, Maps and Photos," Datacenters.com, www.datacenters.com /providers/amazon-aws, accessed April 20, 2020.

38. Alan Satariano, "How the Internet Travels across Oceans," *New York Times*, March 10, 2019, https://www.nytimes.com/interactive/2019/03/10/technology/internet-cables-oceans.html; Nicole Starosielski, *The Undersea Network* (Durham, NC: Duke University Press, 2015).

39. Bridle, *Dark Age*, 61; Starosielski, *The Undersea Network*.

40. pwc, *Global Infrastructure Investment: The Role of Private Capital in the Delivery of Essential Assets and Services* (Price Waterhouse Coopers, 2017), 5.

41. For examples of harbor and canal dredging and construction mainly in the Middle East, see Laleh Khalili, *Sinews of War and Trade: Shipping and Capitalism in the Arabian Peninsula* (London: Verso, 2020).

42. Akhil Gupta, "The Future in Ruins: Thoughts on the Temporality of Infrastructure," in *The Promise of Infrastructure*, ed. Nikhil Anand et al. (Durham, NC: Duke University Press, 2018), 72.

43. Peter Frankopan, *The New Silk Roads: The Present and Future of the World* (London: Bloomsbury, 2018), 89–114.

44. Daniel Yergin, *The New Map: Energy, Climate, and the Clash of Nations* (London: Allen Lane, 2020), 181.

45. For more on this see Kim Moody, *On New Terrain: How Capital Is Reshaping the Battleground of Class War* (Chicago: Haymarket Books, 2017), 59–69.

46. David J. Lynch, "Pandemic Aftershocks Overwhelm Global Supply Lines," *Washington Post*, January 24, 2021, https://www.washingtonpost.com/business/2021/01/24/pandemic-shipping-economy/; Bill Mongelluzzo, "Asia-US Ocean Reliability Falls to New Low," *Journal of Commerce*, November 30, 2020, https://www.joc.com/maritime-news/container-lines/asia-us-ocean-reliability-falls-new-low_20201130.html?utm_source=Eloqua&utm_medium=email&utm_campaign=CL_JOC%20Daily%20Newswire%2012%2F1%2F2020__e-production_E-83030_TF_1201_0617; Cathy Morrow Roberson, "Retailers Turning to Fulfilment Providers for Last-Mile Delivery," *Journal of Commerce*, December 3, 2020, https://www.joc.com/international-logistics/logistics-technology/retailers-turning-fulfillment-providers-faster-last-mile delivery_20201203.html?utm_source=Eloqua&utm_medium=email&utm_campaign=CL_JOC%20Daily%20Newswire%2012%2F4%2F2020__e-production_E-83520_KB_1204_0; Bureau of Labor Statistics, "Warehousing and Storage: NAISC 493," *Industries at a Glance*, January 15, 2021, https://www.bls.gov/iag/tgs/iag493.htm#.

47. Susan Helper, Timothy Krueger, and Howard Wial, *Locating American Manufacturing: Trends in the Geography of Production* (Washington, DC: Metropolitan Policy Program at Brookings, 2012); Joseph Kane and Adie Tomer, *Metro Modes: Charting a Path for the U.S. Freight Transportation Network* (Washington, DC: Metropolitan Policy Program at Brookings, 2015); Liliana Rivera,

Yossi Sheffi, and Roy Welsch, "Logistics Agglomeration in the US," *Transportation Research Part A* 59 (2014), 222–38.

48. Kane and Tomer, *Metro Modes*, 1; William H. Frey, *Melting Pot Cities and Suburbs: Racial and Ethnic Change in Metro America in the 2000s* (Washington, DC: Metropolitan Policy Program at Brookings, 2011), 1.

49. Gallup News Service, "Gallup Socialism," April Wave, Princeton Job #: 19-04-006, April 17–30, 2019, https://www.scribd.com/document/410913616/Gallup-Socialism.

50. Gallup News Service, "April Wave 2," April 17–30, 2019, https://news.gallup.com/poll/257639/four-americans-embrace-from-socialism.aspx; Frank Newport, "Socialism Viewed Positively by 36% of Americans," Gallup News Service, February 4, 2010, https://news.gallup.com/poll/125645/Socialism-Viewed-Positively-Americans.aspxt; Frank Newport, "Democrats More Positive about Socialism Than Capitalism," Gallup News Service, August 13, 2018, https://news.gallup.com/poll/240725/democrats-positive-socialism-capitalism.aspx.

51. On Father Coughlin and the UAW, see Steve Jefferys, *Management and the Managed: Fifty Years of Crisis at Chrysler* (Cambridge: Cambridge University Press, 1986), 61–67.

52. Quoted in *Theory & Struggle: Journal of the Marx Memorial Library*, no. 121 (2020), back cover.

53. Rand Wilson and Peter Olney, "Swarming Solidarity: How Contract Negotiations in 2021 Could Be Flashpoints in the U.S. Class Struggle," *Labor Notes*, January 14, 2021, https://www.labornotes.org/2021/01/swarming-solidarity-how-contract-negotiations-2021-could-be-flashpoints-us-class-struggle.

54. Alex N. Press, "Hunts Point Workers Went on Strike and Won," *Jacobin*, January 23, 2021, https://www.jacobin.com/2021/01/hunts-point-workers-strike-victory-teamsters-local-2020; Chris Geovanis, "CTU Rank-and-File Votes to Save Lives, Continue to Teach Safely and Remotely," Chicago Teachers Union, January 24, 2021, https://www.ctulocal.org/posts/ctu-rank-and-file-votes-to-save-lives-continue-to-teach-safely-and-remotely; Associated Press, "Strikes," https://apnews.com/hub/strikes.

55. Teamsters for a Democratic Union, "O'Brien-Zuckerman and Vairma-Herrera Add More Candidates," January 8, 2021, https://www.tdu.org/O_Brien_Zuckerman_And_Vairma_Herrera_Add_More_Candidates.

56. Nelson Lichtenstein, "Opening the Door to a More Democratic UAW," *Labor Notes*, January 19, 2021, https://www.labornotes.org/2021/01/opening-door-more-democratic-uaw.

57. Daniel Finn, "Can Europe's Center Left Parties Survive Another Crisis?" *Jacobin*, February 14, 2021, https://www.jacobinmag.com/2021/02/europe-social-democracy-pasokification.

58. Helper, Krueger, and Wial, *Locating American Manufacturing*; Kane and Tomer, *Metro Modes*; Kim Moody, "Labour and the Contradictory Logic of Logistics," *Work Organisation, Labour & Globalisation* 13, no. 1 (Spring 2019): 79–95.

59. Cindy Estrada and Chris Schwartz, "Organizing Rural Manufacturing Workers Matters," *The Forge*, October 19, 2020, https://forgeorganizing.org/article/organizing-rural-manufacturing-workers-matters.

60. For a discussion of the problems of taking government by electoral means as a road to socialism, which is beyond the scope of this chapter, see Kit Wainer and Mel Bienenfeld, "Problems with the Electoral Road to Socialism in the United States," *New Politics* 17, no. 4, whole number 68 (Winter 2020): 67–76.

61. National League of Cities, "Partisan vs. Nonpartisan Elections," 2003, https://www.nlc.org/partisan-vs-nonpartisan-elections.

62. Steve Early, *Refinery Town: Big Oil, Big Money, and the Remaking of an American City* (Boston: Beacon Press, 2017).

63. Meagan Day and Micah Uetricht, *Bigger Than Bernie: How We Go from the Sanders Campaign to Democratic Socialism* (London: Verso, 2020), 75–81. An indication of the problems of running without a mass class-based party can be seen in the fact that one of the six DSA aldermen broke from his comrades to vote for the city's police $1.7 billion budget in 2020. He was censored by his DSA chapter, but not expelled, according to Nathaniel Flakin, "DSA-Endorsed Alderman in Chicago Votes to Give $1.7 Billion to the Police," *Left Voice*, November 28, 2020, https://www.leftvoice.org/socialist-alderman-in-chicago-votes-to-give-1-7-billion-to-=police.

64. Day and Uetricht, *Bigger Than Bernie*, 122.

65. Vivek Chibber, "Our Road to Power," *Jacobin*, no. 27 (Fall 2017), insert.

66. For a discussion of why a simple electoral path to socialism in the US is highly unlikely, see Kit Wainer and Mel Bienenfeld, "Problems with the Electoral Road to Socialism in the United States," *New Politics* 17, no. 4, whole number 68 (Winter 2020): 67–76.

67. Hal Draper, *Karl Marx's Theory of Revolution*, vol. 1, *State and Bureaucracy* (New York: Monthly Review Press, 1977), 282.

68. Hal Draper, "The Two Souls of Socialism," in Hal Draper, *Socialism from Below* (Chicago: Haymarket Books, 2019), 41.

# Appendix

1. Cedric Johnson, "The Panthers Can't Save Us Now," *Catalyst* 1, no. 1 (2017): 57–85; Cedric Johnson, "Who's Afraid of Left Populism?" *New Politics* 17, no. 2, whole number 66 (2019): 21–37; John Clegg and Adaner Usmani, "The Economic Origins of Mass Incarceration," *Catalyst* 3, no. 3 (Fall 2019): 9–53; Mark Jay,

"Cages and Crises: A Marxist Analysis of Mass Incarceration," *Historical Materialism* 27, no. 1 (2019): 182–223; Leo Casey, "The Teacher Strike: Conditions for Success," *Dissent*, December 2, 2020, https://www.dissentmagazine.org/online_articles/the-teacher-strike-conditions-for-success.

2. James Forman Jr., *Locking Up Our Own: Crime and Punishment in Black America* (London: Abacus, 2017); Clegg and Usmani, "Economic Origins."

3. Michelle Alexander, *The New Jim Crow: Mass Incarceration in the Age of Colorblindness* (New York: The New Press, 2012), 5, 46, 58–96; Drug Policy Alliance, *A History of the Drug War*, 2016, http://www.drugpolicy.org/issues/brief-history-drug-war; Lewis R. Katz, "*Terry v. Ohio* at Thirty-Five: A Revisionist View," *Mississippi Law Journal* 74, no. 2 (2004): 423–86. The concept of "law and order" as part of capital's controlling ideology has a very long history in the US dating back at least to the anti-labor "Law and Order Leagues" of the 1880s. See David Montgomery, *The Fall of the House of Labor: The Workplace, the State, and American Labor Activism, 1865–1925* (Cambridge: Cambridge University Press, 1989), 209; Daniel J. Walkowitz, *Worker City, Company Town: Iron and Cotton-Worker Protest in Troy and Cohoes, New York, 1855–84* (Urbana: University of Illinois Press, 1981), 233–42.

4. Forman, *Locking Up*, 35.

5. Walter Thabit, *How East New York Became a Ghetto* (New York: New York University Press, 2003), 76–77.

6. Simon Ezra Balto, "'Occupied Territory': Police Repression and Black Resistance in Postwar Milwaukee, 1950–1968," *Journal of African American History* 98, no. 2 (2013): 229–52.

7. Heather Ann Thompson, *Whose Detroit? Politics, Labor, and Race in a Modern American City* (Ithaca, NY: Cornell University Press, 2001), 21, 38–41.

8. Robin D. G. Kelley, *Race Rebels: Culture, Politics, and the Black Working Class* (New York: The Free Press, 1994), 79–93.

9. US Census Bureau, *Historical Statistics of the United States* (Washington, DC: US Government Printing Office, 1975), 415; US Census Bureau, *Statistical Abstract of the United States, 1981* (US Government Printing Office, 1981), 180; US Census Bureau, *Statistical Abstract of the United States, 2001* (Washington, DC: US Government Printing Office, 2001), 191; Bureau of Justice Statistics, *Arrests in the United States, 1990–2010* (Washington, DC: U.S. Department of Justice, 2012), 2. The fairly constant proportion of Blacks arrested over time is particularly significant in relation to Mark Jay's analysis, which attempts to link incarceration to the different periods following World War II. Since both incarceration and overall crime statistics depend on arrests, the constant disproportion of Black arrests points to race as a continuous factor in these.

10. Forman, *Locking Up*, 11–12.

11. Dr. Gary Potter, *The History of Policing in the United States*, Part 1, Eastern Kentucky University, Police Studies Online, 2013, https://plsonline.eku.edu /insidelook/hisotry-policing-united-states-part-1; Dr. Kirk A. James, *The History of Prisons in America*, 2014, https://medium.com/@kirkajames/the -history-of-prisons-in-america-618a8247348. Law and order in the slave South was a different matter.

12. FBI, Uniform Crime Reporting, *Crime in the United States 2016*, Arrests by Race and Ethnicity, Table 21A, https://ucr.fbi.gov/crime-in-the-u.s/2016 /crime-in-the-u.s.-2016/topic-pages/tables/table-21.

13. Forman, *Locking Up*, 176.

14. Andrew Guthrie Ferguson, "Crime Mapping and the Fourth Amendment: Redrawing 'High-Crime Areas,'" *Hastings Law Journal* 179 (2011): 181–89, 226.

15. Loïc Wacquant, "Class, Race & Hyperincarceration in Revanchist America," *Dædalus* 139, no. 3 (Summer 2010): 79.

16. FBI, Arrests by Race and Ethnicity, Table 21A.

17. Forman, *Locking Up*, 198–202.

18. US Census Bureau, *Statistical Abstract of the United States, 2012* (Washington, DC: U.S. Government Printing Office, 2011), 206.

19. Bureau of Justice Statistics, *Jail Inmates in 2016* (Washington, DC: U.S. Department of Justice, 2018), 4.

20. Wacquant, "Class," 75.

21. Paul Jargowsky, *The Architecture of Segregation* (Washington, DC: The Century Foundation, 2015), 25.

22. Jargowsky, *Architecture*, 10, 19.

23. Jargowsky, *Architecture*, 12.

24. Reshaad Shirazi, "It's High Time to Dump the High-Crime Area Factor," *Berkeley Journal of Criminal Law* 21 (2016): 77–79.

25. Jargowsky, *Architecture*, 10–19.

26. Cited in Shirazi, "High Time," 90–91.

27. Radley Balko, "There's Overwhelming Evidence That the Criminal Justice System Is Racist. Here's the Proof," *Washington Post*, June 10, 2020, https://www .washingtonpost.com/graphics/2020/opinions/systemic-racism-police -evidence-criminal-justice-system/.

28. Ferguson, "Crime Mapping," 189.

29. Cathy O'Neil, *Weapons of Math Destruction: How Big Data Increases Inequality and Threatens Democracy* (London: Penguin Books, 2017), 87.

30. O'Neil, *Weapons*, 91.

31. James Bridle, *New Dark Age: Technology and the End of the Future* (London: Verso, 2018), 144–145.

32. Hannah Fry, *Hello World: How to Be Human in the Age of the Machine* (London:

Doubleday, 2018), 153. Similar algorithms, such as COMPAS and LSI-R, are used in sentencing as well with similarly discriminatory results.

33. Ferguson, "Crime Mapping," 191–97.

34. Mara Hvistendahl, "How The LAPD and Palantir Use Data to Justify Racist Policing," *The Intercept*, January 30, 2021, https://theintercept.com/2021/01/30/lapd-palantir-data-driven-policing.

35. O'Neil, *Weapons*, 91–93. New York's stop-and-frisk program was reduced after 2013 when the courts found it unconstitutional, but continued to stop drivers for minor traffic offenses and frisk some forty-seven thousand pedestrians in 2014, according to Forman, *Locking Up*, 212.

36. Moody, *On New Terrain*, 101.

37. FBI, Arrest by Race and Ethnicity, Table 21A.

38. Gallup, "Confidence in Police Back at Historical Average," July 10, 2017, https://news.gallup.com/poll/213869/confidence-police-back-historical-average.aspx?version=print.

39. Shirazi, "High Time," 94–104.

40. Ferguson, "Crime Mapping," 198.

# INDEX

228

# About Haymarket Books

Haymarket Books is a radical, independent, nonprofit book publisher based in Chicago. Our mission is to publish books that contribute to struggles for social and economic justice. We strive to make our books a vibrant and organic part of social movements and the education and development of a critical, engaged, international left.

We take inspiration and courage from our namesakes, the Haymarket martyrs, who gave their lives fighting for a better world. Their 1886 struggle for the eight-hour day—which gave us May Day, the international workers' holiday—reminds workers around the world that ordinary people can organize and struggle for their own liberation. These struggles continue today across the globe—struggles against oppression, exploitation, poverty, and war.

Since our founding in 2001, Haymarket Books has published more than five hundred titles. Radically independent, we seek to drive a wedge into the risk-averse world of corporate book publishing. Our authors include Noam Chomsky, Arundhati Roy, Rebecca Solnit, Angela Y. Davis, Howard Zinn, Amy Goodman, Wallace Shawn, Mike Davis, Winona LaDuke, Ilan Pappé, Richard Wolff, Dave Zirin, Keeanga-Yamahtta Taylor, Nick Turse, Dahr Jamail, David Barsamian, Elizabeth Laird, Amira Hass, Mark Steel, Avi Lewis, Naomi Klein, and Neil Davidson. We are also the trade publishers of the acclaimed Historical Materialism Book Series and of Dispatch Books.

# About the Author

Kim Moody is a founder of *Labor Notes* in the United States and the author of several books on labor and politics. He is currently a visiting scholar at Centre for the Study of the Production of the Built Environment of the University of Westminster in London and a member of the National Union of Journalists, University and College Union, the British Universities Industrial Relations Association, the Labor and Working Class History Association, and the Working Class Studies Association.